BOUNDARIES
Coming of Age in Two College Towns

James C. Stanley

*to Suzette
with warm regards
Peace, Jim
March 2015*

Copyright © 2015
ISBN 978-1-5058-0946-6
Printed by CreateSpace, an Amazon.com Company

All rights reserved. No part of this book may be reproduced or transmitted in whole or part by any means without the written permission of the author.

CONTENTS

Prologue — 1

1. Origins — 3
   A Mistaken Start
   Roots

2. A Place, Too Uppity — 20
   McKinley
   The Night the Lights Were Turned Off
   Leaving Charley

3. Early Lessons in a New Roost — 26
   The Capitol Job
   Liberty Hyde Bailey School
   Mrs. North
   Mr. Burnham

4. The Layout: Home and Neighbors — 39
   The Home on Snyder Road
   The Neighbors

5. The Town — 52
   The College
   Downtown
   Burcham Woods

6. Early Ownership, Pride and Peril — 59
   Collections
   Craftsmanship
   Out of Control
   Fireworks

7. Six Years' Start   74
   Entering the Big Building
   Latitude Reined In

8. Mediocrity   79
   Childhood Ends—Adolescence Beckons
   69 Inches
   "No Gentleman Cs"
   "70% Won't Serve You Well"

9. Rules For Winners and Losers   84
   House Rules
   Points and Ribbons, But No Eagle
   Five-Card Draw

10. Perseverance 101: Patience and Passion   95
    Where Are the Walleyes?
    Save Your Money
    Try 26.2 Miles

11. Perseverance 102: Advanced Course   113
    The 1950s Culture
    A 1932 Car, Rumble Seat and All
    Rebuilding
    The Start
    The Crash

12. The Fair Sex   122
    Grade School
    Mixings
    Teasing
    The Pin
    Separation

13. Fall's Earliest Commitment   130
    Discipline
    The Early Games
    Big George

14. Irreplaceable   137
    1954 Varsity
    Coach
    Working Out on the Farm
    A Difficult Lesson
    1955 Varsity
    Why There?

15. But for the Grace of God   149
    A Terrible Virus
    Unforgiving Bacteria

16. Bad Choices   154
    Just Another Game of Chicken
    Booze

17. Pain: The Absence of Choice   159
    Bias
    A Garden or a Cottage
    The Doctor's Son
    Country Club and Church: The Businessman

18. Speaking Aloud   169
    Content versus Grammar
    Storytelling
    Addressing the Class of 1956

19. Failure   178
    First Days of College
    Engineering English
    A Career Writer
    Saturday
    Closure after Five Decades

20. A New Mistress — 187
    The United States of America Needs You
    People Need You
    Dooley's Influence
    No-Degree Kid
    Selling the New Mistress

21. Premed Competition And Integrity — 199
    Getting into Medical School: A Contact Sport
    The Application
    The Wayne State Interview
    The Michigan Interview
    Acceptance
    The Last Heart Attack

22. A College Sweetheart — 213
    New Freedoms
    Nancy
    A Real Home Away from Home
    The Wedding

23. Beginnings Anew — 227
    Tim and the City of Brotherly Love
    Jeff and Uncle Sam
    Sarah and the Moon Landing
    Balance

Epilogue — 243

Acknowledgments — 245

Prologue

It was not so long ago that I came of age in a college town, a small city just east of our state's capital. This was where I learned to laugh and cry, found joy as a student, played football, owned my first car when only 15, cared a lot for my first girlfriend, and gave a speech at high school graduation. It was from there that I set off to another college town that I call home and a university that I serve today as a professor.

Growing up in East Lansing in the 1950s was, for most of us, a happy time. We were never poor, and our earlier childhood knowledge of society's troubles came from brief segments in a newsreel shown before Saturday matinees at the State Theater, or short news clips viewed on the latest addition to our homes, a black and white television set. Lingering effects of the Great Depression and World War II were not as painful to us as they had been to our parents and older siblings. Time had spared us the vexations of the past. The days were peaceful and the country prosperous.

We were safe. You didn't lock the front door at night or your car at work. The evening's supper table was a place to share the little details of our lives: conflict was nearly invisible. Disrespect for those who governed us, concern about the civil rights of others or gender inequities, simply were not topics of public discourse, much less dinnertime talk. Perhaps we were naïve in those days. These issues, along with the drug culture and greater sexual freedom, awaited us after college.

Facing these changes and the boundaries surrounding them was easier for some of my generation than others. Not all of us had the same opportunities or faced the same obstacles. But my writing is not about our differences. It is about the physical and emotional boundaries that affected my perception of myself and my space in life as I became of age.

1
Origins

At a very early age I believed there must have been a problem with my birth. Perhaps I should have been born much earlier–so I have rationalized. You see most of my friends had siblings who were a few years older or younger. That gave them built-in playmates. That arrangement didn't exist in my home. In fact, I was not sure I was a planned addition to the family.

A Mistaken Start

I think my situation evolved from a mathematical error–a numerical mistake, the result of a miscalculation by a day or so—and in my youth, I suspect I put too much effort in being careful to not further taint what I thought was my erroneous beginning. But that's just the way things were.

My father and mother were both born in 1900. When I came into this world, they were nearing the end of their fourth decade. In those days human procreation was not much of a science. Frequently, a woman would take basal temperatures to find out if she was ovulating and might then conceive—or, perhaps, she would count 14 days back from her predicted "next" menstrual period, to arrive at a dubious estimate of the day she might get pregnant. Avoiding those hot spots lessened the chances of an unexpected pregnancy.

My parents probably weren't trying to have another child at the time of my conception, around New Year's Day 1938. They likely were thinking about each other, rather than about numbers, and that left my embryonic emergence to bad arithmetic. So there I was, planned or not, arriving nine months later on a Saturday night in September, joining a family that included my brother, Bob, already 10 years old.

My conception was never discussed, aside from a comment now and again by my mother's loud-mouthed cousin, Fred, who on more than one occasion called me the *"little surprise."* Great talk for a child to overhear! But, as has often been the case in my life, I was lucky: my mom and dad never made me feel I was an afterthought. After all, I was their last hurrah.

Roots

My family name, Stanley, was another problem I struggled with during childhood. I had schoolmates with the first name Stanley, and I was confused as to what kind of name it really was. In those early days it seemed to me that Stanley was more correctly used as first than a last name. I often wished for a more common surname, like Smith or Brown. I wondered if someone had simply ignored their heritage and just made up a new name for themselves—after all, that was the case with the explorer Henry Morton Stanley, who is best known for the words, "Dr. Livingstone, I presume?" uttered when, after months of searching, he finally encountered the great explorer and missionary in the depths of Africa. The reality was that he actually had no relatives by the name of Stanley. He was an unwanted child of a prostitute in England, and renamed himself after a successful New Orleans businessman he had noticed on the street. I wondered if my name had a similar rogue beginning.

I'm quite sure I was not related to either the explorer or his New Orleans namesake. Nevertheless, my Stanley roots do go back to England. Many years after my childhood, in the mid-1960s, after the death of my father's last surviving brother, Fred Stanley, I discovered among his belongings a small black ledger book containing 19 pages of his writings about the early family history. I think his perspective was more accurate than we tend to see these days in many of the websites that sell information to people hungry to know of their roots. According to my uncle, "Stanley" was first heard as the title of an English Saxon manor called Stoneley, in Staffordshire. It was owned by Henry de Stoneley. His name derived from the words *stone* and *leah*, or *lea*, meaning a stony meadow or field. The history of the property's ownership is more complex.

Uncle Fred claimed that the Stanley family name was coined by Adam de Alditheley, the grandson of William de Alditheley, one of the Norman knights who accompanied William the Conqueror to England and who received a great deal of land as the reward of their conquest. Adam married the daughter of Thomas de Stoneley, Joan, and received a manor as part of her marriage dowry. He subsequently exchanged that manor for the Stoneley manor, whereupon he changed his own name to Stanley to honor the pre-Norman antiquity of his wife's Saxon family. This all occurred during the reign of Henry I, from 1100 to 1135. And that explains why Stanley is my last name.

My more recent heritage also includes a long list of other names, including Baxter, Brackstone, Bloodworth, Blunden, Braday, Colter, Donaldson, Frank, Geist, Keats, Lamphear, Milton, Morgan, Nicholson, Sealy, Schierholz, and Watts. Quite a list, but unfortunately, Uncle Fred never traced those names on my father's side of the family, from the renaissance and Middle Ages to the Stoneley to Stanley name conversion nearly 900 years ago.

Nevertheless, my paternal roots picked up in 1813, when my great-grandfather, red-haired Frederic Stanley, left England at eight years old and laid roost in America, where years later he became a Baptist minister. I'm not sure what happened to the fire and brimstone of his beliefs, but he passed his red hair on to my dad, as well as my brother's son and my youngest son. The other side of Dad's family tree traces back to Joseph Nicholson, born in England during the 1600s, whose great-granddaughter, Elizabeth, married James Blunden, an Irishman, who was my father's great-grandfather on his mother's side.

My mother's maternal roots also go back to the 1600s. They can be traced back to John Alexander, born in England during the late 1680s. Her father, Charles Geist, had his family roots in Germany, but his lineage has been lost.

The parts of my ancestry that are most enlightening to me cover the last 125 years. That's when my grandparents were married: Arthur Stanley to Kate Blunden, and Charles Geist to Ida Alexander. It was shortly thereafter, in the very early months of 1900, that both Mom and Dad—Joseph Dean Stanley and Jeannette Estelle Geist—were conceived.

I never met my grandfather, Arthur Stanley, who died more than a century ago. He owned and managed a general store in Lowell, Ohio, a very small rural town: in addition, he was a photographer and a druggist. Lowell is on the Muskingum River, a tributary of the Ohio River less than 10 miles away. It was then an idyllic countryside town set in rolling hills and enjoying temperate weather. But the proximity to two rivers meant frequent flooding of the environs, destroying businesses, homes, and planted fields. I have seen scores of photos of the overflowing Ohio, dotted with submerged buildings and homes—none of which, fortunately, included the Stanley family home. Many of those photos are fancy mounted prints with "A D Stanley Photography" embossed on their border.

Arthur had married Mary "Tillie" Toothaker when he was in his early 20s. They had two children, Donald and Harold. But in 1884, Tillie died, just three years after giving birth to their youngest. She had just turned 30, and Harold died 10 years later, just as he was entering his teens. Four years after Tillie died, Arthur married my grandmother, Kate Blunden. He was 12 years her senior. Arthur and Kate had three children, Garth, Fred, and my dad. Garth and Fred were born nine and six years before my father arrived. Just like in my parents' family, all of Arthur's offspring were boys.

Arthur Stanley is the only one of my grandparents whose picture I've never seen among hundreds of family photos of Dad's early life. To say that this is surprising is an understatement given that he was the only commercial photographer in Lowell. Years after Arthur died, my grandmother Kate remarried and I often wondered if she might have purged all traces of Arthur to make room for someone else. That's a sad thought, but who knows? In any event, I have no idea what Arthur looked like. That missing piece is something missing in me. More than once I've wondered what he looked like. Did he have a beard? Wear glasses? Did he typically look happy—or serious, as Kate always did? Was he short, like me?

Kate Stanley was one of seven children—four boys and three girls. Two of her brothers became distinguished physicians, including one, an ear, nose, and throat specialist, who spent time in Africa as a missionary doctor. I find it intriguing to think that my genes for science and medicine were there three-quarters of a century before I was born.

Kate was industrious. She was a wiry lady when I knew her and probably had always been that way. After Arthur died, she maintained the general store, and also assumed the job of Lowell's postmistress, a position she held for 12 years, until 1918. This was no small task and involved both posting the mail and delivering it. When she stepped down, my father followed in her steps for two years. Dad at that time had an open-air roadster he called the "blue racer." I've often pictured him flying down a country road delivering the mail in something that resembled a cross between a jalopy and an antique race car.

Dad attended school with a myriad of children in large classrooms where the teacher-student ratio was high—considerably higher than in today's public schools. Shortly after he finished high school, Kate married William Cairns. Five years her senior and a longtime family friend, he was a woolen-goods salesman with a great deal of political clout in Lowell. It was family talk that he had helped Kate obtain the postmistress position. He had courted her for more than a decade before they were married. During that time he became an important fixture in my father's life. I have seen lots of photographs of Dad and grandfather Cairns together—at home, vacationing, and camping. Many depicted their shared interest in the art of fly fishing—something that sustained my father's peace of mind in his later years.

Dad always went by the name Dean Stanley. He never used his first name, Joseph, in my presence, although he preserved the "J" in his signature, "J Dean Stanley." Dean was his father Arthur's middle name—favoring it was, perhaps, a way for him to honor his father and keep a certain measure of his early childhood alive. Or perhaps he just didn't want to be called Joe. Arthur was 49 when my father was born. He died six years later. Dad never said much about his father, perhaps because he had spent precious little time with him.

From the time they were born through their adolescence, my parents lived only 188 miles away from each other, as the birds fly, but their upbringings placed them much farther apart. My mother grew up in the more urban environment of Toledo, Ohio, where her father, Charles

Geist, was a pharmacist and successful drugstore owner. He was handsome and his wife, Ida, was strikingly beautiful. Mother was an only child, and both her parents doted on her. You might even say she was spoiled. She was raised in affluence, surrounded by fancy furniture and linen napkins.

A precocious child, Mom graduated from Toledo's Scott High after having skipped a grade in junior high. Afterward, she traveled east to attend LaSalle Seminary for Young Women in Auburndale, Massachusetts, just outside of Boston. Today it's a coeducational college, but in my mother's time it was one of the more exclusive finishing schools for wealthy young girls from around the nation.

My father never attended college. In his young adulthood he became a whiz at finances—likely a result of his having completed a series of correspondence courses in finance from the Babson Institute (renamed Babson College in 1969) in Wellesley Hills, just outside Boston.

Young adulthood is a time of choices, and I've often speculated on what it might have been like when my father and mother were entering these years. The atmosphere of the East was to my mother's liking. She wrote in her diary about having had a serious relationship with Ellis Waring, a young man in Boston. They were close enough that she wrote glowingly about him. But just when the reading of her diary gets good six pages were torn out that might have explained it all—or not. Photos of my father at the same time, as a young man in southern Ohio, more often than not find him surrounded by pretty girls. I wonder if one of them had been in his life before my mother and if he faced the same boundaries in pursuit of the opposite sex that I faced as a teenager?

When he was 21, Dad moved to Cleveland and worked as a salesman for a wholesale dry goods company. He was "a traveling man," working northern Ohio and living in a rented room in a home owned by a family who knew my mother's parents. It was in the mid-1920s that they introduced Dad to my mother. She was a secretary working for George McGwinn, the vice president in charge of properties at the Union Trust, a Cleveland bank. Mom and Dad courted for three years, fell in love for keeps, and were married in December 1926. Two years later they brought my brother, Bob, into the world.

Mother never worked outside the house after my brother arrived.

Inside the home, however, she excelled. Mother was a serious cook, with a repertoire that ran from yams mixed with marshmallows, to roast beef that gave an appealing aroma to our home for hours before it was served, to her homemade chocolate hot fudge ice cream topping—flavored with real vanilla. She could even add molasses to milk to make a concoction that made you think you were enjoying a drink prepared for royalty.

My parents were not meek, yet I never heard a harsh word between them, and if there had ever been personal disappointment in their marriage, I never sensed it. They had found peace in each other. My mother was my father's biggest supporter and confidante. She made the rules that ran the house, and my father was the enforcer. Mother was the intellectual force behind many of our family's doings. She could discuss matters of politics that were way beyond her friends and she rolled over both men and women as a wicked contract bridge player. She had brains!

My parents' marriage of 34 years was very happy. They could get mushy around the anniversary of their wedding date, sharing a few glasses of wine while listening to Hoagy Carmichael's 1927 composition "*Stardust*" on an old 78 rpm recording. His piano rendition of this piece was an American standard, and according to them, it was "their song." If I asked too many questions about what were they thinking, I got nothing more than a wry smile as an answer.

Much as they were in harmony, my parents were different people, which created choices for me. Depending on the situation I found myself in, it proved advantageous and easy to bounce from one to the other to get the most support, be it a request for money or permission to do something risky.

My family's deepest roots and consequently my own, were very Midwestern—a mixture of hard work and respect for others. They were strong roots, and they came with boundaries.

My paternal grandmother Kate Stanley; Postmistress in Lowell, Ohio, c.1915. Sorting mail in the family's General Store that she maintained after her husband and my grandfather, Arthur Stanley, died when my own father was only 6 years old.

Grandmother Kate Stanley and William Cairns, c.1920. They wed in 1917, a little more than a decade after Arthur Stanley died.

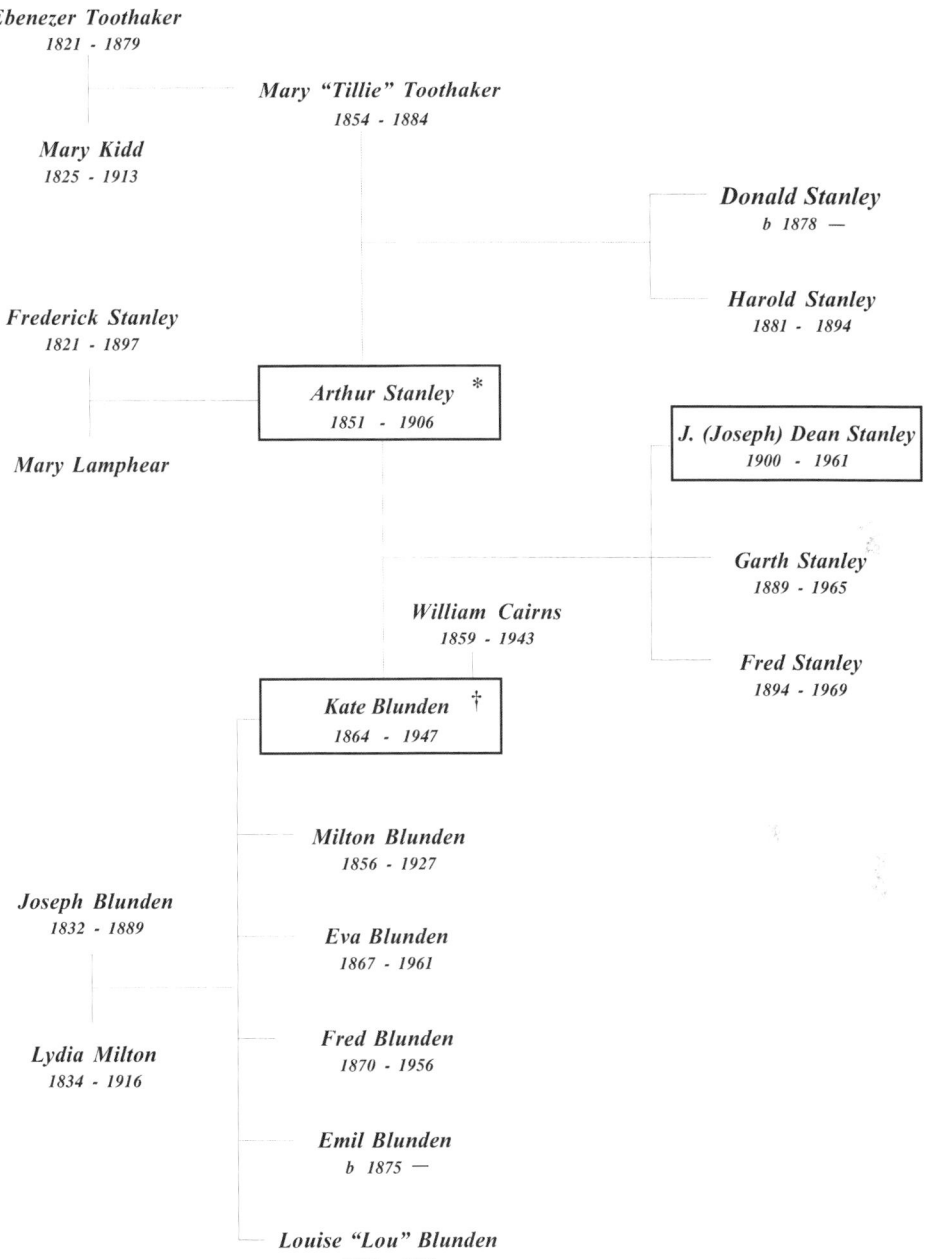

The Stanley-Blunden Family Tree. *Arthur Stanley married Kate Blunden 3 years after the death of his first wife, Mary Toothacher. †Kate was remarried to William Cairns 11 years after Arthur Stanley died.

My maternal grandmother Ida Geist and grandfather Charles Geist, c.1895. They were parents of my mother Jeannette, an 'only child'.

Grandfather Geist's Drug Store in Toledo, Ohio, c.1925.

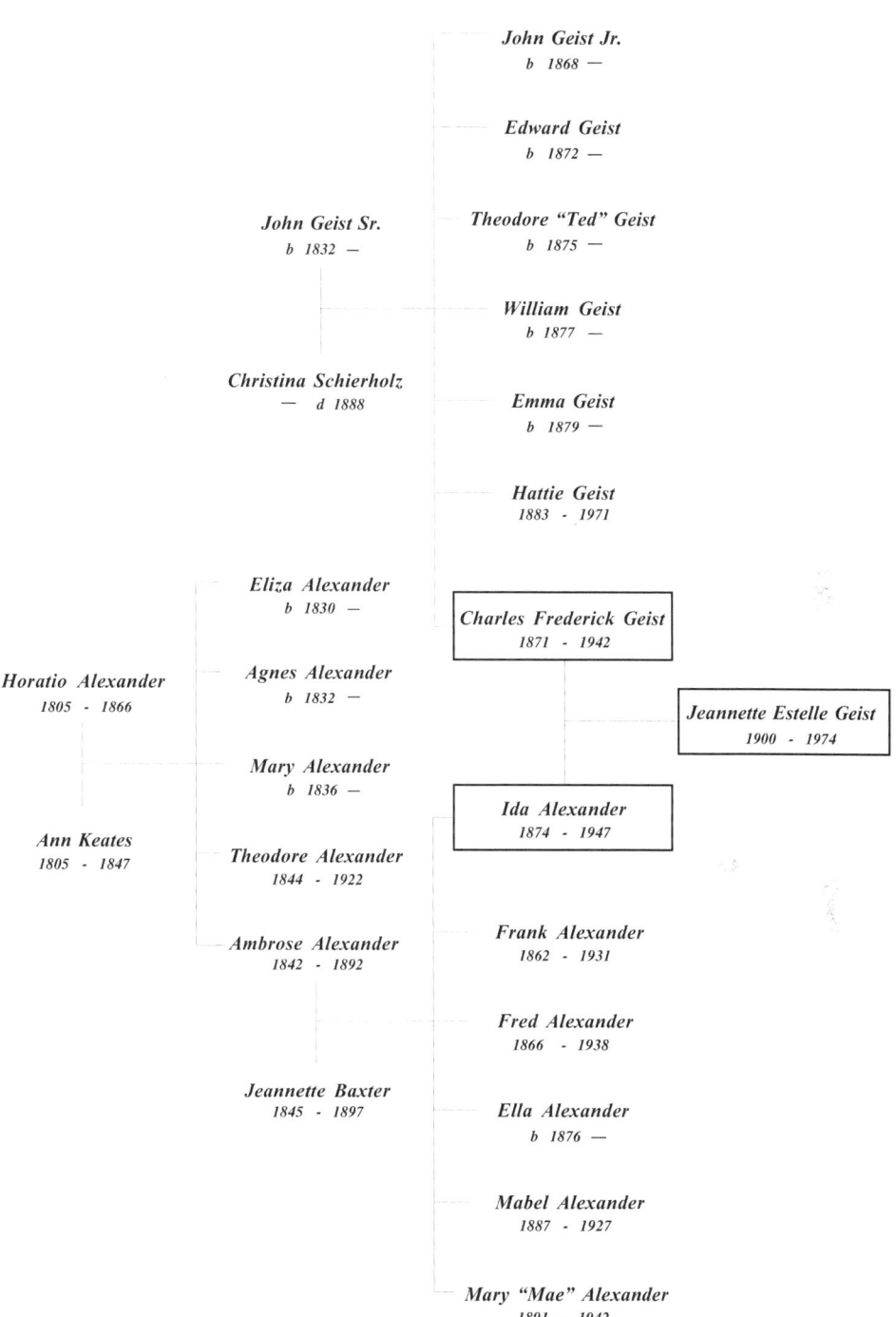

The Geist-Alexander Family Tree.

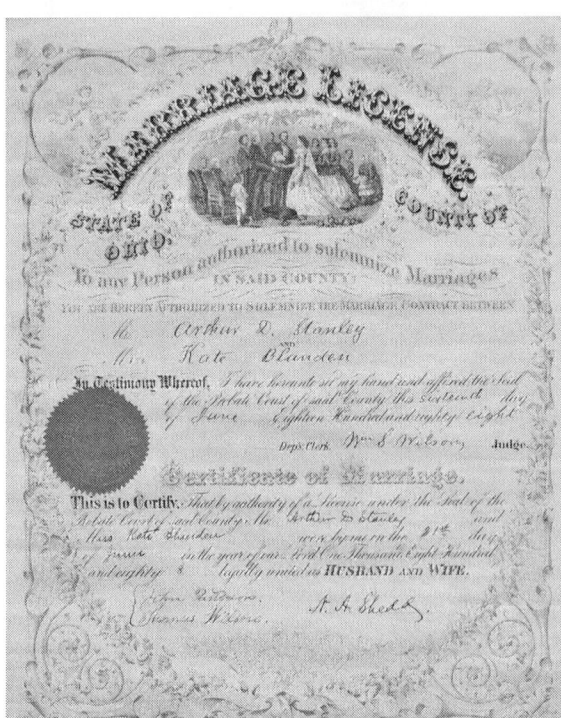

Arthur Stanley and
Kate Blunden
June 21, 1888

Charles Geist and
Ida Alexander
June 20, 1899

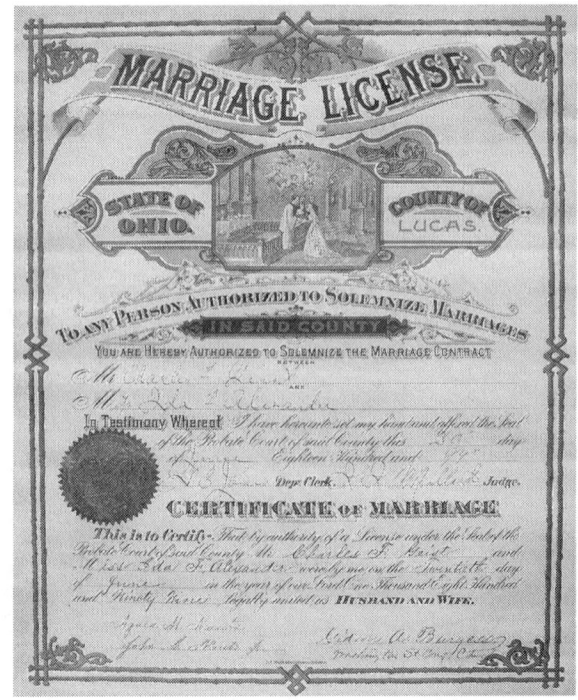

My grandparents
marriages more than
a century ago were the
beginning of our more
contemporary family.

My mother Jeannette Geist in the day's fashion with a bow in her hair in a pensive mood, c.1907.

My father Dean Stanley in fancy clothes with his older brothers, Fred and Garth, under the watch of his maternal grandmother and my great grandmother Lydia Blunden, c.1901.

Dad in the back row (arrow) of his Lowell, Ohio elementary school classroom, c.1907

Dad, his older brothers, Garth and Fred, with his mother Kate Stanley, c.1910.

My mother had a pampered and protected childhood; witness a birthday party with girlfriends, all in white, c.1909.

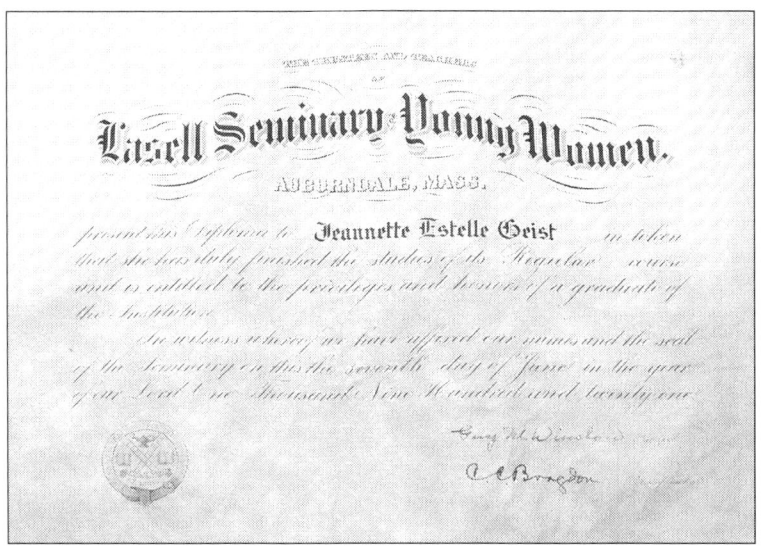

Mother graduated from Scott High School in Toledo, Ohio and then attended a privileged finishing school in Massachusetts.

Mother and Dad as newlyweds in their Lakewood, Ohio front yard, 1926.

Mother and my brother Bob in the family living room before I arrived, 1936.

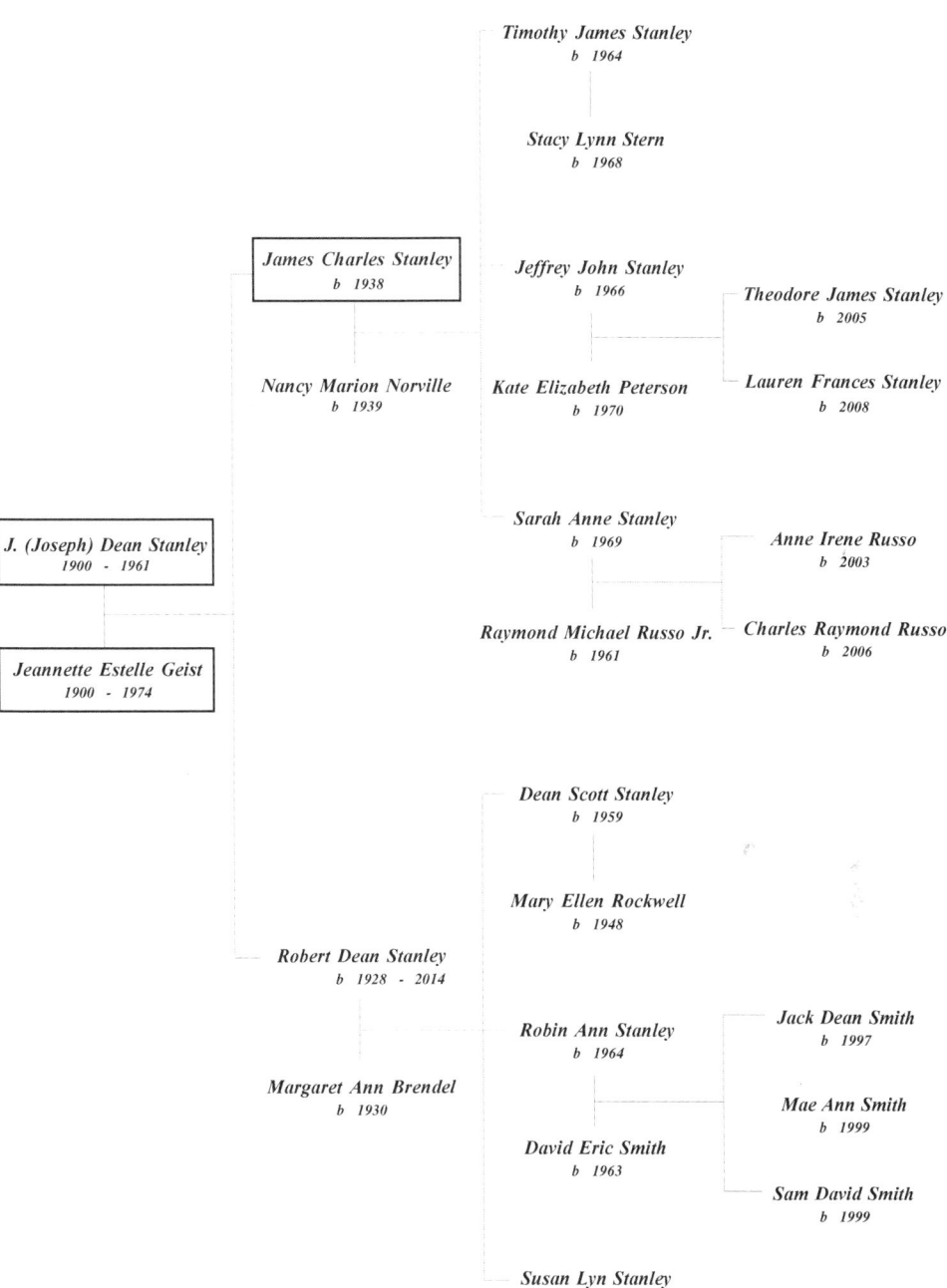

The Stanley-Geist Family Tree.

2

A Place, Too Uppity

Recollections of my earliest childhood are fleeting at best—likely influenced more by old photos than actual memories of those first three or four years. Freud believed that healthy individuals suppress their oedipal conflicts, along with most other memories, as they leave early childhood. There may be some truth to that in my case. A lot of memories of my early years are gone, and I do think I'm emotionally healthy. What I do recall has nothing to do with Freud, but a lot to do with my leaving a place sold on its own social superiority with very proscriptive boundaries.

McKinley

I was born on September 18, 1938, at Harper Hospital in Detroit, and was soon taken to my parents' home in a quiet upscale suburban community on the shores of Lake St. Clair in southeastern Michigan. That roost was a classy red brick house at 254 McKinley in Grosse Pointe Farms. The house is still there and it looks the same today as it did more than seven decades ago.

Some of my childhood vistas remain irresistibly clear, like the dark-green wooden fence posts topped with round balls painted white in our backyard, and climbing rose plants hanging on trellises tied to the fence. To get into the backyard, there was a door right off of the kitchen in the rear of the house, and I remember the three concrete steps I had to navigate up and down to pass between the yard and house. They seemed gigantic. I had to hold on to them tightly at each stage of my climbing down or back up, or wait for someone to help me along.

I also have vivid memories as I grew a bit older of my second-floor front bedroom overlooking our quiet street. My room was always quiet. During summer afternoons the sun's rays were deflected by awnings stretched out over the windows. But warm breezes would sneak in and gently sway the window's glassine curtains back and forth. That's where I took my afternoon naps—in a sleepy corner all my own. It was a pretty neat place. I have faint remembrances of Isabel, a live-in helper my parents adored. I think she spent a lot of time caring for me, reading stories in a soft and sweet voice. When someone rang the doorbell, she would often pick me up and let me look out of my upstairs window to see who it might be.

Our neighborhood streets were lined with full-grown maple and oak trees and our block was encircled with sidewalks laid by workers employed by the Depression-era Works Progress Administration. I remember the walkways, marked by uneven cracks that made a funny click-clack sound when I pulled my red wagon over them. That was a sound not duplicated until I was older and used a clothespin to fasten a card to my bicycle fender brace. The card flapped against the spokes as I rode, creating a noise something like a sewing machine motor.

A few houses down the street were the homes of Billy Sutton and Jerry Martin. They were my first friends. The three of us would dress up, often in play soldiers' uniforms, and go from door to door, helping neighbors load bottles of lard and metal from old toys and flattened tin cans into my wagon. One of our moms usually tagged along. Our chore was to pull these things to the curbside, where once a week grown-ups would place them on a big black truck. They took all of it away to be made into munitions and guns for the War Effort. To us it seemed like a game. But of course it wasn't.

The Night the Lights Were Turned Off

One night our McKinley home was different. As twilight arrived, eerie shadows that I hadn't seen before bounced around our living room floor and wiggled on the walls. Then as darkness approached, the shadows became harder to follow—not as sharp as they usually were. The drapes had been pulled, and as the sky grew dark, the street lights in front of our house didn't come on as they normally did. The lights inside our home didn't come on either. Something had happened.

I was scared of the dark and I wished the early-dusk light had not been blocked by the drapes that my dad had drawn tight. As it was, the orange dial of the radio was the only thing aglow in the whole house. It gave a spooky texture to the room's rose-colored overstuffed davenport and the two matching large reading chairs. I sat on the floor in the middle of the room. The furniture about me assumed the shape of large barricades. I felt trapped.

To make matters worse, a strange man's monotone voice was coming from the radio. My mother's and father's faces appeared drawn as they sat motionless in the room's dim light. Even my brother, who was 14 years old, looked tense. The voice on the radio sounded hesitant and labored, but it never stopped talking. It was WXYZ, but the familiar, resonant voice of Brace Beemer, who portrayed the Lone Ranger at that time most nights, wasn't the one we heard. In fact, the room was so quiet that I could hear everyone breathing. I didn't get it. As much as I wanted to understand, no one was explaining.

It was 1942 and I was only four years old. The country was at war and we lived a stone's throw from the "Arsenal of Democracy"—the converted automobile plants around Detroit where armaments were being made for our armed forces in Europe and the Pacific. Most amazing were the thousands of tanks and B-24 Liberator bombers that rolled off the assembly lines during those times. The auto industry had become a critical contributor to the war effort. And that night my McKinley home seemed too close to the war.

This was a mock air-raid drill and all the lights were turned off. Grosse Pointe Farms was dark and no one was on the street, except those assigned tasks to identify planes that had taken off from Willow Run, a few miles away. You could hear the throbbing of their engines as they passed overhead in the evening silence. They seemed so near. They were our planes, not those of an attacking enemy. But it was wartime and no one my age really knew.

My brother was one of the cadets in the Area Council of Defense, serving as a civilian messenger. He wore a neat white oil-cloth armband with a white triangle inside a blue circle with a red lightning streak in its center. He even had an identification card with his photo on it, in case someone on the street wanted to know why he wasn't at home with his parents. As he sprinted out of the front door that evening with a small book and a pencil in hand, he looked serious, but happy. I was not. Any movement on my part, any attempt to go to a window where I might look out and see a plane myself, was met with my father's stern voice:

"Stay put."

It was easy to recognize what a boundary was that night. It was well defined in that dark room. There would be many more.

Leaving Charley

Grosse Pointe Farms, on the northern outskirts of Detroit, was an affluent community by any standard, and to many people, a wonderful place to be raised. Yet, when I'm asked where I grew up, I always say East Lansing, where our family moved in 1943, when I was five years old. I doubt that at the time, I could have articulated why I dismissed my first hometown, but as I grew older, the reasons became more obvious.

As an impressionable child, I overheard a lot about Grosse Pointe Farm's snootiness, country club affairs, and of course, Grosse Pointe Charley—who ever that was. He was the character jokingly referred to by those who didn't appreciate the elite attitude of Grosse Pointe's citizens. In all likelihood he probably was the fictitious playboy portrayed by an actor in phone conversations on J.P. McCarthy's popular Detroit WJR morning radio program. Grosse Pointe Charley and what he stood for, remained with me: a self-centered, conceited person, unconcerned with the rest of the world. I didn't want to be like that person, and I didn't think I should adhere to the boundaries he set. When we moved and left our home on McKinley, I hoped I was right.

At age 18 months life was joyous and I didn't know what boundaries were. We were living in Grosse Pointe Farms, Michigan, 1940.

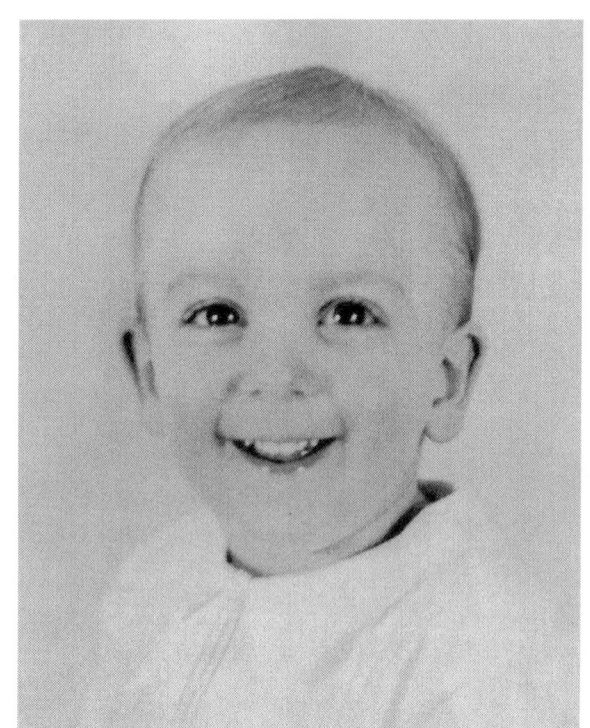

Grandmother Geist playing with me and my Tinker-Toys in the backyard of our home, 1941.

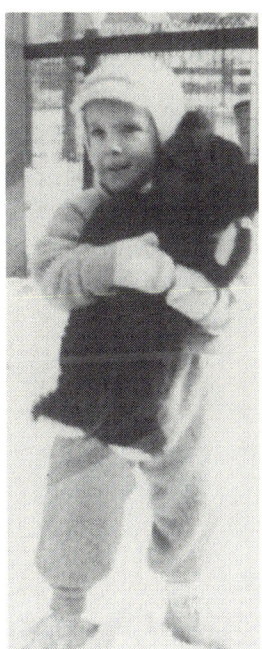  

At age 3 years I liked it all…Winter, Spring, and Summer, 1941-1942.

My first real friends, Billy Sutton on my right and Jerry Marin on my left. Weekly, we helped gather materials, like scrap metals and even cooking lard, from our neighbors to be used to make munitions in support of our Armed Forces fighting in World War II. It was 1943.

25

3
Early Lessons in a New Roost

My first home was easily forgotten. My second home was in East Lansing, a college town where folks talked about some things other than money and material possessions. I enjoyed the culture of learning there. Added knowledge was more prized than a new glitzy trinket. And I liked people who talked about what they knew—or at least what they thought they knew. Many lessons lay ahead.

The Capitol Job

Moving was a big deal for my father. It was a major promotion from his earlier job in Detroit at Stranahan, Harris & Company where he was a securities and municipal bonds salesman. Dad's new position was as the Municipal Finance Commissioner of the State of Michigan. He owed his new job in part to the State Treasurer, D. Hale Brake. An arch-conservative Republican, Brake owned a farm in the small rural community of Stanton, Michigan. A lawyer who had been a State Senator for six years, he was elected Treasurer in 1943. Dad had been President of the Detroit Downtown Republican Club in the early 1940s, when we lived in Grosse Pointe Farms. There is little question that Dad's party affiliation aided his appointment.

With the new job came the move to be near the State Capitol. My father's new duties suited him well, and he worked smoothly with the financial gurus of the state's cities and towns. He quickly became the "go-to" person when it came to municipal finances in Michigan.

That made him a major force in Michigan's growth after the war ended. He wrote many of the bond issues that financed schools, roads, and even airports. A favorite picture on Dad's office wall was a framed *Wall Street Journal* cartoon. It depicted a large, sleepy-looking bear at a cobweb-infested tollgate at the entrance of the Mackinac Bridge. Connecting the state's upper and lower peninsulas, this phenomenal feat of civil engineering was among the longest suspension bridges in the world. Many investors, including the fiscal pundits who populated the pages of *Wall Street Journal*, considered the bridge to be a boondoggle, and they showed little interest in buying the bonds that were issued to support its construction. Work began in 1954, and the bridge opened three years later. My father was the state's fiscal agent for the $99.8 million project, and as it happened, the bridge was a great financial success. The bonds were retired without a hiccup and the tolls and their booths were eliminated. The framed cartoon became a status symbol for my father. It wasn't the first or last time in my life time that Wall Street would be proved wrong. Dad continued as the State Municipal Finance Commissioner for 11 years until 1954, when he established his own consulting firm.

Michigan State Capitol, c 1950. My father's office was on the 2nd floor looking over the manicured gardens toward our new home in East Lansing.

My father's office was next to the State Treasurer, D. Hale Brake's office. Dad was an expert in municipal bonds and securities, serving as Michigan's Municipal Commissioner until 1954. There were many Wall Street trips during those days.

Life was good for my parents in the early days in our new East Lansing home. If you left our neighborhood and ventured west, down Michigan Avenue for about three miles, you entered Lansing. And at the end of the avenue was the State Capitol, its dome lit every night. In the darkness, its floodlights gave the illusion that the building was carved out of ivory—something monumental and eternal. That's where Dad's second-floor office was, looking east over the building's well-kept gardens and manicured lawns and toward our new house.

On Saturday mornings I often got to go to Dad's office. We used to park under the Capitol building itself and I felt a sense of importance when the elevator attendant would welcome Dad in a very formal manner. I would spend hours in the building's rotunda and hallways, gazing at the oil portraits of the state's earlier governors, the circle of battle flags behind glass with their military campaign ribbons attached to the top of each staff, and the fancy signs denoting the executive offices. It was sort of like being in a museum, except for the busy men in suits and ties walking briskly by, to and from their offices and the legislative chambers.

Those mornings were my first introduction to the body politic. I was certain that Dad was a very influential guy. Describing the work he did, Mom used to tell me that he was getting the money to help other people build airports, roads, bridges, libraries, and schools. Of course I thought he must be very rich—and of course he was not. But I was only six years old. I was about to begin my formal education.

Liberty Hyde Bailey School

As we grow older we often talk about how "the snow was deeper when we were kids." That may or may not be true, but there's no question that my childhood was less burdensome than for many of today's young, growing up surrounded by personal stress and societal conflict. My childhood in East Lansing was actually fun. And it started in my first school, a hop, skip, and a jump from my front door.

My elementary education took place in a quintessential school building two blocks from my home. Outside, Liberty Hyde Bailey School might as well have been right out of the movies. Only a little more than 20 years old when I attended, it occupied a small corner of its own large city block. The school was three stories high and sheathed in brown brick. The interior, with its polished granite hallways and its many windows, could have been the model for any one of Norman Rockwell's mid-century schoolhouse paintings.

Liberty Hyde Bailey School is where I found few boundaries and experienced a lot of joy in learning from Kindergarten to 6th grade, 1942 to 1950, It was an iconic building where for the last 3 years I was in the same class room on the front corner of the top floor... but it never got stale!

Each classroom contained neatly arranged student desks with hinged tops and a hole for an ink bottle, which we never had or needed. The teachers all ruled from large dark oak desks that were strategically placed in the front of the class. A gym with a stage served as an auditorium for assembly meetings and school plays.

Every day, shortly after the school bell rang and before our lessons began, we would say the Pledge of Allegiance—none of us had a second thought about reciting the words. For a few years, we brought nickels and dimes to buy War Bond stamps that we would paste into our books until we had the requisite $18.75 to invest in a $25 War Bond—there was a lot of civic togetherness in Bailey School that colored the waning days of World War II.

The American flag was raised every day by one of the Safety Patrol 6th grade students as soon as they returned from manning their posts at five of the busier intersections within three blocks of the school. Bailey School was surrounded by freshly mown grass fields that covered the entire block. It was on those grounds where informal soccer games occupied the remaining minutes after lunch at noontime just before the afternoon bell rang and classes resumed. Competition was in the air, even in those very abbreviated soccer games.

The sidewalk around the block was our race track, being nearly a quarter of a mile in length. Every week, it seemed, there was a new challenge as to who was the fastest in the school. My only attempt to prove I was a fast guy fell flat when Sue Hodge, who would become a close friend in high school, beat me by 50 yards in 5th grade. That day I learned an important lesson: girls can often outdo boys!

Passing through the front doors of the school every day offered us a feeling of belonging. Most of us knew something of Liberty H. Bailey, the scientist, poet, philosopher, and educator whose name was carved in stone above the entrance. Bailey's name had not been picked out of a hat, and indeed he had been in attendance at the opening dedication of the school in 1923. The city's other elementary school at the time was Central School—not much cache in a name like that. Nevertheless, we were quickly labeled the Bailey Brats by our peers across town, who called themselves the Central Citizens. We figured they didn't know who our namesake was.

Liberty Bailey had grown up in the western part of the state and graduated from Michigan Agriculture College. Long before his death in 1955 he had become recognized as an exceptional botanist and horticulturist. He taught at the College for years before becoming the Dean of Cornell University's College of Agriculture. He valued work, and often commented on it:

> *"There is no excellence without labor. One cannot dream oneself into either usefulness or happiness."*

More than once our grade school teachers repeated his words, and we listened. After all, he was an expert on blackberries and pumpkins, and in those days that kind of know-how was a big deal to kids who grew these things in their own backyards.

I won the lotto with my early teachers, who made the learning experience a joy: Miss Brown for kindergarten, Miss Barr for 1st grade, Mrs. Duncan for 2nd grade, and Miss Levinson for 3rd grade. But the most important teacher I ever had was Mrs. North. She was special. For three years I sat in her class, in the same corner room on the top floor of Bailey School.

Mrs. North

Joanna North, next to my mother, was the most influential woman in my life during the first decade of my existence. I was nine years old when I began my first class with her, and she had just turned 40. She taught me in 4th, 5th, and 6th grades. Even today she continues to affect my learning. No one in her classroom received an average education.

She lived with her husband, Arvide, on a farm in Mason, Michigan, the county seat, and she drove the eight miles to Bailey School every day. She had been the sole instructor in a one-room country school for many years. Our 4th grade class was her first teaching assignment in East Lansing.

Although she always had a pleasant demeanor, her graying hair tied up in a braided bun around her head and her rigid stance in those large black shoes made her an imposing figure as she stood at the blackboard or sat behind her wooden desk near the classroom's only door into the hallway. You couldn't sneak in or out without crossing her path. Mrs. North was not one to be challenged—her earlier experience with boys and girls from five to 17 years in age in that one-room school had prepared her well in the art of keeping order in the classroom.

It became apparent after 4th grade that Bailey School did not have enough kids at my grade level for two full classrooms for the next two years. Mrs. North agreed to lead a mixed 4th and 5th grade class the first year. It must have worked well, for she kept the same students for a combined 5th and 6th grade class the year after that. She handpicked the students for each half of these classes, and I found myself in the upper half. I think she was careful to pick those who were likely to be more serious students.

Under Mrs. North's tutelage, learning became a game. Like other teachers, she taught from the book, but she was known for introducing big class projects, and showing us how to take small steps to get them off the ground—always in the right direction. Sometimes we didn't have a clue what we were about to undertake. But she convinced us that when in doubt, just take the next small step. You can't imagine the impact this had on us, as we were just beginning to explore outside our own safe boundaries of family and home.

There were some great projects. One had us learning how different countries govern themselves—but not just from a textbook. Mrs. North divided the class evenly into two groups, each half representing a different form of government—one a democracy with elected officials and a unicameral house of representatives, the other a monarchy with a king and queen and a house of lords. My classmates and I each held an office and we actually carried on as if we were the real thing: making laws, issuing edicts, and negotiating with each other over borders and trade. When we wanted to one-up each other, we had to read how it could be done civilly. What we learned about citizenship—the real and subliminal—became indelible.

Personal finance was another project where Mrs. North's creativity came forth. Her lessons went way beyond the simple story problems used to teach arithmetic in other classes, such as how to count your change when buying a few dime and nickel candy bars with a dollar. Our lessons in finance included understanding the benefits and risks of thoughtful investments.

For that project—this was in 1947—Mrs. North gave us each $1,000 in play money to invest over a period of several months. Some took the safe route and kept their windfall in a savings account with an annual interest rate of 3%. Others invested in bonds that carried a little less interest—but the interest was tax free, and in a few cases the bond's intrinsic value increased over time. The rest of the class, including me, bought stock. We consulted the market values published in the *Lansing State Journal* every week, and if we wanted, we could write to the different companies listed on the New York Stock Exchange to request their annual reports. I bought stock in a major supplier of wood for construction use, Long-Bell Lumber—I have no recollection why I choose that stock—but I made a modest killing in play money.

My investment success was subtly satisfying in that I was silently resisting my father. He never owned a single share of stock his entire life. Although he worked daily with bankers and financiers, he had witnessed a colleague commit suicide by jumping out of a window at the Penobscot building in downtown Detroit after the 1929 stock market crash. It must have hurt him deeply and he must have made a decision to never own stock. Other than this peculiarity, my dad was totally rational. But I was unencumbered by any aversion to owning stock.

There were many other Mrs. North projects, most of them focused on nature and including one about family life. It started with a mock marriage—with a kiss at the end of the ceremony that established a real "yuck factor"—and ended with our first sex education lesson, presented by an attractive student teacher, Miss Davis, who blushed more than any of the rest of us. Learning about sex was serious business, and Joanna North's lessons likely exceeded the prescribed topics in the curriculum for that year—and probably for decades to follow.

Mrs. North made learning beyond conventional boundaries fun and risky inquisitiveness less threatening. It came as no surprise that she became the first Special Education teacher in the East Lansing Public Schools a few years after her tenure at the Bailey School—a long distance from her beginnings in a one-room schoolhouse. Mrs. North lived to the ripe old age of 93. She was ahead of her time, and because of her, so were we.

Mr. Burnham

If Joanna North's influence on me was second only to my mother's during those early years, then on the male side of the ledger, Don Burnham's influence was second only to my father's. The Burnhams lived directly behind us on Beech Street and his children were neighborhood playmates. I shared many hours with his oldest son, David, who was a year younger than me, collecting things: rocks and minerals, butterflies and moths, and even a bunch of the solid elements. We seemed focused on nature and Mr. Burnham helped us set up an informal Beech Street Science Club.

My first independent, face-to-face contact with Mr. Burnham occurred when I was nine years old. I had caught a scale-perfect Imperial moth: a beautiful pale yellow silk moth with a wingspan of nearly four inches. Everyone in our neighborhood knew that Mr. Burnham collected butterflies and moths, and I gave him my moth.

Mr. Burnham had what he called a "relaxing jar" containing cyanide crystals that he used in preparing specimens for mounting. I can still remember the almond-like odor of the jar's contents—similar to the smell of my mother's hand lotion, but deadly. He kept the jar atop of the refrigerator—rather too close for some of us who had only heard of cyanide on spooky radio mystery programs. I thought Mr. Burnham would add my moth to his collection, but a week later he returned it to me on a mounting board he had made of soft pine wood and corrugated cardboard. It was ready to be removed and framed for display in my bedroom. I couldn't wait to show my parents.

On weekends, he would often pile a bunch of kids into his station wagon and we would ride to a nearby marsh or prairie to chase butterflies. There are a little over 50 butterfly species in Michigan and I have collected all but a few Satyrs. Thirty-six of my butterflies are in a display box in the entryway of our home today, from a Giant Swallowtail with a wingspan of four-and-a-half inches to tiny Hairstreaks and a Pigmy

Blue not wider than three-eighths of an inch. During my childhood, collections were the thing: It all began with my Imperial moth. Mr. Burnham got me started.

Donald C. Burnham was a remarkable individual. He attended Purdue University as a mechanical engineering student thanks to his receiving $5,000 as the winner of the Fisher Body model coach contest while attending high school in Indiana. That ornate coach was kept on display in the Burnhams' small upstairs master bedroom. It was off limits to us kids, except when Mr. and Mrs. Burnham were outside and we could sneak in and marvel at its construction. It was under a glass cover and we never touched it. Mr. Burnham had been a gifted craftsman way before building the coach. Years earlier he built model airplanes, including a winner of the *American Boy* magazine contest. The eventual reward of that competition was a meeting with the Prince of Wales and President Herbert Hoover in Washington, D.C.

Mr. Burnham and his wife, Virginia, had five children and they fit the mold of the typical "cheaper by the dozen" family, with a constant stream of neighborhood kids under tow, playing in their near childproof house. They had the first plastic tableware in the town, so broken dishes weren't the constant calamity they were in our house. Their home seemed indestructible, although David and I came close one day.

We were blowing glass bubbles from hollow glass rods, using a small alcohol lamp in the Burnhams' kitchen, with David's mother nearby. The finished bubbles were the little air containing "imps" that would float up and down in a bottle of water when a cap on the bottle was squeezed. We would make one after another and set them out in the garage to cool, a few feet away. Unfortunately, one of the bubbles we had set out to cool, caught a trash can and its contents on fire, making a real mess. Mrs. Burnham helped us put the fire out and we anxiously awaited our punishment later in the day as David's father turned his car into the driveway. The blackened trash barrel and charred junk lay on the cement in front of the garage door as a reminder of our misdeed. As he entered the door he had only one comment to David and me:

"You boys need to be a little more careful."

Mrs. Burnham may have softened him up with an earlier phone call—she was very kind. Other parents in such a spot would likely have grounded us for a few days—I was only 10 years old and David was nine. But Mr. Burnham never discouraged our inquisitiveness or industriousness, and along the way he taught us a lot about personal responsibility.

Mr. Burnham was the Manufacturing Manager and Assistant Chief Engineer of General Motors' Oldsmobile division when I knew him in East Lansing. In 1954, the Burnhams moved to Pittsburgh, where at age 39, Mr. Burnham became a Vice President at Westinghouse, overseeing the nuclear powered Nautilus submarine project. He assumed the Presidency of Westinghouse nine years later and eventually retired as Board Chair. Before anyone in our neighborhood knew about Mr. Burnham's new job, my parents had a very unusual visit by a man from the federal government who asked a lot of serious questions about the Burnhams: Did they have any political peculiarities? Did Mr. Burnham drink or gamble? My parents gave him an A+ as an outstanding citizen. Our community's loss was the country's gain.

I never saw David after their move, but he did well. He attended Princeton University, where he received an AB degree in 1961 that was followed in 1967 by a PhD in physics from Harvard. David clearly had the intellect and scientific bent of his father.

Don Burnham passed away at age 90, probably unaware of the impact he had on me and others living in his East Lansing neighborhood. But I have not forgotten.

Mrs. Joanna North at her desk in our 4th grade classroom on the front corner of Bailey School's top floor. She was also my teacher for 5th and 6th grades and was a major influence in my finding joy in learning, 1946.

Mrs. North's 4th grade classroom with me in the farthest seat (arrow) in the rear near the front windows. The room looks rather bare, but the energy and enthusiasm of everyone there exceeded anything I had experienced before or later in High School.

My 4th grade class photo on the front steps of Bailey School in 1946. I'm standing directly in front of Mrs. North. Mary Ellen Pattengill, with pigtails, was the most popular girl in class. She is standing next to our student teacher, Miss Davis.

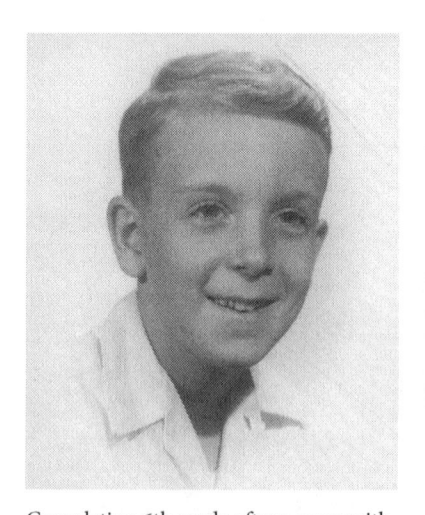

Completing 6th grade after 3 years with the same teacher, Mrs. North, was a confidence builder as 7th grade and Junior High loomed in the upcoming Fall.

Between 6th and 7th grades we traveled to the West Coast and visited five National Parks that opened a new world of wonders to me as an 11 year old, like here when surveying Yosemite National Park. 1949.

4
The Layout: Home and Neighbors

East Lansing was a college town and when we moved there we were surrounded by many who worked and taught at Michigan State. It was a quiet town; other than students, the only time you might see more than five or six people on the main street was Saturday morning, when townsfolk turned out to shop. My home and its surroundings were where I encountered a number of my most important boundaries. I'll do my best to describe what it was like.

The Home on Snyder Road

The house we moved into at 702 Snyder Road in the fall of 1943 was then only six years old—a year older than I was. Hard as it may be to believe, the house where I lived for 13 years looks the same today as it did when I left more than a half century ago.

Comfort and security existed in every corner of our home, a modest two-story wooden frame structure. It had white siding and shutters on its five front windows: two downstairs opening into the living room, and three upstairs for the two front bedrooms. There was a screened-in back porch and a small, attached single-car garage. The house was capped with a pale green shingle roof. And like my previous home, it was on a quiet, residential tree-lined street. The houses in our neighborhood looked similar—they seemed to fit together.

The front door opened into a little vestibule, no bigger than four by seven feet, with an ornate mirror on the wall that we used on the way out to be sure we looked proper. Topping a small wrought iron–legged table with a marble top was an art-deco ceramic bowl where the house

Our home on Snyder Road in East Lansing.

My alto horn and me in my Snyder Road backyard.

keys were supposed to be deposited when returning home. When we first moved in, the walls of the entranceway were covered with yellow wallpaper decorated with repetitions of an English hunting scene—men with little black caps and maroon hunting coats on horses following their dogs, chasing elusive foxes.

The entranceway wallpaper had a modest number of water spots acquired over years of wet umbrellas and coats being shaken out. As I grew older, I felt embarrassed when friends waited for me there, with the water-spotted wallpaper looking like something in an abandoned hotel. The figures on the paper were apparently a favorite of Dad's. But I didn't know that, and neither did Mom.

Years later during a summer vacation from college, I painted the entire entranceway in one afternoon as part of a chore to help out at home. I was only supposed to wash the wallpaper and get rid of the spots, but they were not going to go away, so I asked Mom if I could paint over the wallpaper. She agreed: I bought a quart of lavender paint, and it was done in a few hours. It looked great to me—but not to my father when he came home from work. He didn't bristle, but he firmly told me that I should have called him first. Had I done so, the huntsmen would still have been there. But it was a can of paint and a half day too late.

Our Snyder Road home wasn't a big house, only two rooms on the first floor. The largest was an L-shaped combined living room–dining room. The longest wall was covered with pine paneling surrounding a fireplace with built-in bookcases on either side. I first became time conscious by looking at a two-tone wooden Sessions electric clock on the mantel. A collection of my parents' books added color to the room: my favorites during childhood were a 12-volume set of the *Book of Knowledge,* the *Seven Wonders of the World*, two volumes of *Andersen and Grimm's Fairy Tales,* and neat stacks of old *National Geographic, Saturday Evening Post, Life,* and *Look* magazines.

At the end of the bookcase, near the dining area, was a chair by a small 10-inch shelf that held our home's only phone. It was a prized place, but very different from anything we're used to today. The phone was hard-wired to the telephone lines atop a pole in the backyard. No cell phone service; rotary dialing—no touch-tone numbers, no conference call features. We weren't on a party line—unlike some of my friends' families, who had to ask someone else to please hang up when they wanted to use the phone for an urgent call. Direct long-distance dialing did not exist—you had to call the operator at the Michigan Bell switchboard and request assistance in placing your call—and no area code—just 332-3234 in East Lansing. If the phone rang when you were upstairs, you had to double-time it downstairs before the caller hung up—no answering machines. Of course, we had more patience in those days. The phone's location on that small shelf attached to our bookcases in the corner of the main room of our house didn't offer much privacy.

The living area, with its davenport, easy chairs, coffee and end tables, large RCA floor radio, and tall floor lamps with soft silk shades, was a warm room with scattered red and purple oriental throw rugs covering the hardwood floors. It was open to the dining L, which wasn't really a dining area. When we moved to East Lansing, my mother brought her miniature grand piano, and it filled up most of the dining area. Many evenings, Mother would play the piano for a half hour or so after the dinner dishes were washed and put away—much to my father's delight. It was never enough to get me interested, however—"Chopsticks" was the extent of my talent as a pianist.

The only other first-floor room was the kitchen. One corner had a built-in breakfast nook with padded benches on two sides and two chairs on the others. It was a cozy spot, and it was there that we ate all our meals, except on holidays. On those days Dad would set up a table in the dining area and eating became more formal.

The scariest part of our house was the milk chute. Like many houses of the day, our chute was located on the back wall of the kitchen. It was about 18 inches square with two insulated doors, one on the outside that the milkman would open to leave fresh milk and one on the inside that we would open to retrieve the bottles delivered before breakfast. Three times a week, the milkman would traipse across our yard to get to the milk box. Although I never saw him in our backyard, I heard his milk truck start and stop along Snyder Road. It was the only thing making noise at 5 a.m. in the morning—even the birds were silent.

What made the milk chute scary was that it was also the tunnel I had to traverse when we were locked out of the house. That didn't happen often, but those occasions—perhaps no more than five times total—were memorable. Terror had no equal when Dad pushed on my legs, with my head inside and my shoulders squeezed tightly against the sides of the box until I could push through the door at the opposite end, clamber out, run around, and open the front door for my family. The milk box's steel frame was unyielding and it had been tightly nailed into the wall of the house. It was like a nightmare—I was afraid of getting stuck, unable to go forward or backward. I was relieved when I grew too big for the task and Mom and Dad had to find a place outside where they could hide a spare key for emergency use.

At one time or another I slept in all of our home's four upstairs bedrooms—two in the front, one in the rear, and one over the attached garage. All were small, each with multiple windows covered with glassine curtains, masking their opaque cloth shades rolled up. The rooms seemed inviting, light and open to the outdoors.

My parents lived in the room over the garage when we first arrived in East Lansing—slightly isolated from the rest of the house, and quiet. The room also had two walk-in closets—his and hers. Dad kept more than his clothes there.

Father's closet was where the family's guns and boxes of ammunition were stored—a 30-30 Winchester carbine, two shotguns—one 12-gauge, the other 16-gauge—two target 22-caliber rifles and several revolvers, including a 45-caliber Colt Special and a 32-caliber Smith & Wesson bulldog pistol. Dad was a great hunter, and the carbine and shotguns were there for deer, pheasants, and ducks. I remember a few birds harboring lead shot that I had to be wary of when Mom cooked them as a reward for Dad's outings with friends. The target rifles were my brother's, and he had a slew of National Rifle Association certificates earned from Boy Scout competition. I never put my hands on either of his rifles when they were loaded, but I later became an expert marksman in Boy Scouts as well.

The revolvers were a different matter. No one in my immediate family ever used them. They were holdovers from Grandfather Geist. Following his retirement as a druggist, he joined up with Harry Anslinger, who in 1930, after a successful career as a railroad policeman, was appointed the first commissioner of the Federal Bureau of Narcotics, a forerunner of today's Drug Enforcement Agency. I don't know why my grandfather joined the bureau, but he must have been very patriotic and held strong opinions about drug abuse. We have newspaper clippings describing how my grandfather apprehended some dangerous dealers who were trading in opium, and there's no doubt his Colt 45 entered into it. The bulldog pistol, along with brass knuckles and a blackjack that Dad also kept in his closet, must have been undeclared spoils of one of his arrests. We never talked much about these things—in unregistered hands they were illegal then and still are.

There were no locks or hidden cabinets for guns in those days, at least not in our home. When Mom and Dad were away, the unloaded revolvers became playthings for me and my neighborhood pals. They gave me stature with my buddies, although in retrospect, playing with them was dumb and dangerous. But times were different and attitudes about firearms were certainly more casual.

The largest bedroom looked over the front lawn, which was overshadowed by two graceful elm trees, each twice as high as our house. That bedroom was my grandmother Geist's for a few years after grandfather Geist died and she came from Detroit to be with us. She had just turned 62 when she arrived. Her room always had a sweet smell. She was diabetic and gave herself daily insulin injections using a syringe with needles that she sterilized in the flame of a small alcohol lamp. I used to visit with her before and after school and I remember watching her get ready for her shots. I have never forgotten the hospital-smell of the alcohol, which I liked.

But that smell bothered Grandma. She burned incense sticks to mask the medicinal odor, and the whole upstairs would retain that sweet smell for hours. I forgot what that smell was like until the 1960s, when incense became a popular way for the younger set to mask the smoldering hemp odor of marijuana. Grandma had lots of neat things in her drawers, too, and she used to let me spend hours going through Grandfather Geist's collection of watches, rings, and pins from the different clubs and organizations he had belonged to. Grandmother Geist had a stroke when I was eight years old, and she lived in a nursing home for a few months before dying. I missed her more than my parents ever knew. She was the one person who always had time for me when we moved to East Lansing.

That large front bedroom was occupied by my parents after my grandmother died, but became mine when I was a freshman in high school. Mom and Dad moved back to the smaller room over the garage. I think they liked its two closets. The large front room was big enough for me to display a lot of my collections on bookshelves and still have room for my study desk and floor space to lay out work projects from school.

The smallest bedroom was the second upstairs room facing the front, and that became mine when I was in medical school. By then, it was more of a holding area for things I didn't know what to do with, but didn't want to part with.

The bedroom I liked most was middle-sized and in the rear of the house, with a dormer window looking due west over our backyard. It also had a door leading to a narrow open-air porch over the kitchen, providing a wide view of the neighbors' backyards. Our own backyard was surrounded by a split-rail wooden fence with a tall swing set in one corner and a vegetable garden in the other, separated by dozens of T-roses in between. On each side of the backyard, Dad had planted large garden beds with perennial plants and annuals, backed up by more than 20 trellises for climbing roses. In July and August our yard looked like a page out of *Better Homes and Gardens*.

That back bedroom was the place to be. At night I would push my bed right up next to the window. At age nine, it was my private window to the stars. It was there, too, lying still under the sheets in summertime, that I could track approaching thunderstorms, heralded by the pungent smell of the moist grass when the first drops of rain fell.

A storm's distance could be calculated by counting the seconds between the flash of lightning and the subsequent rumble of thunder. I knew that light traveled almost instantaneously (186,300 miles per second) and that sound traveled a lot slower (about 1,125 feet per second in the summertime). So, when I counted the seconds between the visible lightning bolt and accompanying crash of thunder—"a thousand-one, a thousand-two"—I could figure out how far away the storm was. If I counted up to five, it meant that the lightning came from clouds a little over a mile away (5 x 1.125 = 5.625 feet)—right around Mt. Hope Road, on the other side of the Michigan State College campus.

We could have had another bedroom in the basement—it contained a large front room and bathroom with a shower—but instead my parents turned it into a playroom for my brother and me. Then when I was in high school, Dad took it over for his model railroad. The basement was his private domain, where from a central open area about four by six feet, he would sit for hours at a myriad of control buttons and switches, moving his Lionel trains around multiple tracks. Dad spent days and weeks laying out roads, bridges, and telephone lines, traversing a small city with stores and houses surrounded by tree-covered hills. If my brother, who went on to a successful career as a commercial artist, had the artistic genes, Dad's craftsmanship revealed where they came from.

In the other basement room, my father built a workbench, complete with an electric jigsaw and any other tools one would need to build a bookcase, repair a bike, or fix a window. But that was also where Dad impressed upon me that my most important tools were my hands—or, as he put it,

"Equipment doesn't make the athlete."

I would hear the same thing from him much later, when I was negotiating with him for a new baseball mitt or basketball.

A few words deserve mention about our home's two appendages. The first was at the end of the dining area—a screened-in back porch. I spent many summer days there with friends doing magic tricks, playing cards, and reading books. We had a metal glider that squeaked loudly when rocked too hard, but was relaxing when moved gently to and fro. When rainstorms came we dropped roll-up blinds made of wooden slats one-eighth of an inch thick and three-quarters wide. They smelled like fresh-cut wood when wet with rain, and that lasted for years. On hot and humid days as a child, I got to sleep out there, but I never felt comfortable by myself: small animals, and the foreign sounds they made when scurrying around the bushes at night, scared me.

The other appendage was our small, single-car garage. Its hand-opened doors with loud raspy-sounding hinges announced Dad when he arrived home. No electric doors in those days. The doors were much louder than any approaching car and were completely unresponsive to oiling. I really didn't like those doors. When I was with my parents, whether leaving or coming home, it was always my job to "get the door" —not a great deal of fun in the rain or snow.

The Neighbors

Six homes shared the short city block with ours on Snyder Road. Most of our neighbors were professors at the college—a fact that I didn't appreciate so much at my young age as I might have later on.

Jackson Towne and his wife lived on one corner of the block in a square, two-story brick house, painted white. He had been head librarian at Michigan State College since 1932, a position he would hold until 1959. Mr. Towne was a very formal man, which seemed appropriate for someone who spent most days cataloging books and keeping them in order. He was quite handsome and distinguished, with dark eyebrows and a full head of black hair, combed straight back and carefully parted down the middle. He always seemed to be in a coat and tie, not a speck ever out of place. He was always in control, so much so that most of us, during our early years in grade school, were scared to death of him.

Paul Krone and his family lived on the opposite corner of the block. He was a professor of horticulture at the college, and his academic specialty was the growth and nurture of gladiolas. During the summer the Krones' yard looked like a nursery, with more gladiolas than I have ever seen—or ever will. Like most gardeners and unlike Mr. Towne, his hair was never straight and always seemed a bit mussed, as if he was perpetually en route from tending his flowers. Combined with his round face and large glasses, he looked every bit like your favorite TV grandfather.

Frank A. Hopper and his family lived in the house to our immediate left when we first moved in. Mr. Hopper was a contractor and builder whose specialty was cement structures and sidewalks. He was an expert mason and his name in small block letters, "F.A. Hopper," was set in hundreds of sidewalk squares in East Lansing. After he moved, I used to brag to my classmates that I had known the man whose name was on nearly every sidewalk on our side of town—my first taste of name-dropping, perhaps. Mr. Hopper built 14 homes in his lifetime, and the Snyder Road house was one of these.

When the Hoppers moved on, the new owner was John Hoagland, a young assistant professor of business at the college, who years later achieved world recognition for his contributions to purchasing and supply-chain economics. When he was our neighbor, he was just completing his Ph.D. thesis. While that all-consuming effort was under way, the Hoaglands' dining room took on the appearance of a madman's library. Papers and books were stacked and spread out everywhere: on the table, on chairs, and all over the floor. When the Hoaglands moved to the other side of town, Clinton Cobb, a professor in the college's education school, moved in with his family. He was much more sedate than John Hoagland.

The Zimmermans lived next to the Townes. They were close friends of my parents. Mr. Zimmerman was an architect and his wife was an elementary school teacher; much more about them later.

The home on our right, between us and the Krones, was initially where Donald Wright and his wife lived. Years later, the Clanahans took over. Donald Clanahan was a professor in the college's farm crops department. His specialty was the potato. Thin slices of potato, like potato chips, were strung on strings hanging from the ceiling of his campus office. Each potato had been cut into 15 or 20 slices, following which they were separated a few millimeters by knots on the strings. That, apparently, is how they were studied in those days. It seemed to me that Mr. Clanahan was always quiet. His plain glasses and long, serious face could have convinced you he was the model for Grant Wood's 1930 portrait, "American Gothic." Wood's iconic painting of a famer and his daughter seemed to capture what Don Clanahan represented to me: Midwest morality and the never-ending work of a farmer. He and his wife had five children, including Dorothy, the middle child, who was in my high school class. She was a phenomenal trombonist and on warm nights the neighborhood air was saturated with the mellow notes from her horn as she practiced. Only in a quiet town could this be a treat.

Only one small home faced Snyder Road on the block across from ours. This was where Earl Duke and his wife lived. They were frequent bridge players with my parents and they often celebrated New Year's Eve together. Mr. Duke was an engineer at Oldsmobile. The rest of the block directly across the street from our home was a vacant lot where I could play in full view of my parents. But most of my time after school was spent on the backside of our block.

We had two neighbors whose backyards were separated from ours by a split-rail fence that always seemed in need of repair. The Burnhams' yard was a central gathering place for many of the kids. It was there, during the early evening hours of summer vacations, that we would play kick-the-can and hide-and-seek until dusk became nighttime, the streetlights came on, and we headed home for bed. I'm sure my parents relied on those streetlights more than any clock in the house—and woe to me if I stayed out too long after the lights came on.

The Rasmussens were the other neighbors with whom we shared a fence. Their yard was a great place to hide in: a veritable jungle. Professor Rasmussen worked, I think, in the animal husbandry unit at Michigan State College. He had planted an extraordinary number of trees in his backyard. It looked like a mature woods from the day we moved in. Then the Rasmussens moved out and the new folks, the Olneys, arrived.

Mr. and Mrs. Olney were a strange pair. They didn't appreciate the shade of the trees. As soon as they arrived, they cut down dozens and dozens of trees, leaving only a few along the side of the yard. They replaced the trees with a chain-link, fenced-in rectangle, about 10 by 30 feet, as a run for their boxer dog—a rather unfriendly creature that barked incessantly when we played in our backyards. David Burnham's younger sister, Joan, used to babysit for the young Olney children, although she was only 11 years old at that time. She, like the rest of us, found the boxer scary. This was not a family pet like the Burnhams' cocker spaniel, Sadie.

Mrs. Olney, perhaps in her 30s, was very attractive. She would sunbathe in their backyard for hours nearly every day of summer and got very tan. What remained, however, was an ugly yard—a stark reminder of what had been there earlier. When they eventually moved, we wished they would have taken the backyard with them. I am no zealot for conservation or preserving every bit of nature's green gift to us, but cutting down dozens of beautiful trees that took decades to grow in just a few days seemed criminal—and we kids witnessed it from our own backyards.

EAST LANSING: Late 1940's, Early 1950's

MAP LEGEND

HOMES: Some Of My Schoolmates
JCS	My Snyder Road Home
TA	Tom Astley
DB	David Burnham*
SC	'Skip' Carl
DC	Dorothy Clanahan
MLC	Mary Lou Cole
DD	Diane Denington
FD	Frank Distal
BEd	Betsy Edwards*
BE	Bruce Erickson
TE	Tom Estes
MF	Marcia Ferris
TG	Tom Grimes
GG	Gary Gross*
H	Donna Lou and Francene Hayworth
JHk	John Hecko
ScH	'Scott' Herrick
JH	John Hicks
JHb	Jane Hildebrand
SH	Sue Hodge
DH	David Hull*
JJ	James Jewell
MEJ	Mary Ellen Johnston
CJ	Carolyn Jones
JK	John Kerry
JL	John Leavitt
RL	Ron Lindell
AMc	Annette McDonald
BMc	Barry McDowell
TMc	Tom McIlrath
JM	Jack Moynihan*
LN	Linda Nugent
SN	Susan Nelson
ER	Ed Reuling*
DR	Diane Rinkes
JR	John Robson
DS	Dave Sackrider
GS	Greg Seaman
DSm	Doug Smith
VS	Vicki Smith
JS	Jim Sorber*
MAT	Mary Ann Tinker
TT	Terry Turk
SW	Steve Wilensky

HOMES: Coaches
LA	Lynn Adams
VC	Vince Carillot*
GGk	Gus Ganakas*

OTHER
ELHS	East Lansing High School (Grades 7 to 12)
BSc	Bailey Elementary School
CSc	Central Elementary School
MSc	Marble Elementary School
RCSc	Red Cedar Elementary School
PFD	East Lansing Police-Fire Department
L	East Lansing Library
PO	US Post Office
PC	Peoples Church
STA	St. Thomas Aquinas Church
BD	Business District (Two Blocks Long)
AW	Albert White's Farm and Pond

* During the ensuing years these individuals all moved to a different home in East Lansing.

5
The Town

East Lansing was the creation of the Michigan State Legislature, which in the mid-1800s bought thousands of acres of land to be the site of a new agriculture school. The Chippewa and Ottawa Indians had originally lived on this land along the Red Cedar River. The first white man to settle there was D. Robert Burcham, who became a successful trader in the late 1850s. The land the legislature purchased was heavily forested and much of it had to be cleared to make way for the new school. The first residential development was known as Collegeville. Later it was proposed that the town be named College Park, but this was not to be, and in 1907 it was anointed East Lansing, separated from the state capital by three miles of fields.

East Lansing was a very small community when we arrived in 1943. By my count, there were seven major streets: Harrison, Abbot, and Hagadorn roads running north and south; and Grand River Avenue, Michigan Avenue, Burcham Drive, and M-78 running east and west. M-78 was an extension of Saginaw Street exiting Lansing and in more recent days it carries the tag of Interstate 69. The biggest of the thoroughfares inside the city limits, Grand River Avenue and Michigan Avenue, formed a "hockey stick" dividing the town into two parts: homes and stores on one side, Michigan State College on the other.

The College

The college, founded in 1855 as an agricultural school, was officially known after 1909 as Michigan Agricultural College (MAC). By the time we arrived it had become Michigan State College of Agriculture and

Applied Science (MSC). It became a university in 1955, but the "Agriculture and Applied Science" tag remained in its title for nearly a decade. Since 1964 it has been known simply as Michigan State University (MSU). The campus, located on more than 5,000 acres of wooded land, is interrupted by open rolling fields and divided by the Red Cedar River. Its ivy-covered brick buildings created a sense of serenity and unity in what's commonly considered one of the most beautiful college campuses in the Midwest.

Downtown

The Grand River Avenue–Michigan Avenue passage through the middle of East Lansing was a classic boulevard, with grass-covered islands separating traffic flowing in opposite directions. When we first arrived, these islands, block after block, each contained double rows of elegant, towering American elm trees that had been planted in 1878. The elms' arching branches created a graceful canopy extending for more than a half mile as you entered the city from the south. Walking between the rows of these majestic trees made you feel that you were on an enchanted pathway leading to some faraway place. The view tested one's sense of reality: it was magical. The boulevard stayed that way until I left for college in the mid-1950s. That's when Dutch elm disease felled the lot of them. All the foresters in the world couldn't stop the beetle-spread fungal infection that ravaged all of the city's elms, including the two in our front yard.

The modest East Lansing business district, barely two blocks long when we first arrived, sat opposite the college on the residential side of Grand River Avenue. The central business block was boxed in by Byrne's Drug Store on one corner and the Rexall Drug Store on the other. In between was a smorgasbord of small businesses. When I was a child, any trip to downtown was a treat, especially to the hardware and sporting goods stores. Hick's Hardware had shelves stretching to the ceiling, crammed with boxes of tools and equipment. Looking at and touching all the neat gadgets and gizmos in the boxes was a joy for a kid. The owner, the father of a classmate, seemed to overlook many curious hands including mine. Almost as much fun was VanDervoort's Sporting Goods, next to the hardware store and owned by the parents of one of my brother's classmates. They had everything an aspiring jock might want. I rarely left without a sports trinket of some sort.

The fanciest place on the block was Hunt's Restaurant. It was twice as big as the other stores and was furnished with wooden tables and chairs with cane seats, always neatly placed about the dining room. Hunt's was the only place in town you could sit at a table that had white tablecloths and napkins. I felt special when we ate dinner there every few months. There were no fast-food restaurants in those days.

When I was about 10, I was allowed to go downtown on my own. No parents! At the Rexall Drug Store, as you sat on a soda-counter stool, you could get a Coke made with real syrup and see carbonated water added to the glass. The most adventurous place was Washburn's Smoke Shop, for "Men Only," a hangout for college students, where you could get a snack up front and play pool in the back. If you were older, or acted that way, you could light up a cigarette and not get caught. Most of us didn't last very long inside—Mr. Washburn knew we were too young.

Countering the stale smell of cigarette and cigar smoke at Washburn's was Norm Kessel's Florist, next door. It always smelled fresh. This was where we got our girlfriends' corsages for high school dances and olive wreaths to wear at college toga parties.

Around the corner from Byrne's Drug Store was the MAC Barber Shop. Every few weeks I would wander in on a Saturday morning and await my turn for a haircut. The best part was the wait, the half hour or so that I sat quietly and read *Popular Mechanics* or *Field and Stream* from the pile of men's magazines. No touchy-feely periodicals there—this was a guy's place. Listening to the older college boys talk about their social lives gave me a glimpse of a world quite distant from my own. It was fun. I always had my hair cut short, and usually slickened down with Vitalis Hair Tonic. No ducktail for me—it wouldn't have fit my father's persona, or my own, for that matter.

There was only one place in our city to save your money—the East Lansing State Bank, on the corner of the block opposite the Rexall Drug Store. The American State Bank and the Bank of Lansing were near the State Capitol, miles away. In the late 1940s, Dad helped me open my first savings account with a $2 deposit. It was the destination for the dollar or so I earned with odd jobs and for birthday and Christmas gifts from relatives. All of this was recorded in a small black book issued by the Bank with my name on the front page. It made me feel important. Any bank that would tolerate such a small account today would no doubt eat it up in service charges in short order.

On the other side of the central business block, across the street from Byrnes Drug Store, was a small, narrow shop where you bought new footgear. Shepard's Shoes was owned by the parents of another classmate. The store had a special machine that was a great source of entertainment to all who shopped there. You could stand on the machine's podium-like platform for 10 or 15 minutes and peer into a view box to see the bones of your feet wiggle in your shoes. The soft green light at the bottom of the viewer was like a miniature movie from outer space, your feet suddenly transformed into strange, alien creatures. It was a real fluoroscope, delivering untold amounts of radiation not only to your feet, but to everything around them—certainly too much. But what did we know in those days?

Twichell's Cleaners and Tailors, a few doors away, was another potential hazard. It always smelled richly of carbon tetrachloride. "Carbon tet" was nonflammable, and in fact was commonly used in fire extinguishers. Only one problem: it killed liver cells and was associated with liver cancer as the liver tried to heal itself. Again, what did we know?

The Pig 'n Whistle Gift Shop and the Marjorie Dee Shop were two other stores owned by East Lansing folks where you could purchase little things for your siblings' and parents' birthdays and not go broke. During those early days there were few national franchises competing with the small business owner, and East Lansing wasn't big enough to have its own Sears Roebucks or Montgomery Ward. But we didn't mind.

Evening entertainment didn't require a long drive from our home. The State Theater had the latest movies, and the college's Fairchild Theater was the place to attend lectures and plays. Absent from our quiet city was a tavern. There was no place to get a cold beer or a glass of wine with a meal. There were no stores to buy packaged liquor within the city limits, either. My new found home was dry when we arrived and remained so until 1968. It was then that a public referendum changed the city charter to allow the purchase and service of alcoholic beverages.

Until then, Coral Gables, a nearby popular eating and drinking dive just outside town, was a great habitat that met the social needs of the older college students and the younger adults around town. Many of the day's popular vocal and instrumental ensembles held roost there. Its wooden walls, overlaid with composition board, were covered with newspaper articles, event programs, felt pendants, and political posters that had accumulated over the years to create a collage of interesting historical stuff. Unfortunately, it was a tinderbox waiting to self-destruct, and in 1957 the inevitable happened: Coral Gables burned to the ground. It was replaced a short distance from its original site by a relatively plain brick and mortar building that became home to lots of older city folks, but fewer college students. It was never the same as the old hangout.

East Lansing, like most of Michigan except Detroit, was generally conservative in its ways, but we were a far cry from the Bible Belt, and on Sundays, most of the city slept in. There were two churches, St. Thomas Aquinas Roman Catholic Church on MAC, one of the wider streets in town, and the People's Church, an interdenominational Protestant church, on Grand River. People's Church was where as a youngster I went to Sunday school and my parents went to hear sermons. A few of our neighbors went to Lansing's Methodist and Presbyterian churches, and my Jewish classmates went to the synagogue in Lansing.

My friends and I sort of liked attending People's Church, for the most part: there were lots of inspiring Bible stories and pictures for the Sunday schoolers, with little about Hell and damnation. We found another reason to go to church when we reached 7th and 8th grades. People's Church was the sole sponsor of East Lansing's entry in the Intercity Junior High School Basketball League. There in was the catch: to be eligible for the team, you had to be in church at least three Sundays a month. Whether attendance resulted in greater attention to religion, I can't say.

The evenings were peaceful in East Lansing. The police station, fire department, and city offices were all in a very small red-brick building across from the even smaller, two-window US Post Office. They were located on the third major street, Abbot Road. About halfway down, it crossed the city's fourth major artery, Burcham Drive. At the juncture of these two streets, was where the junior and senior high school building was located, with its circular drive and adjacent Britton Field, where I would play football for four years.

Burcham Woods

Burcham Drive was the big road closest to our home, just one-and-a-half blocks away. Later it would be my direct path to high school, but when we first moved in, it formed the dividing line between our neighborhood and Burcham Woods.

Two open fields separated the woods from Burcham Drive. Both caught my attention. One had a towering oak tree in its center that had died many years earlier. Without leaves and having lost a lot of small branches, its remaining trunk and bigger branches took a menacing shape, like a witch's hand. At our gullible age, stories grew and spread: my friends and I were warned by the older neighborhood kids that the tree might someday reach out and grab us from the safety of the sidewalk. It wasn't until 4th grade that we knew better and could walk by the tree into the woods without being scared. But we didn't tell that to the younger ones following in our footsteps.

In the second field, near the intersection of Snyder Road and Burcham Drive, a cluster of trees surrounded what must have been the foundation of an old building, perhaps a barn. All that remained was a small pool of stagnant water that accumulated every spring from the snow melts, surrounded by a dozen very large granite boulders that must have been dragged in from the field in front of the earlier structure. They made great chairs to sit on. Diana Robbins, who lived at the end of Snyder Road, was one of my classmates in 3rd grade. She and I used to sit there with a couple of friends after dinner in the summertime, where we would talk and listen to the toads and frogs, crickets and katydids having their say—almost if trying to outdo each other. It was one of nature's most dissonant orchestras, uninterrupted by radios or passing cars. Every year this pond was where we scooped up pollywogs in glass jars, taking them home to aquariums where we watched them grow legs, lose their tails, and become tiny creatures that we let out into our backyards to catch mosquitos and other little insects. During those summer evenings, we usually stayed at the old ruin until we could see the first streetlights go on nearly a quarter-mile away, then we hightailed it home. Who wanted to be caught in the field next to the woods when darkness came?

Burcham Woods was a dense stead of mature trees. After traveling one of the few recognizable paths through the woods, you would come out the other side onto Albert White's property, including his farmhouse, barn, and a large pond. Its stagnant water was a great source of little single-cell animals for study in our science classes—like paramecium, which we observed under a microscope propelling themselves here and there with their little cilia-like legs. It was also the place where we took an old wooden door and placed it over three or four logs to make a raft that floated us out into the middle of the pond. I'm not sure how deep the water was at that point—probably not more than a few feet. But once on the water, we thought we might as well be ocean sailors. Amazingly, the Whites never told us to get away from the water. It was probably safer than it looked.

The pond's value to science, and as an adventurous stretch of water to play on, ended when it was drained and the farm sold. Albert White developed it into one of the more upscale residential areas of East Lansing, the Whitehills Subdivision. He became a wealthy and philanthropic citizen of the town. The only reminder of our earlier adventures there was Pond Road.

It was hard to get lost in East Lansing in those early days. There were only four intersections with stoplights when we moved in—but then, we didn't have much cross-town traffic. At night during the summer, with my window open, I could hear a faint hum of cars and trucks moving along M-78, the highway two miles away. Every once in a while a horn would sound and I could imagine someone crossing a lane in front of another car, or perhaps a friendly salute to a buddy going home late at night. It all seemed so far away from our quiet neighborhood.

6
Early Ownership, Pride and Peril

There were many times as a young boy that I tried to separate myself from everyone else. I wanted to be recognized. Some of my friends wore cool clothes, like charcoal grey sweaters with pink shirts and pants whose seams below the knee had been drastically taken in to give them a "pegged" look. Lots of energy spent on fads.

Those of us who weren't clothes hounds got attention in a different way. Many of us collected things, starting with baseball cards and comic books, until we had more than our buddies did. Then we went public, bragging about our accomplishment. Or we pursued laborious or high-risk tasks that generated attention to our accomplishments. It was a matter of personal pride.

Collections

No question about it: collections were separators. Ownership was an essential element of having a collection, perhaps the most important. But good stewardship came next. I took pride in acquiring a complete or near-complete set of anything that could be kept in an album, a box, a bottle, or even cans. Moreover, collections reinforced an evolving compulsion—my sense of competitiveness. I learned the art of negotiating—and a well-honed knack for "trading up." Keeping every piece of the collection in close order so I knew what I had and what I needed defined boundaries that in later years would serve me well.

My first real collecting started with stamps when I was eight years old. That was when my brother was in Japan serving with the occupational forces at the end of World War II. He would send letters home in official U.S "overprinted" air mail envelopes, different from the ordinary stamps of the day, and none of my friends had them. So by chance, I had something pretty neat that I could trade. I quickly branched out. The 1938–43 presidential regular postage stamps, with face values ranging from ½-cent to $5, were still in use, and a modest number of commemorative stamps celebrating important events or people were easy to gather from discarded envelopes on my own. In the beginning, it was just a game.

My father changed that. Initially, he gave me a Scott's catalogue that not only told the story of the individual stamps, but assigned a monetary value to each. Imagine having neighbors who gave me cancelled stamps from their old mail that had actual cash value! My father also gave me a dozen or so cancelled stamps that had been out of circulation for years. And he had lots of them: following in his mother's steps, he had been the postmaster of Lowell, Ohio, and he must have become smitten. He subsequently collected every stamp issued from 1919 to 1937, except for the rare, 1923 rotary-press 2-cent Harding stamp.

Dad also had a lot of uncancelled stamps in blocks of four, and an inch or so of sheets of the 1935 imperforate National Parks series. There was a story behind that series: President Franklin D. Roosevelt, a serious stamp collector himself, had received them as philatelic favors for himself and political friends through Postmaster General James A. Farley, who had been his campaign manager. Farley had access to stamps in sheet form before they were perforated, and he obtained many sheets for the president's personal use. When this improper behavior became known, additional imperforate sheets of the National Parks series were issued to public collectors. Dad bought scads of them.

When I was 11 years old, my father gave me all of his stamps, and I began to make my own albums. The only problem was that the stamps he gave me had become so valuable that they always had to be locked up. Today they're in our bank's safety deposit box. But before they got there I learned a lot of "rat-facts" about events and people through my collection. For example, Washington's bicentennial stamp, issued in 1932, was an easy reminder of his birth date: 1732. Did you know that 1.732 is the square root of 3? Sounds dumb, perhaps, but I remember it to this day because of Washington's birth date. Collecting stamps had quickly morphed into a lesson in politics, culture, and science.

My most ambitious collection was an attempt, undertaken with David Burnham, to sequester each of the solid elements. My interest may have been piqued by my father, who gave me a 2' x 3' poster of the Periodic Table of Elements that he purchased from the State College Bookstore. Some elements, such as the common metals—iron, copper, mercury, magnesium, lead, aluminum, and tin—were easy to acquire. We also collected small bits of tungsten, sulfur, carbon, and iodine. Other items took some finagling with an East Lansing jeweler—silver, gold, and even a 3mm square piece of platinum—all for only $2. He must have had a soft spot for two grade-school kids wanting to take on such a big project. David's dad even got us small pieces of chromium and nickel from the vats where Oldsmobile bumpers were plated. We never completed our collection, but we were on a roll.

The Periodic Table hung on my bedroom wall like a religious painting—after all, it offered a view of the world that seemed complete to me. All of this was years before either David or I were exposed to high school chemistry. On our own, we had learned about the atomic mass, neutrons, protons, and electrons of the common elements—the building blocks that compose our physical world and bind it together. I still have the cardboard box in my basement containing my prized elements. Why would I ever want to give them away?

Butterflies were a different sort of collecting, and much more physical. It was Mr. Burnham who in 1948 got me started when he mounted an Imperial moth that I had caught in our backyard. Collecting butterflies continued into my adult life. Nearly a quarter of a century later, in the early summer of 1975, my wife Nancy and I enrolled in a University of Michigan adult education course, "The Natural History of Butterflies." I had just begun my academic career as an assistant professor of surgery, and the course offered a breather from my busy schedule. The class met in a rickety third-floor classroom of the Natural History Building, a venerable campus structure where years earlier I had taken undergraduate courses in comparative anatomy and mammalian endocrinology.

Warren H. Wagner Jr., known to his friends as Herb, held forth as our instructor. He was a distinguished professor of biology and world-famous botanist whose writings on phylogenic relations in the evolution of ferns not only advanced the science of plants, but made him a cult hero to students and a revered scientist amongst his peers.

Herb Wagner was also an enthusiastic lepidopterist, something that fit well with his interest in plants. He had written or coauthored 20 papers on butterflies and possessed an extensive collection. His course met for six weeks, in the classroom and laboratory from 7 p.m. to 9 p.m. on Wednesdays, and in the field to collect specimens on Saturday afternoons. It was pure joy.

Herb was an outrageous performer who engaged every soul in the classroom. His energy was contagious, particularly for one of his students, and one of the medical school's most beloved faculty, Edgar A. Kahn. Dr. Kahn, affectionately known as Eddie, had just retired as a member of the neurosurgery faculty, which he had headed from 1950 to 1969. He was a legend, and remains so today. Independently wealthy, Dr. Kahn was the son of America's foremost industrial architect, Albert Kahn. He was also the oldest in our butterfly class at 75 years. Less than a decade earlier he had been the attending faculty on my first rotation as a surgical resident. Dr. Kahn was wiry, 5' 6" tall, hyperkinetic, and just sufficiently hard of hearing that he spoke a little louder than everyone else.

The inaugural class began with Dr. Wagner bringing in a half-dozen Schmitt boxes containing hundreds of Sulfur butterflies, arranged in rows, from a pale yellow (caught in early spring) to a dark golden orange (late fall). Fifteen minutes after he had begun to explain color variation in a given species, in walked Eddie Kahn—and not quietly. The steel-legged chairs that furnished the classroom made a creaking sound on the old wooden floor every time they were moved, and it was unlikely that Dr. Kahn heard the clatter he made as he rearranged his chair in the row directly behind me. Nor did he realize that his whisper to me was an announcement to the class:

"Jim, Jim Stanley, what the hell are you doing here?"

What might have been very upsetting to most lecturers if coming from anyone else merely provided Dr. Wagner with the opportunity to introduce Dr. Kahn to the class. Late or not that night, Eddie Kahn was treated like a visiting dignitary. In fact he was. It was a fun start.

Eddie Kahn blossomed in the class. One night he let all of us know of his amazement at learning that the iridescent blue of the Morpho butterfly's topside wings was not because of blue pigment. When he viewed the wings with a polarizing microscope, he was flabbergasted at the absence of any blue color, and in his excitement, and in a voice loud enough to be heard on the street, he managed to tell everyone in the lab about it. Of course, the blue color is due to light being refracted on microscopic ridges along the surface of the wing's otherwise colorless scales. Dr. Kahn was also mesmerized by metamorphosis: the process by which the caterpillar loses its wormlike characteristics to become a chrysalis, from which weeks to months later emerges a graceful butterfly. Neither he nor I had a clue about the cellular or molecular underpinnings of what was one of nature's most dramatic events—but then that was why we were in Dr. Wagner's class.

Eddie Kahn marveled at the senses of these small creatures. On one of the class's Saturday outings we explored a bog on the outskirts of Ann Arbor, where the Spring brood of Baltimore Checkerspots had residence. Dr. Kahn arrived in his Mercedes sedan with his wife, Rose, an internist at the university, and I pulled up behind him with my wife and two sons in tow, in our older Volvo station wagon. As the outing progressed, our youngest, Jeff, caught a Monarch that Eddie had trouble running after, and he gave the butterfly to him. It was shortly thereafter that an appreciative Dr. Kahn struck up a conversation with Jeff, bits of which I overheard. As the two climbed down an embankment, this silver-haired icon was asking our youngest son what the butterfly's antennae were for.

Jeff: "That's how butterflies know where they are." Indeed, the segmented antennae or feelers in these small creatures provide a sense of balance and smell.

Dr. Kahn's reply was a proud, "That's right, son, they're neurosensory organs." Eddie was in his element. I think Jeff got it.

Herb Wagner was instrumental in my maintaining my collection. Prior to his class, my mounted specimens were in an array of cardboard boxes, all containing Naphtha balls, usually used to keep pests from devouring wool clothes when stored over the warm months. Herb knew I wanted to be a serious collector and he gave me a dozen or so air-tight, wooden museum-quality boxes that continue to hold some of the butterflies I caught in the 1970s. They were scale-perfect then and remain so today. As for Eddie Kahn, for the next decade, until his death in 1985, whenever we would meet he would ask how my collection was going. He knew I was off to a demanding career as a surgeon, but my part in his life was established in the time we shared as classmates in Dr. Wagner's course on butterflies.

In the years to follow, I stepped into Mr. Burnham's shoes, grabbing our children and a handful of the neighbors', along with Nancy, and heading into the open fields surrounding our subdivision where we would chase butterflies. These weekly excursions were a lesson in observation and the beginning of a life-long hobby for some. Over the ensuing decades, from May to October, I always had a butterfly net in the back seat of my car, and on occasion could be seen pulling over next to a field where the hill-topping flight of a swallowtail caught my attention and became the object of a chase. Some sight: a young doctor in a white shirt and tie running after a speck of color! Butterfly collecting made me a much better observer of the little things in life.

Some butterflies have perfected the art of mimicry. Birds avoid eating tasty Viceroys, for instance, because they look like Monarchs, which have a disagreeable taste and odor and contain toxic cardiac glycosides that are ingested by the caterpillar when it feeds on milkweed before metamorphosis takes place. Other butterflies have developed wing patterns that scare off predators, like the spots that look like eyes on the forewings and hind wings of the Buckeye. And if you can't scare your enemies, hide from them: the underwings of many butterflies are so drab that they fit in with the local underbrush without notice—for instance, the brown and black underwings on the opposite side of the Morpho's blue wings, or the Anglewing's underwings, that look decidedly like bark or dead leaves. Pretty neat tricks for such small living creatures.

Many other collections always crowded my East Lansing bedroom: insignia patches, pins, and service ribbons from the armed forces that I kept in a wooden box; rocks and minerals in large New Era potato chip

Butterflies

Seashells

The Elements

Rocks and Minerals

Prized Youthful Collections: Intact more than 6 Decades Later.

cans; coins in blue Whitman folders; seashells in clothing boxes; pressed leaves in notebooks—all with little handbooks and catalogues, worn bare as I read them over and over. An awareness beyond the boundaries of my home was evolving because of my collections.

Craftsmanship

Doing something that someone else can't undo is often very rewarding, and even when the product is modest it creates a sense of pride. Doing something well completely on your very own is especially satisfying: it becomes a part of your creative soul. You can start or stop on your own without input from others. You have control of your labor. When I was nine years old, I got this kind of satisfaction from building model airplanes.

Anyone my age who has built model planes knows the drill of painstakingly starting with some simple materials and a plan, adding hours of cutting, gluing, and finishing until the plane sits there, exhibiting not a clue to the uninitiated of the step-by-step, detailed construction under its surface. My passion was building stick-models of the famous planes of the early part of the 20th century: the aircraft of World War I—the Curtis Hawk, Fokker, and Spad—and the more contemporary Valiant and Piper Cub.

My models had balsa wood-stick frames covered with a paper shell, all put together by following a tightly prescribed plan. The pieces came in kit-boxes. Step one was to place the individual wooden strips on a piece of wax paper that covered an illustrated drawing of the plane's skeleton. I cut the balsa parts to size with an X-Acto knife holding a #11 blade. X-Actos had been introduced in Poland as surgical tools, but because of difficulties in sterilizing them, they never took hold as such. The knife felt comfortable, nevertheless, and was my first exposure to exact cutting. The wood strips to be glued together often needed to be held in place by pins pushed through the plans into the underlying composition board. I usually glued a few pieces together after dinner, checking things out in the morning, and adding a few more pieces before heading off to school.

I'm sure my parents got a whiff of that wonderful acetone-based glue each morning before they heard me moving about my room. It was years before "glue-sniffing" became a sport for getting high in the drug culture days of the 1960s. I don't think I was ever affected by the clean chemical odor of the glue, but I did like the smell. Who knows? My days often started off happily. Another great odor connected with this hobby was from the banana oil I applied to the paper glued to the completed frame. When it dried, the paper gradually shrank and became taut like the skin of a drum. The last touch was to paint the paper shell with clear dope. That paint was the last of the trifecta of smells accompanying my model airplane projects.

The stick planes I built were very well balanced and could glide for long distances. Most were propelled by the unwinding of a quarter-inch rubber band anchored in the rear of the fuselage, passing forward to where it was attached to a hardwood propeller. Twenty or 30 turns of the rubber band before it was released gave the propeller enough pull to create a glide path of 20 to 30 feet.

Over two years I made six of these stick models. I flew my planes at the vacant lot at the corner of our block, and on summer days, at the school grounds. But for the most part they hung from strings tacked to my bedroom walls, where I could admire them day and night and show them off to my friends. Later in my teenage years I built planes of solid wood, usually StromBecker models, and flew them with small gas-powered engines and U-guide wire controls. But stick models were my first passion. I was proud of my handiwork: they were my possession alone, and in their making I didn't need anyone's help.

Out of Control

Why all these words about model plane building? First, these creations took hours of hard work that most might not realize. Perhaps more importantly, they later gave me a deep, visceral discomfort when something of my own making escaped my control.

The Zimmermans lived two doors from our home on Snyder Road in East Lansing. Art Zimmerman was an architect for the State of Michigan; his wife, Helen, was a grade school teacher in town. They had no children. My parents were among their closest friends and on three occasions when Mom and Dad were out of town on a business trip, I would stay at their house. And what a home it was—not made for kids like me. Helen had a collection of teacups on every end-table and shelf and not a speck of dust anyplace amid their provincial furniture. I was on more than my best behavior when I was in their home.

Helen was a shirt-tail relative of a very prominent Smith family from the east side of Michigan. They were descendants of Chris Smith, who with his two sons in 1922 founded a manufacturing firm, later known as the Chris Craft Company, that made elite wooden motorboats. They were the gems you saw at the lakeside, often popped up in the movies, and were frequently featured in fashion wear ads. One of the Smiths' sons also got housed at the Zimmermans when his parents were traveling, and he wasn't always on his best behavior. The Zimmermans put us together as playmates, even though he was three or four years older and we really didn't have much in common. One thing for sure, he seemed to have little appreciation for things that belonged to others—perhaps because he had so much of his own.

Whatever the case, when he heard about my planes, he insisted I bring them to our screened-in porch where we had been playing. As soon as I arrived with two of them, he grabbed my favorite, the Piper Club, and with a quick wind of the prop, he let it fly right into the living room. It stopped when it slammed into a large mirror over our davenport, falling broken to the floor. The major wing spar was broken in two places and the wing's ribs were torn from the overlying paper. Even the tail assembly rudder was bent in half. I'm not sure I could have wrecked it more thoroughly if I had dropped it from the city's 150-foot water tower. To say I was upset would be an understatement. But he was not the least bit apologetic. He insisted on trying to fly my other plane. Not a chance.

My father, who witnessed the whole thing and sensed I was about to blow a gasket, suggested we all climb into the car and take a quick tour of the State Capitol building. My neighbor's relative had done more than break something that wasn't his. He had, in one quick move, destroyed a creation I had spent hours and days bringing to life—as close to perfection as a nine-year-old could make it.

That day was another turning point in my childhood. Whatever I was to create in the future, I would protect from the uneducated and ignorant. It may have been a selfish shift, but I didn't want another's thoughtlessness to destroy something I took pride in completing. I liked finite doings—things that started with me, stopped with me, and stayed with me. I was going to be possessive, but happy.

Fireworks

Other attempts at being recognized by my peers didn't require the hands-on efforts that came with collections and crafts. One of these was about fireworks. Children always like bright things and excitement, I think. Sometimes we reveled in the predictable loud noise that came when we used a small rock to strike the red paper for our cap-guns, with its bits of embedded gunpowder. I can still smell the metallic odor from the expended paper.

The fascination with lights and noises that starts in early childhood at times ran away with us, especially when we got our hands on matches. Probably more often than our parents would have expected, we would get hold of a book of these little incendiary devices, light the whole pack, and jump back with delight at its three-second flare.

"Don't play with matches."

That was a common admonition to all of us as youngsters. But it only fed our curiosity and registered less as a warning than a challenge.

I'm not sure what got into my father, but one day he acquiesced when I asked him if we could build a flare out of match heads. I was probably seven years old. After cutting off the red tips of at least 50 packages of paper matches and stuffing them tightly into the cardboard cylinder from a finished roll of paper towels, I was ready. In front of our house after nightfall, Dad lit the top match with a burning stick. The flames rose up five inches or so. It was so much better than a few matches at a time. I was enthralled.

My interest was whetted. Skyrockets, firecrackers, and aerial bombs were illegal in Michigan unless you had a public permit. Since we were too young to get permits, the only way we could get our hands on real fireworks was to persuade someone who traveled to Ohio, where they were legal, to buy them for us. I was never successful going that route.

So without store-made fireworks, I took to making my own. The answer lay in the simple chemistry set I received when I was nine. What a lark! One of the most important substances in the set was powdered magnesium. That stuff would burn fiercely with potassium nitrate as an oxidizer to accelerate the flare. It was the perfect mix for a flash explosion.

The brilliant, bright light of burning magnesium was mesmerizing. It was like a string of flash bulbs. The whole room would light up, even during the daytime. When I ran out of the metal powder in my chemistry set, I resorted to whittling small ribbons off a magnesium tray in my mother's kitchen cupboard with a sharp knife. If she only knew! It was addicting.

My father was tolerant of my experiments, but as I grew older, a little bolder, and wanted to make bigger explosions, he told me a story that set me back. It was about a young man named Daniel (Danny) Dodge. He was the son of John F. Dodge and his wife, Matilda. His father died when he was only three years old and it's possible he never was told not to play with matches.

Danny Dodge was the heir to the Dodge Motor Company fortune. In 1938, the year I was born, he was 21 years old and reportedly worth more than $10 million—perhaps $150 million in today's money. Naturally, most of his friends considered him to be very lucky. He was on his honeymoon at a lodge he owned on Manitoulin Island in Ontario when luck deserted him. Danny had wed Laurine MacDonald, a 19-year-old native of the island, less than two weeks earlier in a fancy ceremony at Meadow Brook Hall, his family's home near Detroit, which his mother and his stepfather, Alfred Wilson, had built a decade earlier.

On that fatal day, Danny found himself toying with dynamite sticks that had been left in an old piano box. They were probably leftovers from excavating the lodge's basement. At the time he was in the carriage house and had thrown a lit stick from the garage, when either sparks from the stick or something else ignited an unseen pile of nearby dynamite. Danny, his wife, and two others were seriously hurt. He was knocked unconscious by the blast, mortally injured.

I'm not sure it was true, but my father told me that Danny Dodge had nearly blown his arm off. It was reported that his wife and another woman who worked at the lodge put tourniquets on his limbs to stem the bleeding. Others at the lodge loaded him into the back of his 250-horsepower speedboat and they headed across Lake Huron to the town of Little Current, where medical help was available. The weather was horrific and the boat had to plow head-on into four-foot chop to make the passage.

Then it happened. Danny stood up in the back of the boat, and either fell or jumped overboard into the cold waters of the lake. The others frantically circled about in the stormy waters. They said they saw him but couldn't reach him. He drowned. His waterlogged body was found 23 days later. That story, told to me in my father's most graphic manner when I was only 10, stuck. I never again played with fireworks, either store-bought or handmade. But there's a bit more to the story.

Meadow Brook Hall, the place of Danny Dodge's wedding, was a palatial, 110-room Tudor mansion surrounded by nearly 1,500 acres of rolling hills. In 1957, his mother gave the entire estate to Michigan State University. It has since become part of Oakland University and the house itself is used for special events, fundraising affairs, weddings, and the like. I have been there many times. It's a wonderful place, with Mrs. Wilson's and her family's furnishings kept intact in each room. My most important visit to Meadow Brook occurred three decades after my father's warning. It was a very unusual weekend.

I was an assistant professor at the University of Michigan and was presenting a paper on renal artery disease at a three-day meeting of hypertension experts from around the country. At the time, I didn't know that the Wilson estate and Meadow Brook Hall had belonged to the Dodge family or had any relation to the story my father had told me. You might imagine my emotions when I learned that the room assigned to me had been Danny Dodge's. For two nights I slept in his bed, trying to fall asleep with my head on the pillow and my eyes on a nearby Norman Rockwell sketch of an early airplane. It was an original. Those were restless evenings. It had been a long time since my father's warning, but his words echoed that night:

"Don't let what happened to Danny Dodge ever happen to you."

I didn't forget. Nor had my father. When he was a young teenager, he had been burned when a canister containing TNT exploded while he was standing over it. A group of his friends had gathered a few pounds of black powder, likely left over from mining operations in the area, and lit a fuse before running to safety. When it failed to go off, Dad went to check it out. The ensuing explosion caused extensive superficial burns to his face, hands, and arms. He spent months that summer wrapped in dressings soaked in tannic acid, prescribed by a local physician who had developed an interest in similar injuries during World War I. Dad was left with black pocks of powder scattered here and there under the skin of his arms—and a determination that something of that sort would never happen to one of his own.

My children never got chemistry sets and we never had fireworks around the house. We watched July 4th celebrations from a distance. We were safe.

7

Six Years' Start

My introduction to high school was a time of personal turmoil—as it was for so many kids. I quickly lost the comfort of my old grade-school friends and instead had to form new friendships with schoolmates from other parts of the city.

Entering the Big Building

The number of students in my new school seemed immense, stretching from 7th to 12th grade. We had no middle school or junior high in East Lansing in 1950. As 11- and 12-year-olds, we were just thrown into a population at vastly different stages of adolescence. Although we suddenly had older role models to emulate or ignore, as we wished, they often bumped into us without warning in our new school's hallways. At the start we didn't know where our boundaries were.

It didn't take long to recognize how different the next six years would be. Moving from one room to another every hour with a different teacher was the biggest change. And grades, sometimes based on a curve, generated competition that was not always peaceful. Other things were different, too: my voice changed and girls became more than playground teammates. Social differences emerged, sometimes painfully. All of this happened in what appeared to me to be a gigantic place, so huge that the first few weeks seemed like a visit to a cavernous warehouse in another world—not at all like my old haunts centered around the same elementary school desk with the same teacher every day. None of us exhibited a lot of moxie or confidence in our new station.

East Lansing High School on Abbott Road was built in 1927 and was

Six Years' Start 75

East Lansing High School. where I passed through 7th to 12th grades and walked the halls from 1950 to 1956 before graduating and speaking at our class commencement.

a ripe 23 years old when my classmates and I started 7th grade. It was a long, three-story building behind a wide field of grass, bisected with a narrow circular drive from Abbott Road that passed in front of the school and exited to the south onto Evergreen Avenue. The building had all the accoutrements of the day: a small library; physics and chemistry rooms with central black-top tables for experiments; a home economics room with stoves and sewing machines; a tiny auditorium with an even tinier balcony for school plays, concerts, and assemblies; and a gymnasium for physical education classes, basketball games, wrestling tournaments, and of course, class dances.

A multitude of rectangular and square classrooms for didactic teaching comprised the bulk of the building. The front-center door led into a short hallway giving access to the principal's and school administrators' offices, keeping nearby raucous behavior to a minimum as we first entered the building. Later, a two-story addition was tacked on to the building's north end that contained classrooms where I took art and mechanical drawing.

Another big difference in our lives that first year related to our hallway lockers. They gave us a newfound sense of privacy that, in my case, was only breeched once. I haven't forgotten that occasion. We all had combination locks, but you had to shut the door tight for the lock to engage. One day early in the year, Vicki Smith left her door ajar as she headed off to class, and a few of us took all of her books and gym equipment from the bottom of the locker and piled them onto the overhead shelf—so precariously that it would all fall if it were not for the door to hold everything in place. When Vicki returned at noon and opened the locker, her possessions fell unceremoniously to the floor with a clatter that everyone could hear—especially the perpetrators who stood by smiling. I was standing next to her and had a grin on my face. Not smart on my part. Vicki hauled off and slugged me in the face—just once. But for the next week I sported a black eye—received from a girl, no less. Locker doors were always shut after that day, and everyone treated Vicki Smith with a lot of respect. I, of course, was embarrassed.

The majority of the entering 7th grade class arrived from one of East Lansing's two established elementary institutions, Bailey School and Central School. But our class also had students from the new Red Cedar School on the other side of the Michigan State campus and a few from Marble School, whose kids were from more rural areas.

Gender-wise, my class was a bit of an anomaly. When I first entered the big building there were 47 boys and 65 girls in my class, and when I left six years later, there were still 47 boys but, by then, 78 girls. A more normal distribution would have been just a few more girls than boys. Our predecessor, the class of 1955, had 59 boys and 55 girls, and the class of 1957, 65 boys and 68 girls. There was no obvious explanation for why our class was different.

East Lansing High School was a hike from my Snyder Road home—seven-tenths of a mile each way, to be exact. For five years until my senior year, when I had a car to get me to and from school, I had to walk or ride my bike, whether rain or shine, sleet or snow. I had a new bicycle in those days, replacing an old and rusted one inherited from my brother Bob. It was a cool scarlet and grey Schwinn that my parents gave me in 7th grade. The trek to school was always the same: one turn to the left and one turn to the right. Those trips, by my calculation, amounted to at least 1,120 miles over those first five years. They were never a burden, perhaps because the destinations of school and home were both happy havens.

My mother used to watch me start off to school every morning with John Leavitt or Dave Hull, peering at us until we disappeared with our first turn two blocks away. Some of her parting admonitions have never left my mind: "Zip up your coat, you'll catch pneumonia," or better yet, "Stand up straight when you walk, don't let your shoulders stoop. You'll get arthritis." After almost 50 years of bending over patients on the operating-room table, it seems I am always a bit stooped-over, but no big-time back trouble to date.

In 1956, my graduation year, a new high school for the upper-class students opened its doors on Burcham Road and our old school became the junior high. It remained that way until 1996, when the city completely renovated the building to become the Hannah Community Center, serving the entire East Lansing community to this day. It was named in honor of John Hannah who was president of Michigan State University from 1941 to 1969 and whose children, a few years younger than me, had sat in the building's classrooms.

Latitude Reined In

The first unexpected challenge I faced in my new school came the initial week of 7th grade, with my homeroom teacher, Alexander Purvis. Mr. Purvis was an exchange teacher from England and he usually wore cardigan sweaters or tweed coats. He had thinning hair combed off to the side and the pale, pasty cheeks of someone who had never been outside in the sun, suggesting a rather meek personality. He looked the role of a "Brit."

We were in the process of electing classroom officers, and some of us guys got together on who we would vote for. We had to give a nudge to a few of the others who didn't initially see it our way and that often led to rather loud and animated discussions. There was no conspiratorial murk—it was just backyard politics to us, something that "everyone did." That day, however, we were within earshot of Mr. Purvis and our antics did not sit well with him.

Although he was usually quiet and composed, what we didn't see was that when pushed too far, Mr. Purvis could become quite stern. He detested cliques, conspiracies, and crowd manipulation, and while our attempt to round up votes might have been acceptable to us, it wasn't to him

Mr. Purvis had lived in London and experienced the fires and destruction wrought by the cluster explosions of Germany's incendiary buzz-bombs dropped on his homeland during the war. It was a long stretch, but without much warning he admonished us not to march down the path of the Nazi leaders who a decade earlier mobilized and controlled the German people for their own perverse cause. Mr. Purvis believed we were attempting to coerce our classmates to vote for our slate, rather than allow them their own independent judgment. And that was not going to stand in his class.

Whatever the fairness of his analysis, Mr. Purvis established himself as a strong teacher. He lost his pallor. After a half-hour of his forceful soliloquy, we all understood. The need for transparency as a marker of freedom was a simple concept. That was my first week in the big building: new opportunities, but also new boundaries.

8
Mediocrity

As adolescence approached I found myself constantly being judged and it was an uncomfortable feeling. My childhood had been rather carefree and personally unchallenging. But with my teenage years came a realization that just showing up and being there was not going to work.

Childhood Ends—Adolescence Beckons

In 1946, after the last days of World War II, we were once again in Middle America: eating, working, and sleeping like everyone else. With the war behind us, there was no more collecting lard and scrap metal, or even milk weed pods to be used for life preservers, and no more watching my parents count the rationing stamps needed to buy meat, butter, and gas. When the soldiers returned from overseas they were greeted by an explosion of new jobs and career choices. The country had grown in their absence. Kids such as I felt the difference too: the rules of life seemed less onerous—at least, parents' expectations of their children seemed modest. It would have been easy and acceptable to be average in those days. But that was about to change.

Dad gave me lots of freedom to explore during grade school, but as high school neared, he began to set some subtle boundaries. For one thing, he never let me forget to respect my name. As I was entering my teenage years, whenever I went out for the evening, he would remind me:

"*Don't forget your name is Stanley.*"

He was not hinting that I should consider myself a bit special or better than someone else. He was just passing on a not-so-subtle reminder to keep my nose clean and stand tall. Trouble was always just around the corner. My father knew that. He did not want me to do anything dumb or regretful.

69 Inches

I was never the biggest or strongest and certainly not the first picked when we divided up to play ball as kids. Sometimes I was the last picked, bypassed until I was the only one left. That always hurt, but even being one of the middle choices gave me a certain angst. After all, if I was in the middle, I was also halfway to the bottom, where I was likely to be overlooked.

I wasn't always ignored, even though there were times I wished I had been. In fact, unless you've gone through it yourself, it's difficult to grasp the pain of being taunted by the others when you're not big enough to push back. The old cliché, "Sticks and stones may break my bones, but words will never hurt me," is just not true. More than once I had to listen to "Stan, Stan, the garbage man; stole a pig and away he ran." I never found out where this came from or exactly why some of the older kids laid it on me, other than as entertainment for themselves. The sound of their laughter as I turned away from them is still with me. My response was to run home and hide in my bedroom, hurt and not wanting to tell my mother or father what was bothering me.

Feeling self-conscious didn't stop as I entered high school. To this day I wish I had been born in December rather than September—I would have started school a year later, making me a year older than most of my classmates and, presumably, closer to them in size. It might have made it easier for me to be more competitive, especially in the football, a sport I loved. My classmates, in general, were bigger and stronger. I never have gotten over a coach's quip to my dad during a post-game dinner in the school cafeteria, catered by the parents of the football team.

"He needs more meat and potatoes."

I was a junior and I certainly ate, but not much happened until my senior year, when I finally reached 160 pounds. Even then I wasn't as big as most interior linemen and brute force was not going to carry me to success in football. But I learned to compensate for my stature by playing on the edge. When I could get away with it, I would straight-arm an opposing player up the middle, and that quickly equalized any difference in our sizes—more often than not, taking him to the ground. I was only flagged once for this. But it felt good to lay someone bigger than me flat on his tail. Nevertheless, I was still small.

When I was 17 years old, my lower-extremity long-bone epiphyseal plates closed and I stopped growing. I was as tall as I would ever be: five-nine, or 69 inches. I rationalized that wasn't so bad—the average height of an adult male in the United States at that time was exactly 69 inches. But population-based statistics didn't help me much. Reality set in when I went to college and most of my friends were taller.

At times I wondered if the rest of the "short guys" just lived in some other part of the United States. But this farfetched notion blew up years later, when I was called to serve in the army after my internship. I joined other well-educated physicians from all over the country at Camp Bullis in Texas for basic training. When 60 of us lined up by height in a company formation, I found myself the second shortest. The shortest, as it happened, was Woody Allen's psychiatrist. Unbelievable: the only recruit who was shorter than me was a guy from New York City who talked incessantly about Allen's peculiarities. His banter was inappropriate, but I'm glad he was there. He kept me from being last!

"No Gentleman's Cs"

Although my size was not under my direct control, my studies certainly were. My father would not tolerate my coasting through a class without trying and settling for being an average student. That became obvious as I entered 7th grade. His edict, which I heard many times in the succeeding years:

"No gentleman's Cs."

This was his definition of mediocrity. Dad probably knew I could pass through some courses without working up much of a sweat. However, bringing home a C was going to require a lot of explanation—more explanation than I could comfortably muster. It was easier to work hard and do better. I never received a C in high school. Dad had clearly marked off a boundary, and I heeded it.

"70% Won't Serve You Well"

I received further lessons about mediocrity in my industrial art class, better known as shop class. Lynn Adams was the teacher. He was also the athletic director, my freshman football coach, and my track coach. He was a goal-oriented taskmaster and a rigorous instructor, both in class and on the field. I got to know him well, as I was his student every year of high school.

Mr. Adams always wore a light blue dress shirt and a solid colored tie. His suits were neat and his appearance was more that of a businessman than a teacher. His round face, accented by thinning grey hair combed straight back and silver-rimmed glasses, repeated itself day in and day out, from the time my brother ran track for him a decade before I did, to the day of my graduation.

Mr. Adams exhibited no elite mannerisms; he was just a solid teacher and an honorable man. He was also the glue of the school, holding the longest tenure of any of the faculty. He often was recognized as the ballast that helped any number of teachers facing classroom struggles and students with study problems.

He abhorred mediocrity, and often reminded classes before an exam that there was always room at the top. Clearly, he expected everyone to try to get there. One day, after returning an exam on which a majority of the class had done poorly, Mr. Adams became indignant. With a distasteful grimace, he warned us:

> "Seventy percent may be passing in this class, but being correct 70% of the time won't serve you well if you work at the bank."

He was right. There is little value in just passing, especially if the stakes are high, as they often are in life—a lesson I was reminded of decades later, when teaching young resident surgeons how to operate. Just passing in the operating room won't do it. Mr. Adams had defined mediocrity: it was 70%. It came as no surprise to me when the athletic field at the new high school was named the Lynn C. Adams Stadium. That was a small honor for a teacher who was much more than a leader in athletics.

Keeping my grades up might have convinced me that I was not average, but life had other boundaries to remind me that I wasn't so great. I recognized this and became competitive within myself. I wanted to find excellence. It was at times much harder than I thought it might be, and that was painful.

9

Rules For Winners and Losers

Certain rules help you survive: they are big deals. Others keep you comfortable. Some rules seem to exist to help others more than yourself. As a kid, separating the important rules from the trivial ones was difficult. My childhood and adolescence exposed me to a variety of rules, and I didn't always recognize their value until later. Many became boundaries of my everyday life—at home, at school, and elsewhere.

House Rules

Our home, no doubt like most of my friends', had a lot of rules: edicts from parents. These were real rules to be heeded, not the thin guidelines that many families offer to recent generations of children. Some of these rules were simple:

> *"Eat the rest of your vegetables and then you can have another glass of milk."*

Most were said repeatedly and never written down, yet they were every bit as clear as if set in stone. They were probably in my best interest: brushing my teeth, washing my hands, buttoning up my coat on cold days, getting a good night's sleep.

Some were strident, but wrong:

> *"Don't read in the dim light; you'll hurt your eyes."*

It took me nearly two decades to debunk this endlessly repeated admonition from my mother, which compelled me to trade a soft spot on the floor for an uncomfortable chair at the dining table where the light was better. It proved to be an old wives' tale. During my third-year medical student ophthalmology rotation, I learned that while reading in poor light may tire your eyes, it will not harm them. How upset my mother would have been if I hadn't followed her advice—yet, how painful it was to sit on that hard dining room chair!

Other rules were meant to keep order in the family and keep others from having to expend an inordinate amount of energy on my upkeep:

"Clean up your room first, and then you can go outside to play."

I heard that one at least every other day for years. I probably had one of the neatest bedrooms in the neighborhood, and certainly the neatest in our home. In that regard my behavior approached the American Psychiatric Association's definition of an obsessive-compulsive personality disorder, at least as it pertained to organizing my piles of bedroom junk. But my mother had no time to be constantly straightening up anything of mine. That was my job, and the rule was that I did those things before moving on.

House duties that benefited me were often laborious but tolerable. Work rules assigned to me that might have been more appropriately applied to others felt like punishment. I rarely differentiated the two as a child. As I grew into adolescence, however, most rules became part of a game. I learned to use them to my advantage. It took a while.

Points and Ribbons, But No Eagle

An important institution helping me find my way from childhood to adolescence was Scouting. The Boy Scout motto, *"Be prepared,"* was easy to embrace and made great sense to me in school and in dealing with family and friends. Why would anyone want to be unprepared for anything? And the Scout Oath was a reminder of the oft overlooked characteristics of being a good and useful human: *"On my honor, I will do my best, To do my duty to God and my country; To obey the Scout Law; To help other people at all times; To keep myself physically strong, mentally awake and morally straight."* And of course, the Scout Law reinforced the creed: *"A Scout is trustworthy, loyal, helpful, friendly, courteous, kind, obedient, cheerful, thrifty, brave, clean, and reverent."* These were frequent reminders of what was expected of my behavior.

Try these on a child of today's more liberal culture and see if they fit!

Established in the United States in 1910, Scouting had existed for less than 35 years when I first wore the blue uniform as a Wolf in Den 2 of Pack 201, but its emphasis on achievement was already a familiar part of the culture. We took pride in advancing to the Bear and Lion ranks and in all the little arrows sewn on our uniforms for well-defined projects, which our den usually completed during meetings after school at the home of Dick Childs, a classmate. His mother was our den mother. Cub Scouts introduced me to a not-so-subtle message—"Work results in rewards." Today, personal growth often seems to be measured in personal satisfaction, rather than personal accomplishment. But that was not for me in those days.

I was a Cub Scout in Den 2, Pack 201, and a Boy Scout in the Panther Patrol of Troup 21 at Bailey School.

After three years as a Cub Scout, I became a Boy Scout in Troop 21. That was in fall 1949, when I was 11 years old. Troop 21 started at Bailey School as World War II came to a close. We were the new kids—the third troop in East Lansing, following Troop 12 at Central School and Troop 2 at People's Church, the oldest of the three, which had been founded in 1921. During the school year we had weekly meetings from 7 p.m. to 9 p.m. Dues were a nickel a meeting, which got you marked as "present" on the scribe's books. If you maintained perfect attendance for a year, you got another award: a small gold star with the number of years you had gone without missing a meeting. My gold star had a "3" in the center of it: just being present counted. But you needed more.

Three lessons embodied my growth as a Scout.

Lesson #1 was simple: Learn the rules. Elementary and junior high had plenty of rules, but most were simply what you were expected to do to stay out of trouble. If a reward was to be had in school, it seemed far off and at times ethereal. Not so in Scouting, as I learned at the 1952 Little Valley Forge Camporee.

The camporee was a mega-five-day camping adventure in southern Michigan for hundreds of experienced Boy Scouts. It started off with the raising of the American Flag, followed by a broadcast of Irving Berlin's "God Bless America," sung by Kate Smith, a generously proportioned entertainer who had sung her signature song to millions, including the armed forces overseas and homeland television audiences. The camp's speakers projected her voice at a deafening level. The ground seemed to shake. Everyone got it: patriotism was the thing. This was Americana at midcentury.

Each day there were organized events: some taught us how to rough it in nature, some to challenge our physical and mental capacities, and others to relax. The former included a compass course and knot-tying competition. The latter was fun and included swapping patches from different camping events, jamborees, and scout-o-ramas with kids from other councils. These were all sewn on our unofficial vest that for some of us was a kaleidoscope of color and a real source of pride—like the decals that our suitcases acquired from faraway places we visited with our parents or the pins from sporting events we wore on our school jackets. They all had their designated place.

Greg Seaman, Frank Distal, and I represented the Panther Patrol of Troop 21 at the camporee competitions. We were by now pretty skilled campers and thought we could hold our own in some of the contests, but discovered we had an additional advantage: we knew the rules by which the competition would be judged. While these rules were available to all of the scouts, we paid more attention. Such simple items as airing out your sleeping bag every morning and keeping a pail of water near your campfire—just in case—got you points, even if they made little practical sense. For instance, you could lash a long stick to two short ones planted in the ground and use it for a stand to hang your wet boots so they would dry out quickly. That was good for two points. It hadn't rained for weeks and no one was walking around the dusty campsite in wet footgear. Nevertheless, we built the stand and earned points that no one else got.

Then there was the shower, made by lashing three eight-foot sapling trunks together, like the tent poles of a teepee, and finishing it by hanging a large coffee can with holes punched in the bottom, with another can, intact, hanging above it. If you filled the top can with water, then tipped the water into the perforated can by pulling an attached rope, you had a working showerhead—and 10 points. Who would ever need a shower next to their campsite, when every day we all paraded into a modern building in the center of camp to shower and clean up? But we built the shower and got points that no one else considered.

The result was that we won the award for best patrol at the camporee: we picked up points in all the expected ways, but at the same time we completed an assortment of more unusual tasks that were listed among the judging criteria: the "rules." As an award, we received a great pendant to hang on the top of Troop 21's scout flag, which we displayed at our weekly meetings. It was an important lesson. Knowing what's expected of you, and working to meet those expectations, has real value: something good to remember as we entered our turbulent teenage years, when getting distracted from the rules was easy.

Lesson #2: Always figure out the simple way to make a tough task easier. Morse code, using dots and dashes, had always held great prestige within Scouting. The catch is learning the code. My contemporary *Boy*

Scout Handbook had nothing in the way of tips, just a table of the letters of the alphabet and the corresponding dots and dashes. Luck came my way in the form of my older brother's *Handbook*, an earlier edition with a single page of cartoon-like drawings for each letter, making them easy to remember. For example, the letter "A" was accompanied by a round apple hanging from a straight branch (a dot-dash), while accompanying the letter "R" was an old-fashioned roadster car with an accentuated round front tire, then a straight running board, followed by the round rear tire (dot-dash-dot).

This form of mnemonic learning was a treat. The drawings for each letter were so easy to absorb that after a few hours I had the alphabet code down cold. Greg Seaman and I walked away with first place in the camporee signaling competition. My brother's old *Boy Scout Handbook* had given us a simple way to make a tough task easy.

Ten years later, in 1960, as a freshman in medical school, I came across something similar. We were learning the 12 cranial nerves: olfactory, optic, oculomotor, trochlear, trigeminal, abducens, facial, auditory (now labeled the vestibulocochlear), glossopharyngeal, vagus, spinal accessory, and hypoglossal. For the uninitiated medical student overwhelmed with a host of rat facts, naming these 12 nerves in order was a challenge. But the pain was lessened by a saying that someone in our past had circulated: "On old Olympus's towering top, a Finn and German viewed some hops." The first letter of each word gave a clue to the name of the nerve.

Mnemonics are a great help for recalling the more complex words, and there are many other examples, some rather risqué. Take the vestibulocochlear and vagus nerves, and make a sentence with the words virgin and vagina and any other words beginning in o, t, a, f, g, and h. Some sayings were so politically incorrect that most of us wouldn't admit they helped us become doctors. Today, in caring for the elderly who are experiencing the first signs of forgetfulness, a doctor or family member can help them maintain their recall using similar associations, mnemonics in both words and pictures—not too different from what I first learned in Scouting.

Lesson #3: Never shirk at getting the essential things done first. Seven months after being a Tenderfoot—the first level of rank in Boy Scouts—

I advanced to Second Class Scout, and after an additional seven months, I achieved the rank of First Class. After that, merit badges became the basis for advancement, and three months later I was a Star Scout, and a Life Scout eight months after that. Six months later, just two and a half years after entering Boy Scouts, I had 28 merit badges and held the highest leadership position a boy could hold in the troop. I had become the Junior Assistant Scoutmaster.

I had two great scout masters. John McIntosh was a graduate student at Michigan State and along with some of the dads, he led us on phenomenal camping trips to Rose Lake, a four-mile hike from our homes with our gear on our backs. William Sharp was my second leader. He had just joined the East Lansing Police Force. As a scout master he had the patience of a saint and helped many of us get over the bumps of early adolescence. In 1963, he left the police force to entered business, but East Lansing was the fabric of his life. Bill Sharp later served on the School Board for 12 years and on the City Council for 13.

In 1952 the rule was that you needed a total of 21 merit badges to reach Eagle Scout, including several required badges. The one I had yet to receive was swimming. I was a crummy swimmer and rather than go over to the pool at the college or the YMCA in Lansing to practice, I procrastinated. One day at a time, I put it off, until finally I waited too long. The rules for becoming an Eagle Scout were revised to include a whole new set of required merit badges, such as Citizenship in the Nation and Citizenship in the World. I became discouraged for there was no way for me to easily catch up when school activities were competing for my time. I was wiped and quit scouting. I was in 8th grade.

I was—and still am—proud to have been part of the scouting movement. I still have the cards for each merit badge and rank, signed by the council staff, H.J. Ponitz and C.A. Neiz, to remind me of many happy days. But they also remind me of what I missed: becoming an Eagle Scout.

I didn't think too much about it until my last years as an undergraduate at the University of Michigan. My roommate at the time, Ron Gregg, was president of the student government. He had also been an Eagle Scout. Every day he would lay his Order of the Arrow sash on top of his dresser and place his Eagle Scout badge on top of it. The Eagle badge

The opportunity to achieve on your own and advance through the Scouting ranks generated a modicum of self-confidence. I became the Junior Assistant Scoutmaster of my Troup when 13 years old and I had 28 merit badges on my sash, but I was one required merit badge short of becoming an Eagle Scout; a regret I carry to this day.

was almost like a religious medallion for him, and clearly something of immense personal value and importance. I was impressed with Ron, for what he was doing as a student and for having achieved the highest rank in Scouting. The two may have gone hand in hand.

Many other successful people have attributed a portion of their achievements to their Scouting experience. Some are politicians, some writers, others explorers. Among the 12 astronauts who traveled to the moon, 11 were Boy Scouts, including Neil Armstrong, an Eagle Scout who was the first human to set foot on the moon. For my generation, the most significant boundary to escape was the confines of Earth, and a bunch of scouts did it. I remain a little envious of those who don't let conventional boundaries hold them back, like gravity or, in my case, swimming. But I learned my lesson, and I can't think of a steep challenge that I have dilly-dallied over since my days as a Boy Scout.

Five-Card Draw

A deck of 52 cards was my first introduction to quick counts, predictions, and "going for it" with a calculated risk. Playing cards was going to require more than luck. I also had to know and follow the rules. It all started with the game of fish in my early childhood and progressed to canasta as my teenage years approached. Most often I played cards with neighborhood friends, but on occasion I'd join my parents when family plans were aborted, such as a rained-out picnic or canceled trip to the movies.

One evening, lightning struck a transformer, leaving our part of town without electricity. A card game by candlelight that night unmasked my intensity and desire always to win. We were playing canasta, my mother, father, and I. The deck had been frozen for a long time, and it looked like one of us was going to pick up the whole lot of cards with the last few moves. Dad did it, raking in the pile. The game was over. My reaction, in a dark and very silent living room, was loud and unrehearsed:

"Damn!"

That was the first time I can recall that my parents heard me swear. Cussing at school, in the locker room with guys, might have passed my parent's attention, but not at home. I was 11 years old and got a quick earful from my mother. Dad was silent. I rarely heard a cuss word leave his lips, but I was confident that he too could swear, especially when he was with his political buddies and Mom was not around.

Two lessons learned. First, while an appropriate use of a cuss word could express my emotion better than a much longer exposition using less offensive language, I should first think about my audience and be sure they will get the point before uttering anything. Second, in games of pure chance, I was not always going to win. In the long run, my rate of success—like anyone's—would tend much more toward the average. So when it came to cards, it seemed wise to pick a game in which some additional element of skill could make a difference. As the years passed, that game turned out to be poker. Here was a contest in which it was important for me to know my cards, hedge my bets according to the odds, and know when it made sense to bluff—or not. Poker gave me confidence. As a teenager, I was never a mediocre poker player.

I am not sure when our regular poker games started, but by the time my friends and I were juniors in high school, we were spending a couple of hours a few nights each week playing cards. It was a social thing, but it also met our need to compete at a relatively low level of risk—for some of us, anyway. Usually, four or five of us would gather about a kitchen table or basement recreation table and play either five-card draw or seven-card stud. We solved a lot of school problems during the hours we sat together, but we were serious about the game, and serious about winning.

We usually played in the kitchen at Scotty Herrick's or in the family room at Gary Gross's home. We also spent lots of time in Ron Lindell's and Jack Moynihan's basements. On a number of occasions, when my parents would go to New York City for the weekend, the whole gang would come over to our house and we'd set up two tables and play until 2 a.m. or 3 a.m. in the morning. These sessions, during our senior year, included a few cases of beer bought by a classmate's older sibling. The house would be a mess after two nights, but everyone chipped in to clean up. When my parents returned on Sunday, Mom often said:

"Thanks for cleaning up the house. You didn't need to." If she had only known!

Most of the games were strictly for fun. We played by house rules, and frequently the dealer would call deuces or one-eyed jacks wild. Some of us got the hang of the game quickly. I bought a copy of *Oswald Jacoby on Poker*. He had published a lot on card games and was a world-class bridge player. Some of his suggestions on betting and improving the odds of assembling a good hand may not have held up under strict scrutiny, but everyone knew I had read the book, and sometimes that persuaded them to back away from my betting, figuring I understood something they didn't. A short read and loud talk about something new often creates an illusion of knowledge and competence. I usually got away with it.

A half-century later, I often find it difficult to listen to someone pontificate about something I know they don't know much about. But in the early 1950s, the reissued 1947 book by Jacoby served me well by reinforcing my bluffs and guiding me to bet an appropriate amount of money given the cards I held.

We played for small stakes, usually a nickel ante and limited bets with raises up to a quarter. But sometimes the pot got rather large, and losses caused nerves to fray. A few of us were regular winners: Scotty Herrick was an astute player, Jack Moynihan and I always did well. But a few others were always on the short end—not because they got the short deal, but because they just didn't get the game. They didn't know, much less use, the rules.

One evening, David Sackrider made a series of outlandish raises before the last card was dealt in a seven-card stud game. Two of us had exposed cards that favored us—in Scott's case, four spades, and in mine, four hearts. If just one of our three down cards was of the same suit as our up cards, one of us was likely to have a flush and win. It was possible that Dave held a low-rank straight, but that assumed all three of his down cards fit. Of course, he could have found himself with three of a kind or two pairs, or even four of a kind or a full house after the last card was dealt, but the odds of that were not as good as either Scott or I getting a flush.

Dave had already lost nearly $10 and he couldn't afford to lose more. Most of us considered it a bad evening if we dropped $2—to lose $10 was crazy. Scott and I told him as much, and we weren't bluffing or trying to bolster our position. But Dave couldn't see this. He had run out of pocket money and was desperate to borrow from us to stay in the game. Upset, we told him he would have to leave the game if we won. He agreed, called the bet, and lost. We forgave the loan and he went home.

More than a half century later, I was quoted in an Ann Arbor newspaper on the best way to keep a competitive edge: "Keep learning, take risks, don't fear failure." That was something I learned playing cards in my youth. Failing at poker, when it occurred, never made me afraid. You have to take risks to win. But you have to understand those risks. That night long ago, Dave Sackrider didn't.

My poker winnings my last two years in high school were over $400. Interestingly, however, I didn't play poker or gamble in college or later in my adult years. Perhaps my studies and training required too much time, leaving precious few hours to make a long night at the card table attractive. My short career as a poker player taught me that while being lucky is fun, it doesn't guarantee success, and bad luck doesn't make you mediocre. But knowing the rules means knowing not only what you should do, but what you should not. If you don't know when not to do something, you will not win and it won't be by chance. You will simply lose.

10

Perseverance 101: Patience and Passion

It's sometimes said that the three keys to success at any task are perseverance, patience, and passion, and that the first is the hardest to master. Perseverance is easy enough to practice when another task isn't competing for your time and attention. When it is, perseverance can be painful and the task may fall undone. But then, nobody wants to be called a quitter.

This was the case, especially, when I was growing up. Time seemed to move more slowly. When my patience was challenged, there appeared to be few consequences to abandoning a task. That was not always so when I was older.

My first memorable lesson in perseverance involved fishing—specifically, having to wait long hours on the water without a bite. This early experience was relived, a half-century later, when I trained for and ran my first marathon.

Where Are the Walleyes?

Before I was born, my parents often took trips to the National Parks out west. They loved the outdoors. After World War II, in the late 1940s and early 1950s when I was around, we would spend a week each summer camping and fishing on the five-mile backwaters of the Manistee River, behind the Hodenpyl Dam, which was part of the Huron-Manistee National Forest in Northern Michigan.

Hodenpyl Dam was a major hydroelectric power plant built in the mid-1920s, and owned by the Consumers Power Company. They, along with the U.S. Forest Service, also owned the surrounding shoreline of the backwater. That kept the entire body of water free from development. No cottages or racing power boats disturbed the native quiet. When we camped there we were likely the only ones living at water's edge. My family had been given permission to enter the protected land by a friend of my father who was an executive with Consumers Power. We might as well have been vacationing in the wilds of Alaska or Canada. We were alone.

The Manistee River had originally cut through a glacial moraine. After thousands of years this created a deep valley with steep surrounding hills. When the dam was constructed and the adjacent land was flooded, those hills represented abrupt drop-offs of 70 to 150 feet into the backwater's deepest reaches. The water surrounded by dense conifer and hardwood forests always looked peaceful, but for a novice, this was no place for offshore wading or casual swimming. It was a treacherous body of water by any measure. But the fishing was great.

Setting up camp there provided us with a serene view of the pond created by the dam. It was really like a big lake, more than two miles wide. It also gave me a feeling of isolation. The nearest civilization was the village of Mesick, Michigan, a good five miles away by infrequently traveled back roads and seven miles by water if you put in upstream just outside the village.

We spent our nights sleeping in an umbrella tent that my parents had purchased at the J.L. Hudson Company in Detroit in the late 1920s. It was made of indestructible canvas and had screened windows on each side and a large front door, all of which zippered up tight at night when we were inside. My parents slept on a metal spring mattress and my brother and I on air mattresses, each of us in warm woolen sleeping bags that my mother had made sometime in the 1930s. You could hear the field mice at night, scurrying around the tent's perimeter, squeaking and scratching at the immovable object that had invaded their home turf. But they couldn't get in.

Our amenities were few: a Coleman lantern and stove, a steel icebox for our perishables—stored away from the tent, lest a bear wander in—wooden chairs with canvas seats and backs, and a folding wooden table to eat at. Our prized possession was a 12-foot, flat-bottom, canvas-covered Penn Yen boat that we tied to the top of our car for the trip from our home to the campsite. It had a small, two-and-a-half-horsepower Mercury motor to get us around the backwater—perfect for trolling during the late afternoon fishing.

The most audacious camping equipment was a wooden toilet seat attached to two 2x4 boards that kept the seat from falling into a hole my father dug in the ground: real class. Our private latrine was located behind some bushes 50 feet from the tent, and every time we used it, we shoveled a little dirt from the pile next to the hole to cover our doings. That kept the bugs away—except for the yellow-jacket bees. They were always present, dirt or no dirt, and they were scary. Even today, just thinking of those bees buzzing around my bare butt gives me the shakes.

Once a day, we took our boat across the pond to fill three thermos bottles with water from an artesian well near the dam. It was always cold and tasted better than the chlorinated city water back home. The aquifer, a hundred feet or so beneath the surface, was highly pressurized, and it would likely never have run out, but we always turned off its faucet that was attached to a thin pipe sticking three feet or so above the ground. I always wondered how deep it went.

Hodenpyl Dam was about three-quarters of a mile across the water from our campsite. There were no other human beings in sight or sound, and at night the only unnatural thing we heard was the distant horn signaling that the gates of the dam were being opened, to warn anyone downstream that a torrent of water was about to come their way. The sound was like a foghorn and its short blasts, three in number, came shortly after darkness enveloped our campsite. It was an eerie sound in the dark and stillness of the approaching night. We heard the horn again every morning, as if calling to the generators to restart pumping electricity to the homes and businesses in Northern Michigan. Of course when the gates were opened, we never saw any drop in the water level above the dam—there was simply too much upstream water compared to what was passing through the turbines inside the superstructure of the dam itself.

Our campsite was very quiet, which must have been why Dad loved it. When things got too hectic at the office or at home, he would recite something that probably meant he hoped for a little quiet:

"All I need is a little peace, calm, and contentment...and a little time to cogitate."

Fishing was a comfort to my father and something at which he had spent hours with his stepfather Cairns. Most days my father, my brother, and I would put out in our little boat an hour or so before sunup, with a dense fog still hanging over the water. During those early morning hours Mom would stay in camp, straightening up things.

When we set off, curtains of white mist, like a soft blanket, extended from shore to shore. Being on the water was like being on a cloud. We seemed to glide silently along the surface, cutting through the mist as we moved to the deeper holes offshore, where we knew the fish were waiting for us. We didn't hear anything other than the quiet putt-putt drone of the little outboard motor, and then no noise when it was turned off and we began the morning's fishing.

This was when perseverance came into play. I would hold my line between my thumb and first finger for hours, waiting for the little jerk signaling that a fish was nibbling at my minnow or earthworm bait. I wanted to be the one who snagged the first fish, and my hope was that it would be a walleye pike, not a small, undersized bass. We were usually silent, not wanting to spook the fish—as if they could hear us or feel the vibrations of our voices.

The silence went on, minute after minute, then hour after hour, until the sun was up and the fog was gone, at which point the fish were more likely to rise to the surface where insects might be afloat. After a few hours sitting quietly in the boat, all I wanted was for any fish to take my bait and get hooked. But it seemed to take forever. Many mornings, the long, boring wait left me wishing I'd stayed ashore. The fish, especially the walleyes, must be some other place—an opinion Dad categorically rejected.

Be patient, Jimmy. It's still early."

We almost always caught our daily limit of small-mouth bass and blue gill fish, and maybe every other day a walleye. Sportspeople of that era in Michigan's freshwater, river-fed lakes usually saw the walleye and northern pike as the best catch of the day. When I would reel in a fish, and when my pole would bend in a near U-shape bringing in one of these prizes, my father would remind me that this was what I had been waiting for, and wasn't I glad I had persevered? The same was true later in the afternoon, when we spent hours trolling with the favorite artificial lures of the day, June-bug spinners. Nothing happened fast, but if you didn't persist, clearly nothing ever would. Perseverance was a core value of successful fishing, and I was slowly getting it.

The countryside surrounding the river's backwaters was punctuated by Mesick, a charming little village that some writer should give a place in contemporary literature. If you hold up your left hand and pretend its backside is Michigan, the village would be halfway between the first and second knuckle of your forth finger. It is located in an area originally populated by the Potawatami Indians, headed by Chief Kautawabet, whose name meant "broken tooth." Of course, in his time there was no Mesick or Hodenpyl pond, just the fast-flowing Manistee River.

Mesick in the days we camped nearby had no stoplights or restaurants and only one gas station. There was a bait and tackle shop and a small variety store. At one end of the town was the Joseph Lumber Company, which sold a modest amount of wood supplies to builders. The yard was owned and managed by Mrs. Joseph, who had lost her husband years earlier. For infrequent travelers needing a place to spend a night, she maintained five small 20x20-foot, single-room tarpaper cabins. We stayed there a few times rather than pitch a tent on the backwaters. Each cabin had two beds, a small gas stove, a sink with running water, and a stall shower. But the toilets were a stone's throw behind the cabins—real outhouses—that were ever so cold in the predawn mornings before we set out to fish.

In summer, the people of Mesick watched movies once a week, projected on a wooden screen about 15x20 feet in size, located across the road from Mrs. Joseph's residence, the lumber yard, and her cabins. No cars, just wooden benches to sit on, like bleacher seats, and plenty of room to sit on the ground with your blanket. There were no indoor movie theaters within easy driving distance. I never knew for sure, but I had a feeling Mrs. Joseph and her family built the movie screen and benches for the folks of Mesick. This was postwar America, and maybe 25 or 30 people at most found their way to the open-air theater to watch motion pictures on Saturday nights, all proud to be together with the tourists like us who had wandered into town. Seeing others was a treat

Mom and Dad camping at Yellowstone National Park, c1935. Note the umbrella tent... it became a family heirloom.

My wife Nancy and I camped on the backwaters of the Manistee River behind the Hodenpyle Dam near Mesick, Michigan during the first two summers we were married, 1962 and 1963. We were following in my parents footsteps, sleeping in the same family umbrella tent, eating at the same folding table and sitting on the same folding chairs, that they vacationed with more than a quarter-century earlier.

Dad fishing in Northern Michigan with two of his financial buddies from Wall Street, c1950.

My catch of the day, a Walleye, caught when trolling on the Manistee River, 1948.

after days of camping by ourselves in the wilderness. The next day, Sunday, we would break camp, pack up and head home to East Lansing—in those days a seven-hour drive.

Dad thought highly enough of the Hodenpyl dam backwaters that for a few years after we first camped there, he regularly invited business acquaintances from Wall Street to stay in Mrs. Joseph's cabins and go fishing with him. The experience "invigorated" them, he said—whatever that meant. His guests were probably more accustomed to staying at upscale resorts on the east coast, but they must have liked it. They fished there with my dad many times.

Nancy and I spent our first two summer vacations after we were married on the same backwaters of the Manistee, in the same tent and at the same campsite—in fact, we used the same Coleman stove and gas lamp, chairs, and mattresses. One thing was different. We inherited the two family sleeping bags made by my mother, with their wool outer shells and inner flannel lining. Each had its own zipper, and each was for one person only. That wasn't going to be very romantic, so we redid the zippers to create one giant sleeping bag that we could crawl into together. Needless to say, it was a great way to snuggle. My mother understood.

Nancy and I didn't always land a lot of fish, but when we came off the water at dinner time without a catch, we warmed up a can of corn beef hash, grilled a pound of bacon, and opened up a bottle of wine. Sitting alone with nothing but the chill of the oncoming night about us and enjoying our one-star gourmet meal was just fine. Camping on those waters was still special.

Fishing is a solitary pursuit, best enjoyed by those who have lots of patience. By the time I was a teenager, my patience had been tested fishing many places other than in Hodenpyl's backwaters, and it was no different out west in Colorado or Wyoming. But fishing near Mesick was my first real lesson in perseverance. At the same time I learned that some endeavors require a philosophical attitude. Fishing offers no guarantees of success. Even when I did everything correctly, luck often made the difference. In fact, the more luck the better. That's been true my entire life.

Save Your Money

For some reason, I thought a small kid like me could still be very good at archery—and I was anxious to prove it. In the late 1940s the East Lansing City Park had haystacks with canvas bull's-eye targets, and during the summer, several of my friends and I would sit for hours watching the college students and adults practice. There were no fancy rigs in those days. The most sophisticated bow had recurved tips, but lacked today's pulley mechanisms and other features that increase the arrow's velocity and lessen the drift as it makes its way to the target.

Patience always requires an expenditure of time. I was nine when I made it known that I wanted a bow-and-arrow set. But wanting something and getting it when you were a kid were often poles apart. Although my parents told me that when I became a teenager I could have a set, I didn't want to wait. One good substitute for time, I realized, was money.

Dad agreed that if I really wanted a bow I could save my money and buy one for myself. That would cut a couple of years off my wait and it started me on a saving spree. My weekly $1 allowance for helping around the house and yard was a start. Then at age 10 I got my first real job delivering the *Lansing State Journal*, which brought me a few more dollars a week. That, and no spending on cheap toys, comic books, or candy, made the difference. I had saved a little more than $40.

A new sporting goods store, Beaman's, had just opened in East Lansing, owned by the parents of a schoolmate a year older than me. Beaman's had a huge variety of hunting and fishing gear, and a small supply of the newly introduced Bear bows, made of a laminated birch wood. Fred Bear was a leader in archery equipment who lived in Northern Michigan and his bows were very popular. I bought mine for $42. It was a 40-pound bow that took a lot of effort for me to string, but it was cool. I also bought three target arrows and two hunting arrows.

It had taken me nearly a year to save my money, and at times my patience was challenged by tempting side attractions, but I stayed the course. For the first time, perseverance had paid off in a reward to myself. It was worth the wait.

Try 26.2 Miles

Fifty years later, the lessons in perseverance I learned at a young age became important as I took on a very personal challenge. In early April 1995, my wife and I were vacationing in Cozumel, Mexico. Our daughter, Sarah, was going to run the Boston Marathon two days after we returned home to Ann Arbor. She had asked us to come and cheer her on, but after a week away from work, I felt I needed to get back to the office. But Nancy suggested I should think about it—after all, Sarah was our only daughter and how many times do your kids ever run marathons? My wife only needed to say it once. The office could wait.

We left on a Sunday morning, the day after returning from Cozumel, on a flight to Logan Airport in Boston. Once on board, the first thing I noticed was that most of the passengers seemed different. They were younger than the usual travelers and most were very trim. They were runners. My extra six inches of girth made me feel morbidly obese—and, to say the least, I was a little self-conscious. Then I noticed one of my colleagues from the anesthesia department across the aisle, and we struck up a pleasant conversation, which he ended with a statement that stuck with me:

"Jim, I didn't know you were a runner."

Obviously, I wasn't. I hadn't given much thought to my own fitness, but clearly I couldn't have sprinted more than 25 yards or jogged more than 100 yards without being winded. My friend looked great. I was out of shape. I knew it and I didn't like it.

Sarah ran well and I felt a rush of pride as she raced down Boylston Street across the finish line of the 99th Boston Marathon. That night we had dinner at the top of the Hub, at a corner table looking out toward the Massachusetts Institute of Technology and Harvard on one side and downtown Boston and the harbor on the other. The infectious esprit de corps of the runners and their families at the restaurant, and at the airport the next day, registered with my subconscious. I felt a little envious. Oh, to be young again!

Two weeks later, Sarah called with an improbable query:

"Dad, why don't you run in the 100th Boston with me next year?"

My first thought was that this was absurd and simply out of the question. I hadn't done anything athletic since high school and regular exercise wasn't a part of my life.

"You must be out of your mind."

Sarah's voice changed; it was obvious she felt let down and perhaps sad that she had suggested something she should have known I couldn't do. Sensing this, and remembering how happy she had been a few weeks earlier, I said I would think it over. I said nothing to Nancy, but in the next few days I took stock of my physical and mental state. Both of my parents had succumbed to heart attacks, and my older brother had recently undergone coronary artery angioplasty. Who was I kidding? I was at risk. It was worth a try.

The 100th Boston Marathon had provision for entry by way of a lottery, and both Sarah and I sent in the $40 with our application. I was a bit scared just thinking about how out of shape I really was. We would not be notified if we made it until six months before the starting gun was fired, but I didn't wait to hear. There was a lot to do if I was to run Boston.

I asked Kim Eagle, a cardiologist at the university, if he could arrange a cardiac stress test for me before I started running. I told him that I hoped to run Boston. As I recall, he said I needed more than a stress test—perhaps a psychiatrist and an orthopedist. Given that I was out of condition and overweight that may not have been bad advice. But I was determined to persevere. I began by passing up the bagels at teaching conferences. It was simple arithmetic: one bagel was 100 calories, which equaled a mile of vigorous walking or jogging, and I didn't have enough free time to add a lot of extra miles to my busy schedule. That understanding helped.

By the time the postcard came, announcing I was "in", my weight had dropped 20 pounds and I could jog at a conversational pace for about two miles. I felt great, and I had a goal: to run the Boston Marathon at age 59. Sarah didn't get in through the lottery, but she agreed to run with me without a bib number, as an unofficial runner. "Bandits" were not a favorite of the sponsoring Boston Athletic Association, but neither was joining the race unofficially a cardinal sin.

My training quickly made a difference. I managed to shed a total of 45 lbs. Those who hadn't seen me for a while probably thought I was ill, but I felt great. At the 1995 American College of Surgeons Clinical Congress in New Orleans, I ran into an old fraternity brother and medical school classmate, Richard Kremer, who I hadn't seen in years. I was walking with Cal Ernst, a close friend and possessor of a rather dark sense of humor. When Dick said I looked like I had lost weight, Cal didn't hesitate to reply:

"Actually, since his last round of chemo, he's put a few pounds back on."

Dick was silent and clearly troubled—and when I told him I was in great shape, didn't have cancer, never had any chemotherapy, and had lost weight training for the Boston marathon, he punched me hard in the stomach.

I usually kept my mouth shut about what I was up to, but not always. Two colleagues on the university's anesthesia faculty were superb runners. Patrick Benedict had run marathons in the two-hour-and-40-minute range. Hailu Ebba, who was completing a fellowship, had been a junior medical student on my service years earlier. A superb athlete, Hailu had run the 1,500-meter race in the Olympics for Ethiopia and had run more than one marathon in less than two hours and 20 minutes. At Oregon State University, where he competed head-to-head with Steve Prefontaine who was attending the University of Oregon, Hailu became the Pacific 10 Conference champion in the mile in 1972, 1973, and 1974. He and Prefontaine were the best runners in America in those days. To top it off, he was the first college student to run the mile in less than four minutes—3:57.8, to be exact—a life's accomplishment in and of itself.

One day in the surgeons' dressing room, Hailu asked why I had lost so much weight. I'm sure he already knew. When I braggingly replied that I was running Boston in something like three weeks, four days, and 14 hours, he gave me an embarrassingly big hug in front of our colleagues. He clearly was proud of my commitment.

> *"Why don't you come out on Sundays with Pat and me? We run five or 10 miles and afterwards have a cup of coffee."*

Hailu and Pat were running six-minute miles, while my jogging speed was a little less than twice that. When I declined the invitation, it was understood. But I was proud of what I had accomplished in just a few months, and sometimes I even allowed myself to express it publicly. Once was with Jeff Stross, a senior internist at the University, who stopped me in the hall one day a few weeks before the run.

> *"Why in the world are you running a marathon at your age?"*

My reply was simple:

> *"Jeff, you know, you get a medal when you finish!"*

He walked away, convinced I needed serious counseling. But I was healthier than I had been in years and I was relentless in my training, determined to avoid a cardiac event like the one that had ended my parents' lives. That was the real reason, not the medal, but getting a medal made a good story.

When I arrived in Boston the Friday before the run, I was ready. Weeks before I had read Hal Higdon's book, *Boston: Celebrating the 100th Anniversary of the Boston Athletic Association Marathon*. On Saturday, Sarah, Nancy, and I drove the course in a rented car to give me an intellectual understanding of Monday's run. Sarah was going to meet me at the 10-mile mark in Natick. But during the four hours I sat by myself in the athlete's village at Hopkinton High School awaiting the start, I realized just how alone I was, even in the midst of 19,000 other runners. All the training and focus was worth it, I figured, even if my only thought was to finish.

The weather was perfect, near 52 degrees at noon. When the Massachusetts State Trooper sang "America the Beautiful," I could feel my heart pound and my eyes welled up with tears. When the gun went off, it took me nearly 12 minutes to get across the starting line, but we were all wearing electronic chips on our shoes, so no one's time was compromised by starting in the middle of the pack.

For the first four miles I felt like a sardine in a packing house. The pace was faster than my usual, near eight-minute miles, but my adrenalin was up and I felt good. I saw Nancy in Natick at the 10-mile mark, holding maize and blue balloons high above her head, and it was there that Sarah, wearing a running outfit identical to mine, joined me. She was my coach for the next 16 miles.

The wind blowing off the bay and into my face was cold as we neared the finish and ran past the Citgo sign and over the last vertical challenge, a bridge, to enter downtown Boston. The streets were littered with little white Dixie cups that once held water to keep the thousands ahead of us hydrated. I was too tired to avoid them and they cracked like thin ice beneath my feet. I was euphoric knowing I was going to finish.

Cordoned off from the street, the crowds cheered and the music rang in my ears. "*Keep it up, you're looking good*" was a repeated refrain from the thousands of bystanders, mile after mile after mile. I was almost there, and with all the cheering, I couldn't help but think this must be how it felt at the Olympics.

Sarah and I crossed the finish line together on that Monday, April 15. She had prodded me to get off the couch, get in the lottery, and run with her. The hundreds of miles of training were a blur, but running with my daughter under the balloon-embellished finish-line banner in front of the Boston Public Library was an unforgettable moment.

My time of more than five hours was OK and close to what I had expected for my first marathon, only a few years away from my seventh decade. I picked up my medal, a gold-rimmed medallion with a blue enamel field containing a gold unicorn, the symbol of the Boston Athletic Association—but considering what it had taken to get me there, it might have been a medal for extraordinary military valor. Seven months later, on November 3, I ran the New York City Marathon. That's another improbable story.

My daughter, Sarah, and I crossing the finish line at the 100th Boston Marathon in 1996.

I first met David and Linda Upton when he was a patient of mine, and their reaction to my new pastime was unique. David had married Linda six years before I resected his aortic aneurysm. He did exceedingly well following his operation and I became friends with the two of them. We shared an interest in healthy living, mine related to running fitness while theirs revolved around alternative medicine and diet. They had taken over a small vineyard in western Michigan, Tabor Hills, and saw it evolve into a maker of fine wines and a place for wholesome organic food. The Uptons and their family owned the Whirlpool and Kitchenaid Companies, a big part of the western Michigan economy. After completing Boston, I sent them official t-shirts from the run and a photo of Sarah and me at the finish.

David and Linda shared my excitement over the next six months as the New York Marathon approached. I ran this one alone. Nancy and our two sons, Tim from Palo Alto and Jeff from Iowa City, came to cheer me on. We holed up at the Plaza Hotel across from Central Park—not the most inexpensive digs in town, but running the marathon was a celebration and I wanted to live it up.

My wife's and sons' only glimpse of me was in Brooklyn, at the nine-mile mark. But later that night we had dinner at Tavern on the Green, a glitzy, touristy, but cool place for me to be seen with my second marathon medal draped around my neck. The boys went home the next morning and Nancy and I checked out of our room later the same day. You need to know the Plaza Hotel to understand what happened next.

We had been hotel guests for only two nights, but when we got to the desk our bill was printed up, and printed up, and printed some more. Almost six pages, but the price seemed right: $1,760, not bad for two nights in two rooms at one of New York's elite hotels. When I asked for a copy of the bill, however, the well-dressed gentleman behind the check-out desk seemed genuinely flustered and excused himself. He returned after a minute and said the bill was on the credit card and we were OK. I already knew that—I had given him our credit card when we checked in. All I wanted was a copy of the bill.

As it happened, my oldest son, Tim, had been using his computer during of the afternoon of my run, and a $1 charge was added to his hotel bill each time he signed into a different search. But at the time I hadn't seen the bill and didn't know that. When I quietly demanded a copy of the bill, the gentleman disappeared again. By that time there were a few more guests in line, none too happy about the wait. Nancy sensed that and went to look at some items in a nearby display window. I was alone at the front of the line and I was uncomfortable. After another few minutes the gentleman walked out with a well-appointed young lady who he introduced as the credit manager. Really, what was going on?

She proceeded to tell me that the bill had been taken care of:

"It's all on the Richards' account."

It was a mistake—evidently. I told her I wasn't a Richards, wasn't on

"Looking good" at Mile 9 of the New York Marathon in 1996. It was my last 26.2 mile run.

a business trip, and that I had just been in town to run the marathon the day before. She looked flustered. I wasn't going away.

Then the truth came out. She said that they were supposed to be silent unless I persisted about the bill, and only then were they to tell me,

"Your fairy godmother hoped you had a good run."

Richards was Linda Richards, David Upton's wife. That was her maiden name, and our stay at the Plaza had been her treat—which only figured. Linda, with her deep commitment to healthy living, was anything but sugar and spice and everything nice when it came to consuming junk food. Next to watching what one ate, she respected those who worked hard at physical conditioning. She and David had decided to reward my commitment to getting fit.

Persevering, which I'd learned first under Dad's watchful eye on the

Manistee River, was still central to my way of living. All three of our children had run marathons. After my own first run in Boston, and after a long, hot soak in the bathtub, I called Tim, our oldest, in Palo Alto.

"Timbo, I finished Boston!"

After a 10-second pause came his response:

"Incredible."

That's exactly how I felt.

11

Perseverance 102: Advanced Course

Fishing, saving money, and running weren't difficult for me. But my personal power of perseverance was tested much more seriously a few years into my teens, when a task arose whose goal was more distant, my ability to succeed untested, and the price of failure too painful when compared to earlier challenges requiring a modicum of perseverance.

The 1950s Culture

Sitting next to my father in the front seat of the family car during frequent Sunday outings in the country was one of the joys of my childhood. I felt a sense of freedom as we wandered for miles, in no hurry to get somewhere. I liked the idea that I could explore distant places, many for the first time. And I was captivated by our family's car, an oversized Pontiac sedan. There is little doubt that these drives fed a veritable quest to own my own car. Perhaps because of this, it was no surprise that when I was 15 years old, before I was old enough to get a driver's license, I bought my first car. I certainly didn't need a set of wheels and we weren't rich. But it was the culture.

The American automobile was one of its defining elements of the country in the mid-20th century, especially emblematic for young adults returning from service overseas. Big, fast, and glitzy cars represented not just freedom but a conspicuous reward for all the sacrifices Americans had made abroad and at home. Gas-guzzling cars were OK too in those days, as long as they looked good. The car you drove became a personal statement as to who you were.

I, too, wanted to be seen, but perhaps in part because of where I was growing up, I wanted more than that. Michigan's economy in the early years following World War II centered on the automobile. Stronger metal alloys, complex electronics boosted by the introduction of transistors, and easily molded plastics, pushed the envelope for producing bigger and better cars. A multitude of new designs, both in body and engines, were coming off the lines, and there were no foreign imports to compete with them. If you were a science-oriented youth where I grew up, the prospect of designing and building cars offered plenty of excitement. I was going to be an automotive engineer and I thought owning my own car might get me there sooner.

A 1932 Car, Rumble Seat and All

Only two of my junior-year classmates could drive to and from school in their own cars: John Hicks, in his lavender 1936 Ford truck, and Jim Sorber, in his 1939 Ford coupe. One day Jimmy was in the countryside looking for old cars that might provide spare parts for his own car. He came upon a farmer in DeWitt, Michigan, about a dozen miles from East Lansing, who had a 1932 Plymouth coupe for sale. Miraculously, after two decades on the road, it had no rust. Being a Chrysler, it had many engineering features unavailable on other cars of the same age, like hydraulic brakes and a reliable electric starter. I needed no prodding. Two days after Jimmy reported it to me, I bought it for $40, cash. It was a bargain.

My car came home, towed behind Jimmy's—because, although it didn't have any rust, it also lacked a battery. In fact, it didn't run—hadn't for nearly a year, according to the farmer, who had stored it in his barn and covered it with grey house paint on more than one occasion. We parked it in front of my home. There was no room for my new acquisition in our single-car family garage—that was for Dad's car. I had mentioned my pending acquisition at the dinner table the night before—I'm sure my parents heard me. But my carefully couched words must not have fully registered.

My father arrived home later in the day when I was not at home. Lucky for me—it gave him a chance to think about how he was going to deal with me and the car. When I walked in the front door around 6 o'clock, he quietly put down the evening newspaper and made a quiet pronouncement:

"If you bought it and intend to fix it, you pay for it. It's yours."

The message was clear: It was not his or the family's car and I had just purchased a modest liability. On the other hand, he didn't call my new project off. I think he knew it was a step toward my becoming an engineer.

That car became the biggest project of my young life. Only dogged perseverance was going to allow me to finish the rebuilding of this car. And I was on my own.

The 1932 Plymouth coupe was a classic. It cost $610 when new, with a $20 option for freewheeling, a feature that disconnected the drag from the engaged clutch when you wanted to go faster than usual speeds. My car had that. It had a low-profile roof, so it didn't look top-heavy like the Model T Ford and other coupes of that era. And it had a roll-down back window that allowed you to talk to passengers in the car's two-person rumble seat. It had four-wheel hydraulic brakes and a four-cylinder, 65-horsepower engine that could get you going at 50 or 60 miles an hour on the open highway.

It had been a gem when new, and to my eyes in 1954, it had not lost any of its luster. Only it didn't run. The next step was to rebuild it.

In the ensuing months I spent hundreds of hours taking my car apart and putting it back together, with my own hard-earned money—except for a $2 can of grinding compound that my father bought one day on his way home to help me seat the new valves. I think he had a slip of the mind that day, but I was not about to remind him of his earlier words as to who was paying for the car.

Rebuilding

I can't imagine a 15-year-old today completely rebuilding a car built 20 years ago, but in 1954, taking on a 1932 car was much simpler. There were no complex parts, and the farmer had included a 90-page owner's instruction book describing in detail everything about the car—radiator hose diameters, clearances of valve tappets, clutch plate dimensions, size of the brake pads, and much more—all in simple words with accompanying illustrations. This little paper manual was the same guide that auto mechanics used, but it was equally understandable to laypeople like me and my father.

Dad was great help in getting my car in running order, often after dinner during weekdays and all day on many weekends. I tried to absorb every element of mechanical engineering the car and the instruction book had to offer. Not bad for a high school junior and a businessperson who, during the day, worked with paper and a calculator, not socket wrenches, screwdrivers, and pliers. Most of the car's engine bearings

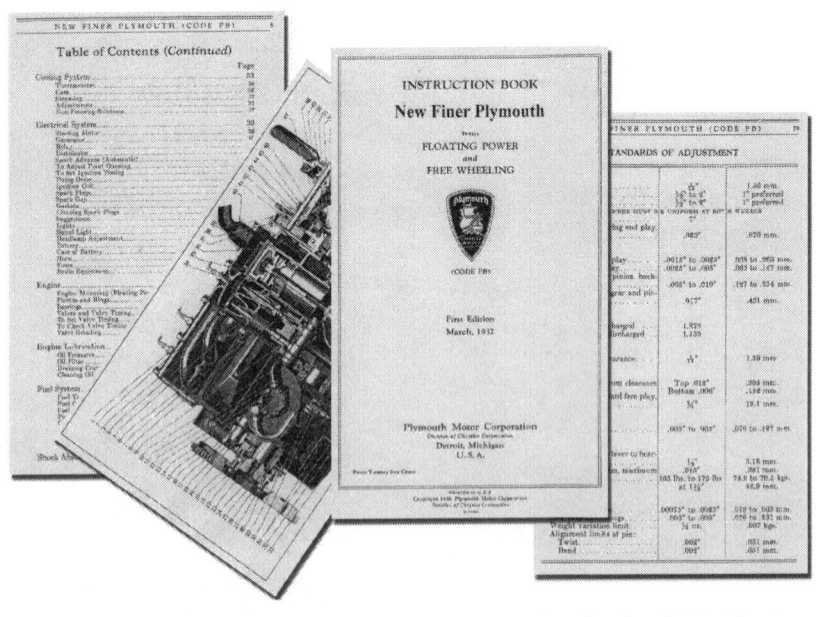

The guide for the restoration of my first car was a 25-cent handbook published by the Chrysler Corporation that accompanied the car. It was full of details, clear and simple instructions on maintenance and simple repairs. All owners possessed it…and no doubt most probably used it. They don't make car care so easy today.

and valves were frozen from disuse and needed replacing. A major overhaul was in order.

A week after I purchased my car, we pushed it into our backyard under a large swing set where I could start to take it apart. We jacked it up on cement cinder blocks, so the wheels could come off and I could work on the brakes as well as the undercarriage with its drive shaft, rear end, and exhaust system. It looked a little like a lost soul—all alone by itself. But that back corner of the yard became a regular gathering place for me and my friends, and of course, Dad.

When winter felt imminent, we moved the car into our small attached garage. By now, Dad had bought into the project, and never once did I hear him comment on the inconvenience of having to park his car in the driveway, even when the snow came. The garage was a great place to work—almost like my own mechanic's shop. I kept my tools out on a small bench along with my radio. When I worked at night, I listened to southern disc jockeys broadcasting from Tennessee and Texas: unreal characters from the decade preceding Wolfman Jack, who became the father of late-night rock and roll, broadcasting from Mexico across the river from Del Rio, Texas. Great sounds: Bill Haley and the Comets with "Rock Around the Clock," Fats Domino and "Ain't that a Shame," and the Platters singing "The Great Pretender."

Night after night, it couldn't have gotten much better than that. Even my father recognized the top ten songs of the day—I think he sort of liked them. Certainly, my friends' parents weren't listening to that kind of music. We usually kept at it until Mom would open the door and let us know it was almost 11 o'clock and we needed to come in, clean up, and hit the sack.

Step by step, we rebuilt my car: new piston rings, valves, crankshaft bearings, gaskets, and a coat of flat black primer after bumping out a few small dents in the fenders and hours sanding off the many coats of grey house paint that had protected the car from rust. The original upholstery on the front seat, however, as well as in the rumble seat was in great shape. I often wondered how many people had ridden in it, and for how long.

The Start

By late April 1955 the snow had melted and spring had arrived. The car was ready to go: new running gear, new rubber on the wheels, and a full tank of gas. We pushed it out of the garage and onto the street in front of our house, where it had first landed some nine months earlier. Its rebuilding took about the same time as a baby's gestation. I was anxious about how it would start—a bit like a parent expecting the birth of a child.

I turned the ignition key and the engine kicked over and started. But when I goosed it with a little push on the accelerator pedal, it sounded like a threshing machine. The car jerked erratically, 50 feet or so, down our quiet street with me behind the wheel. Embarrassed and upset, I turned the engine off. Dad kept cool. He opened the hood, reread a page in the owner's manual, and switched two of the spark-plug wires. We had crossed the ignition wiring for two of the car's four cylinders. When I restarted the car it sounded like a well-oiled sewing machine. Success!

Dad and I and a few friends rode around East Lansing and Lansing for hours until sunset, then came home to a dinner celebration. I felt the freedom of my earlier childhood rides in my Dad's car that day. Dad was happy and proud. Mom was ecstatic: no longer would we be late for meals or miss church on Sunday mornings because we were working on the car. A month later, it was painted by a professional who had worked at Chrysler in the 1930s. He was the real thing, and after painting the car a light grey, he did the pin striping of the body and the hood's louvers: just like new.

The car became my companion on many trips around Michigan with a number of my high school friends: to the Interlochen Music Camp, where some of my classmates were studying, and on weekend trips to Saugatuck on Lake Michigan, where we listened until the wee hours to live performances by well-known jazz musicians like J.J. Johnson and Kai Winding. During the remaining days of high school over the next year and a half, I rejoiced in showing off my classy little coupe. It was my personal statement of who I was.

Part and parcel of rebuilding my car was my desire to become an

My first car, a 1932 Plymouth Coupe with a rumble seat, bought from a farmer for $40 when I was only 15 years-old. I wasn't old enough to drive by myself the day it was purchased. My dad and I rebuilt it and took it for out first ride in 1955. It was a time when my ambition was to get an undergraduate degree in mechanical engineering and a master's degree in metallurgical engineering and become a leader in the automotive industry. That would prove to be a shortlived goal.

automotive engineer. I was certainly inspired by my backyard neighbor, Don Burnham, who was at Oldsmobile during the halcyon days of the '88 and '98 Rocket cars, and by another Oldsmobile engineer, Elliot "Pete" Estes, who lived kitty-corner across the street at the end of our block and who, within a decade, would become president of General Motors.

With such role models, I wanted, unavoidably, to be the best—first, by getting an undergraduate college education as a mechanical engineer; second, by obtaining a master's degree in metallurgical engineering. A defining moment came the same year I began work on the Plymouth: I read Walter P. Chrysler's brief autobiography. The career of this great entrepreneur convinced me that stellar engineering would trump the chrome-plated trim and gaudy body designs that were emerging from Detroit at that time. I wanted to be the one to create the next generation of American cars. But my 1932 Plymouth would not be taking me on that journey.

The Crash

My car met its end on a snowy road during the late fall of my sophomore year in college—in 1957, just three years after I had towed it home. That day, a Friday, I was driving from Ann Arbor to East Lansing with two fraternity brothers packed into the front seat. Dates with three Michigan State coeds awaited our arrival. Jim Boylan sat in the middle next to me—he was on the university swim team. John Robson, a high school classmate, sat next to the passenger-side door.

Instead of taking the ever-busy M-16 highway, I decided to travel on M-39, a picturesque country back road with little traffic. We started what was meant to be a scenic drive with a light autumn wind behind us, but ominous clouds soon darkened the afternoon sky and snow started to fall on the leaf-covered road—a bad combination. My 18-inch wheels with their narrow tires were no match for the slick surface. I had little traction and I knew it. We had encountered few opposing cars that afternoon, but fate was not on our side as we neared East Lansing.

My car slid sideways into the oncoming path of a new Buick. Everything seemed to be happening in slow motion for the few seconds before we hit. The rising dust from the floorboard and the loud noise of the collapsing steel on the right side of the car were followed by an eerie quiet surrounding the three of us and the wreckage of the two cars, both totaled. That silence is as clear to me today as it was a half-century ago. It was broken by a voice:

"Are you OK? Can you hear me? Are you OK?"

And then I heard the sounds of sirens from the police cars and ambulance.

Lots of people we didn't know seemed to be looking at us before we were put in the ambulance and taken to Sparrow Hospital in Lansing. John's pelvis was fractured; Jim's shoulder and my thighs were badly bruised. Perhaps we were lucky to be alive, but this didn't ring true to me at the time or in the ensuing years. I was cited for driving too fast for conditions: 30 miles an hour at the time of impact. Indeed, that was too fast. I walked with a limp for weeks, but Jim never swam again for the University, and John was out of school for months as he lay in traction, waiting for his pelvic fractures to heal.

John had been attending the University of Michigan on a naval scholarship. His father, a distinguished obstetrician and gynecologist, had served in the South Pacific during World War II as a physician. Following graduation in 1962, with a degree in mechanical engineering, John accepted a commission as an officer in the navy. He attended flight school in Pensacola, Florida, where he got his wings, and for the next three years he served in uniform. He volunteered for an assignment to Vietnam and spent two years on the attack aircraft carrier *Ticonderoga* as lead officer of the deck. John sent many planes off the decks of the carrier into harm's way, and he felt the pain when all did not return from combat. Many of the country's homebound could not understand the patriotism of John and others during combat in those years. But serving as a doctor in the army at the same time, I could.

That accident in fall 1957 could have been worse, but it was bad enough, and it has haunted me over the years. It's possible to think of it as a simple reminder that bad things can happen to good people, and we were good kids. But I have never been too sure that it was that simple. I had not anticipated or asked for the events of that day. I should have been more careful.

12

The Fair Sex

Where would we be if it weren't for sex? Clearly, it's designed to perpetuate our species. For the youth of the 1950s, it was also forbidden fruit, hidden behind a definition of morality many generations in the making. Somewhere along the road, love was added into the equation, and this made getting beyond many of the day's boundaries a little more bearable—but it created the additional pitfall of confusing sex with love. We may still do so today.

Grade School

The intermingling of the genders received very little encouragement in the 1940s. Childhood romances were generally dull. We didn't have the media and Internet exposure of explicit coupling that today's youth often use as guides. Certainly, the occasional naked body from a far-off land, which we saw in the *National Geographic,* didn't shed much light on the subject. And there was not much social engineering in schools in the form of sex education. That left me and my generation to our own devices. Bit by bit, we picked up the lore, until, by the time adolescence arrived, we thought we had figured it out.

Being smitten by someone of the opposite sex in grade school was a start. Girlfriends were cute and fun and that was more than enough. The big deal was to carry her books home after school, and if you were really lucky, you got to hold her hand along the way.

These successes didn't just happen: they required foreplay. In the bright daylight in our classrooms, we would compose our romantic thoughts on scraps of paper and pass them to someone we liked and who we hoped liked us. The messages were not too detailed.

"I love you. Do you love me? X O X O X Yes or No."

Nothing was indirect in those days. I haven't forgotten the circled "Yes" from Kay Ellen Pattengill in 4th grade. She was a knockout: round face, pug nose, big brown eyes, neatly braided pigtails, and an impish smile. Kay Ellen would have fit the role of the ideal eight-year-old in any of today's television sitcoms. Everyone liked her. The only problem with her "Yes" for me was that another half-dozen boys got the same answer. She moved a year later and it took a while for some of the guys to recover, including me.

Two years later, in 6th grade, I did better. I had a real girlfriend, at least for a month or so. Mary Ellen Johnston was pretty and very smart. She must have bathed with a scented soap, because she always smelled good—sort of a combination of flowers and fresh bread. I remember how happy I felt when I walked with her to her home on Abbott Road, five blocks from Bailey School, usually hand in hand. One day we stopped in her backyard, hugged, and kissed on the lips. At that age—I was 11 and Mary Ellen a year younger—that was a "happening." Mary Ellen was in 5th grade in a combined classroom that we shared. Her mother was a high school French and Spanish teacher and she would often offer us a snack when we got to her house. Her father was very sick and was often homebound with severe rheumatoid arthritis. Her home always seemed very quiet.

When winter came the after-school walks gradually stopped and so did our close friendship. I have often wondered if Mary Ellen remembered that kiss. I'm sure it was her first too—we were both exploring something new. It was a start.

Mixings

Things soon accelerated. Everyone attended class parties and dances in 7th, 8th, and 9th grades. There was little pairing, but the boys learned to wear suits and the girls got fixed up with frilly dresses, white socks, and saddle shoes, vintage 1950. Later, when partnering came into vogue, our class's nearly two-to-one preponderance of girls made it easy for us guys to find dates, but the girls suffered. Some of the girls' parents figured this out and responded by sponsoring dances away from school, with pre-parties that guaranteed their daughters a date. To most of us these affairs seemed contrived and many of us didn't feel comfortable moving around the dance floor with an arranged date. But things were on the move.

Teasing

Courtship didn't always start with mutual admiration. As soon as we realized that girls were important we found ourselves acting out, in both obvious and subtle ways, to gain their attention. Junior high girls were often taller than we were, and many of them were clearly better students. Perhaps to even the playing field, we found ourselves involved in outlandish pranks and jokes at the expense of the opposite sex.

Home economics class unmasked many gender differences. It was a mandatory class for everyone, boys and girls together, and it was fertile ground for teasing. Jean Cargill, the teacher, was excellent, and she did a yeoman's job keeping order most days. The class involved just what you would expect—sewing, cleaning, planning balanced diets, cooking, and budgeting for a household. Each topic, whether consciously or not on our part, revealed gender gaps. The guys made bags for their gym clothes and the girls made aprons. Some of us became proficient with sewing, and to this day, in the operating room, I often resort to words I first heard in home economics—basting, scalloping, gathering, etc.

Cooking was where class often grew disorderly. Other than reading about cookouts in Boy Scout manuals, the guys didn't have a clue how to prepare food—and especially how to bake. One day we got a great idea when making muffins from scratch. The proper ingredients—flour, sugar, salt, and yeast—were all in containers about the room. So were the supplies for cleaning up afterward, including soap.

Unknown to the girls listening intently to Mrs. Cargill, we added LUX soap flakes to the girls' batter. It was no surprise that their muffins came out with the flavor of something stale and bitter. Aside from those of us who had done the dirty deed, no one could understand, and we weren't about to enlighten the class and get in trouble. I think we were more interested in the girls' reactions to our prank than in the results of their cooking.

Not everybody was fooled. One of my classmates, Francene Hayworth, figured out that my muffled laughter was tied to the yucky taste of her baking efforts. She sat across from me at a work table with drawers in front of each of us. My laughter abruptly halted when Fran kicked the rear of my drawer and it rammed into my midgut. All was fair.

Harmless gender-heavy pranks continued for the next few years, until two of us stepped over the line.

My steady girlfriend and I often double-dated with Sue Hodge and Barry McDowell during our senior year in high school. Barry had just moved to East Lansing and he arrived with a great car, a Nash whose front seats reclined, making the car into a bed. Sue and I had been friends since grade school. She had an inviting smile and an upbeat personality to match. Her home was off a short street that burrowed into the college campus, and it was there that she and I played a prank that would not be considered so funny today.

There was no question that Warren Richards, a speech teacher who also oversaw the junior and senior plays, had an unusual fondness for one of our senior classmates, Vicki Smith. Vicki was an outstanding student, very popular and quite attractive. Whatever the reason, she drove Mr. Richards' new Oldsmobile hardtop around the school every noon hour for several weeks. We wondered out loud about her being the teacher's pet. Jealousy was not in the air, but the jokes about the two of them ran rampant.

How we came up with the idea escapes me, but one day Sue and I drove down to Lansing City Hall and took out a marriage license in our names, filled out in ink from a fountain pen with the City Seal affixed. All we needed was a blood test and someone to officiate and we would be on our way. But we had something else in mind. I remember sitting in Sue's kitchen with a piece of cotton dipped in Clorox, bleaching out the ink until we had a blank certificate. We then typed in Vicki Smith's and Warren Richards' names and addresses. The next day we borrowed a key from an unsuspecting student working in the principal's office that unlocked the bulletin board attached to the wall in the school's main corridor. Up went the marriage license. Then we hid the key.

Disbelief and laughter were the response from the students as they mulled about the hallway, soon joined by the visible angst of the school's office staff as they searched for and finally found a second key and removed the document. Sue and I kept our part secret for decades. It was a practical joke, well done, but of course we had stepped over a certain boundary of decency. Vicki didn't deserve being hurt. But Warren Richards' unsettling favoritism toward a young girl in his class was despicable and he deserved worse.

The Pin

Being a varsity athlete in any sport at East Lansing High carried with it a certain nonathletic advantage as regards the fairer gender. Going steady was one of the things upper-class guys and girls did to validate their attachment to each other. There were many ways to declare this, the most common being for the girl to wear the boy's ring on a necklace chain or for both to simply proclaim that they were going steady. Varsity players had a different, distinctive custom, cooked up, no doubt, by an especially libidinous jock years before I attended high school.

Everyone who lettered on a varsity team became a member of the Varsity Club. We each received a little, gold-plated "E" pin, about three-eighths of an inch in height. You could wear the pin on your sweater or shirt. But it had a special appeal for our steady girlfriends. The move to going steady was sealed when you placed your "E" pin on the inside of your girlfriend's bra. Of course, she wouldn't continue to wear it there, but before it found its place on her own sweater, it had its start next to her bare breast. Now, that was some move!

The open sexual life of many of today's teenagers didn't exist in the 1950s. Nevertheless, by the time most of us in the Varsity Club got "pinned," we and our steadies had managed to get our paws all over each other, with few surprises or regrets. My own steady and I were no different than the others. The "E" pin just gave us an excuse.

Separation

I received a more definitive lesson in relations with the opposite gender in college, when they assumed greater seriousness and the possibility of being hurt grew exponentially. Finding yourself paired with someone with whom you would share the rest of your life was not a game of puppy love or casual sexual exploration. It was the real thing.

The popular culture of the time contained plenty to pique our interest in sex, although much of this was tame by today's standards—like the 1956 movie *And God Created Woman*, featuring Brigitte Bardot, for example, or *A Certain Smile* of 1958 starring Rossano Brazzi and Joan Fontaine. And who among us that same year didn't mark the pages containing the heated scenes of passion in our copies of *Peyton Place* by Grace Metalious, just so we could reread them without suffering through the boring parts? Sex appeared to be where one's imagination met reality, but it was always accompanied by a lot more anticipation than action. Boudoir escapades for us were almost unheard of.

Most of us left our homes, comfortable and relatively mature, to enter college at a distance from parental oversight, and sex was certainly one of the issues hovering over this change in our lives. The only governance mechanisms controlling boys' hormones were their own morals, as problematic as they might have been. The biggest change for me was having no hours and no one constantly reminding me my name was Stanley. It was time to find out exactly who I was—not so much to redefine myself, as I was comfortable with my ambition to succeed as an engineer. Perhaps that was a saving grace, for in matters of love I did not fare so well during my freshman year and the beginning of my sophomore year in college.

I was separated from my high school girlfriend, Annette McDonald, who was a student at Ohio Wesleyan while I attended the University of Michigan; although I cared for her a lot, our close relationship of nearly three years rapidly dissolved. This may have been of her or perhaps her parents' doing, but suffice it to say I was left in the lurch and felt deeply rejected. It took me many months to recover. (There will be more to tell of my friendship with Annette in a later chapter.)

I don't remember the exact circumstances, but early in my sophomore year I had a date with a very cute freshman coed. We had met at a mixer in October 1957, and for the rest of the school year we hit it off. Ginny Sinclair had strawberry blond hair, big brown eyes, and an infectious smile. There was a lightness to her being. She had been president of her class at DeVilbiss High School in Toledo, Ohio, and she exuded confidence. Ginny lived her freshman year at the Stockwell dormitory and she pledged Kappa Alpha Theta, the sorority situated next to my fraternity, Sigma Alpha Epsilon, where I was living.

Ginny and I had coffee dates, study dates, went to formal dances, toga parties, and visited each other's homes. We were serious. Then one night when we were alone, cuddling and sharing intimate things on my fraternity's rooftop porch, she said she had decided to attend the University of Madrid in Spain the next year. I felt like I had been placed in a vacuum and I was suddenly alone with my own thoughts: another separation that I had not anticipated.

There was little I could say, however. Ginny was a very complete young woman who didn't make decisions on the dash. Everything she did made sense, even working part-time at Miller's Ice Cream Parlor on South University, just for fun. We agreed to never let our friendship cool—we cared too much about each other. Ginny and I saw each other every week during the ensuing summer, before we were to be on separate time coordinates. Her departure was bittersweet; she was excited, and I knew I would miss her.

It was the second time in a year that I felt emotionally down, even though it was no reflection on how Ginny and I felt about each other: nevertheless a sort of de facto rejection that was painful.

The next fall I had the distinction of being the only one to have foreign phone calls charged to my fraternity house bill—to Madrid. But the phone calls and letters became less frequent as the months passed and we both sensed a degree of separation. Ginny didn't come back to Ann Arbor during the nine months of the school year. When she finally returned from Spain she asked me to visit her at her family's Port Clinton summer home on Lake Erie, just to see "where we were." It was not to happen.

Shortly after Ginny and I had met, she had arranged blind dates for two friends of mine from Michigan State: Gary Gross, whose father owned two radio and television stations, WJIM and WGFG; and Peter Frenzel, whose family were prominent in Indianapolis business circles. The two girls she fixed them up with were Ginny's roommate, Gretchen VanDys, a nursing student, and Nancy Norville, who was in Ginny's sorority pledge class. While Ginny was away, Nancy and I had begun seeing each other. She was about to become the most important person in my life. (More about Nancy and our future together in a later chapter.)

Gender issues had created an entire new set of boundaries that were best approached with care. Crossing some of them were gut-wrenching and passing through others were joyous.

13

Fall's Earliest Commitment

Competitive high school athletics was one of the most visible personal commitments a boy could make when I was growing up—especially team sports. For many of us, the sport was football. What appealed to me was the competition: you either made the team or you didn't. You either started or you sat on the bench. You either won or you lost. It was rather simple, and it all came together on Friday night at game time.

Discipline

My father had played semi-professional basketball in the 1920s for the Ohio Blue Streaks, and he was not a wimp when it came to sports, but he questioned my driven behavior and that of my teammates, from late summer through the last football game in November. I only heard him comment on it once, but he meant it:

> *"They don't build statues to high school football players."*

But I wasn't in it for a statue. I liked the idea of sucking it up and moving out. I liked the discipline. And make no mistake about it, our football field, with its stubble grass and pebbles rising to the top of the soil for air, was a sacred place for this experience. It started in 9th grade, and for the next four years, there was little else that mattered for 11 weeks of my life. It fit and I fit.

In our town during the 1950s, discipline wasn't something we needed to learn in the classroom. School work was easy; our teachers were interested in us and we were interested in learning. You could almost always succeed if you applied yourself and worked at it. Getting 100% on an exam was not uncommon. But for an athlete, that wasn't good enough. On the playing field we were expected to give 110%.

Playing football with commitment required little reinforcement in East Lansing. The message in the tile wall of the locker room put it simply: *"Winners never quit, quitters never win."* I saw it on the way in, on the way to the field, and on my way home. If I didn't get it there, I got it on the first page of our playbook, with more emphasis: *"Sweat, sacrifice, and a little extra effort"* and *"It never rains or snows in East Lansing".* Simple clichés to some, perhaps, but to neophyte athletes in the 1950s they were more. We read those words every day of the season. They were like a religion—we believed them.

Football was tough—you competed nonstop with yourself as much as with others. Practice twice a day in the 90-degree August heat before the season, push-ups until we tasted the grass and dirt, wind sprints until we couldn't breathe, and bruises as well as cuts were all part of the game. Nothing was expected to get in the way—not school work, friends, family, or pain.

The Early Games

Football had already become something other than a game of backyard catch when I was nine years old. Three days a week during the fall I was part of a radio show on the Michigan State College campus with a couple of 5th grade classmates. We were guests on *Book Club*, a WKAR radio program from 4 to 4:30 p.m.. It was broadcast from a small studio inside the Fairchild Theater building; college students majoring in communications read children's stories aloud to a group of kids like me, who listened and asked questions when prompted. Dick Childs, who lived a few blocks from my home, and I often walked to the broadcast studio together.

On the way home we always walked by the MSC football practice field. What got our attention first was the noise. We could hear yelling and the sounds of the players colliding with each other, all punctuated by the coaches screaming orders and blowing their whistles. This was a few blocks from the stadium, behind a long chain-link fence with canvas tarps draped over it that kept us from seeing inside.

One day Dick and I snuck in to watch. No one asked us to leave, and subsequently the MSC football practice became a regular stop for us after the radio show. A week later, we were asked if we would like to help clean the players' cleats when they came off the field, using miniature rakes that were easy to hold in our small hands. I can't remember exactly how this came about—the invitation to help may have been from a harried student equipment manager who recruited us to do his work. But we were quickly on board for the rest of the season, maybe three or four games. Not only did we get to attend practice on weekdays, but were allowed into the stadium and were part of the team's bench for Saturday home-game days.

Cleaning the cleats of All-Americans like the halfback George Guerre and end Lynn Chandnois was a thrill—strange as that may sound. They were genuine celebrities, their game pictures usually gracing the Sunday sports section of the *Lansing State Journal*. Guerre was my kind of guy— 5' 7" and 157 pounds. He had started at the University of Michigan in 1942, and after enlisting in the Army Air Corps he became a decorated flight navigator before returning stateside and enrolling at Michigan State, where for the next three years he was the team's leading rusher. His taller teammate was Chandnois, who could play both sides of the ball, offense as well as defense. Following graduation he played for the Pittsburgh Steelers and is still ranked second in career kickoff returns in the National Football League, behind only Gale Sayers.

The players were nice to Dick and me, as was Clarence "Biggie" Munn, who was in his first season as the team's head coach in 1947. How much cooler could it get—standing on the sideline watching a long run, the players coming over to catch their breath and have me clean the dirt stuck between their cleats? All the while I could hear everything the coaches were saying to them. I had the best seat in the entire stadium. No trash talk, no cussing—the coaches were in control. It all made sense.

I'm not sure I really understood the game in those days, but the players' intensity stayed with me until I had a chance to don pads myself. I played football for four years at East Lansing High School, and by then there was no second guessing my knowledge. I understood the game.

But what I remember most from that first season were not the practices or the games, but about a player named George.

Big George

Solely because of football and alphabetical seating, George Sheridan became a close friend during my first year in high school. He was only a year older, but had led a more difficult life than I had. George lived in a small house supported by his mother, a nurse, who often suffered abuse from her alcoholic husband, George's father. A pharmacist with three drug stores in New York, he had lost everything in the Depression, and things had been hard for the family ever since. Drinking may have eased his loss, but it only made matters worse for his family. George frequently confided in me that he had to step into his father's path to prevent him from hurting his mother. I was unable to respond in a way that might have lessened his load—he had a different degree of responsibility than the rest of us had ever experienced. George was, by no choice of his own, one tough guy, and as one might guess, one tough football player.

As a starting member of our freshman football team, George was dominant. The biggest of the 27 of us who suited up that year, he was respectful of authority and had a special admiration for Lynn Adams, our coach. One day in mid-October, however, George was truant for the afternoon practice, when earlier he had been in the coach's class. When Mr. Adams queried the team as to his whereabouts, someone said it was the first day of pheasant season and George had gone hunting. Poor George—someone had squealed. No matter how important he was to the team, he was in trouble.

The coach was insufferable that afternoon, the rest of us paying the price for George's hunting excursion. Just before an extra set of wind sprints at the end of practice, George pulled up in his ramshackle car, right next to the field. We all knew something ugly was likely to happen when coach saw him. No one moved. The next few minutes were surreal.

George got out of his car with a great big smile on his face and two pheasants in one hand. He simply walked up to Mr. Adams and gave the birds to him.

"Coach, I had a great day. These are for you."

As quickly as that, he touched the soul of a seasoned teacher and hardened coach. Mr. Adams, with a pensive smile, thanked George, blew his whistle, canceled the wind sprints, and sent us to the locker room. That day, our coach became the father George wanted.

George was a guy's guy and that occasionally caused trouble. He was huge—an imposing 9th grader weighing over 200 pounds. He walked with an unintentional swagger. He wasn't fat, just big, with a barrel chest and big belly and hands with stubby fingers that always looked rough with cuts here and there. He had street smarts and certain trigger points best left untouched.

We all knew the warning signs. When perturbed, George's round cheeks would turn red, his long black hair would fall over his eyes, and his gaze became intense. His breathing would turn measured and he didn't waste time or energy on talk. He rarely flinched or backed down, and few wanted to get in his way.

Fights in the school hallways or outside the building were a rarity in East Lansing, but George provided the exception. One day Kenny Slotnick, a 10th grader who fit the title of the school bully, verbally lit into a small 9th grader over a seat in the cafeteria. Kenny was like an animal on the prowl. Carrying a reputation as a looming menace never fazed him; he seemed to gleefully accept the tag.

George, who was nearby, did not buy what was happening.

"Pick on someone your own size."

Without a second's pause, Slotnick invited him to repeat that outside. George didn't say a word but walked out the back door, ducked when Kenny took a swing, and with one motion landed a doozy of a right to Slotnick's face, knocking him to the ground and quickly finishing the matter. Kenny's conceit was short-lived and the maniacal glean in his eyes was gone. No one screwed around with George. Many of my classmates could be fun on a picnic, but on a tiger hunt, George was the man.

By the way, if you hadn't guessed, I was the small 9th grader.

Not everyone saw George the way I did, however. George smoked—perhaps not so uncommon for a teenager today, but most unusual in 1952 at East Lansing High. He could often be seen leaning rakishly against his car and taking a long drag on a cigarette, with a smile on his face and accompanied by a cloud of smoke. He was at peace with the day's affairs. Unfortunately, one day when George was lighting up near his parked car after school had let out, a teacher saw him and reported him to the principal, Lee F. Kinney.

The students characterized Mr. Kinney, rightly or wrongly, as "The Owl"—not because he was wise, but because of his looks. Matching the few strands on top of his head were thick black rows of hair running from front to back on each side, a few inches above his ears. These rows often stuck straight out and from the front, looked every bit like owls' ears. To complete the look, he wore dark horn-rimmed glasses that made his eyes look bigger than they really were. He was a sight.

George's infraction prompted Mr. Kinney to hand him a three-day suspension from school. There was a shared instinct among my friends that this was a raw deal. George hadn't been smoking on school property, but rather on a public street, long after school hours. A classmate, Eddie Reuling, and I decided to let the authorities know we thought his treatment was unfair and unjust. The next morning we arrived in the high school's administrative offices, where we met with Dorothy Stophlet, the assistant principal. She listened. George was back in school that afternoon. We were sure we had done the right thing.

I mentioned the day's happenings to my parents at dinner that night, with a certain bravado. But my pride in helping George didn't resonate. Far from being proud of me, my father lectured me that George's doings were none of my business. He ended the conversation with an analogy: When he had worked in an oil field and a barrel got loose and started to roll, the smart worker got out of the way. I couldn't agree. George wasn't a barrel and I wasn't in the way of anything. I promised myself that if I ever had kids, I would always be supportive if they ever took a moral stand for a friend.

George left East Lansing High after our freshman year. He later married his grade-school sweetheart, Mary Burke. For many years I didn't hear much about him. You can imagine my pain when a decade later, in 1962, my mother sent me a page from the *Lansing State Journal* with an article about George and his family. They had been living in a small house at Lake Lansing, a few miles from East Lansing. A fire had burned their home to the ground. It was Palm Sunday. He and Mary lost everything, including one of their two children. But George had a tough spirit. He and Mary rebuilt their home, and a little less than a year after the fire, they had their third child.

Years later, this giant of a man developed diabetes and lost a leg. Then in 2000 he lost his life to vascular disease. Life had never been easy for him.

My closest memories of George, however, revolved around playing football and the good times we had together. Through him I learned what difficult times can really be. He was indeed a friend.

14

Irreplaceable

Like many adolescents, I had an inflated sense of my own importance. At times I thought I was so valuable as to be irreplaceable. Understanding that this was not the case was difficult. This reality became clear when I was playing varsity football.

1954 Varsity

When varsity practice opened my junior year, 10 of the 46 boys in my class suited up for a new coach, Vince Carillot. He brought a new culture and high expectations to East Lansing. But some things remained the same—and anyone who has played high school ball will recognize what I'm talking about.

Those early weeks of the season brought a certain smell of freshly mowed grass, like a recently cut alfalfa field. And there was the unforgettable coolness of the air at game time on Friday nights. Sometimes other smells come back, too. One is the effect of sweat and dirt on our jerseys and pads after a few days of late-August practice, rendering them malodorous enough to compete with dead animals. The stuff not only stank but it was wet every day when we suited up. Nevertheless, once workouts started, no one noticed the smell. After practice, the hot showers washed us clean, and the smell of the Wintergreen rubbing liniment that soothed sore, overstretched muscles gave us a fresh lift heading out of the locker room.

Joining the varsity team included certain rites as the seniors introduced us into the locker-room pecking order. One rather painful stage involved what definitely was an off-label use of Wintergreen liniment. Its active molecule was methyl salicylate, which causes vasodilation of the skin's capillaries, bestowing a sense of warmth: great for aching muscles. But a little dab in a neophyte's jock strap hanging in his locker was something else. Fifteen minutes after suiting up for practice, the unsuspecting player's scrotum felt like it was on fire: painful for the recipient as he started practice, but a quiet laugh for the upper classmen behind the coaches' backs. All in all, it was innocent fun, and it took the edge off our pain as we pushed our bodies to the limit.

There was a mystique about playing varsity football for East Lansing High, its major component being a sense of privilege and pride. This was the real thing. We all knew we were going to be part of a winning team. Our seniors in 1954 included a few standouts, most notably Greg Montgomery, a tall redhead who went on to Michigan State as a quarterback, and Demetrious Spanos, who was ahead of me as a pulling guard. Demetrious was a rough and tough player who made the All-State team. Our record my junior year was blemished by a nonconference loss to Mt. Pleasant High School in the season opener and a later loss to Three Rivers High School that dropped us to a final 6-2 record and second place in the Twin Valley Conference. Being second was not what Coach Carillot had in mind for us as we looked ahead to our senior year.

Coach

Vince Carillot ate and slept football: magazines and newspapers at his home were covered with "Xs" and "Os." He knew how to build a football team and he quickly became an icon to his players. He was born in 1929 and attended Michigan State College, playing football for Clarence "Biggie" Munn until an ankle fracture kept him off the field. Fortunately, he found a place next to the coach as a graduate assistant for the rest of his collegiate career. Munn, in his day, was one of the game's innovators. He popularized the "multiple offense," with its unbalanced line and single wing formations to compete with the then more conventional straight-T offense.

Coach Carillot brought his mentor's new offensive plans to East Lansing High. The most obvious difference was the unbalanced line, where the two guards lined up together on the same side of the center. I played one of those positions. One of these guards would frequently pull and move behind the line, blocking down field at a distance from where they started when the ball was hiked. This innovation increased the number of running options, much as in today's spread offenses. Most pulling guards were faster than the usual linemen employed in straight-T offenses. They were also required to go one-on-one on many plays, making their athleticism a pivotal factor in the success of the play.

After his graduation from college, Vince Carillot coached for three years at Concord High in mid-Michigan, where his team won a Class C-D State Championship. He was then recruited to East Lansing High. During his six years as head football coach there, his teams won two Class B State Championships. His overall high school coaching record was 74 wins and 6 losses, for an amazing 92.5 winning percentage.

He then returned to his alma mater, Michigan State, as an assistant coach working for Duffy Daugherty. In 1970 he accepted the head coaching position at the University of Tulsa. Two years, later he returned to his home state as an educational analyst to the Michigan House of Representatives.

Then Vince did something unheard of for a college-level football coach: he earned a PhD in the economics of higher education in 1982 from the University of Michigan—the home of the Wolverines. Imagine a Spartan from Michigan State, being educated at an archrival school! It was a good move: Vince subsequently became vice president for business and finance at Eastern Michigan University. He lived across the street from me in Ann Arbor before retiring to Savannah, Georgia.

Vince Carillot was an exceptional coach, a committed educator, and a rigorous taskmaster. He could be dismissive toward anyone who did not give it their all in practice or in the game. When you played for him you became a competitor and were better for the experience. Some of us didn't know how important that was at the time, but we were very lucky.

Working Out on the Farm

Most of the team started working on their physical condition months before formal practices started in late August. Jack Moynihan and I were both second-string guards our junior year and were eager to start as seniors. We thought it was a done deal. Each summer Jack and I, along with several other classmates, worked at the Farm Crops Research Division at Michigan State College, laboring in the fields along Mount Hope Road, on the western fringe of the college campus. The job provided much better physical conditioning than working in a store or office.

We also got paid, but not much. Starting at 80 cents an hour before our sophomore year, we received a 10-cents-an-hour raise each summer, topping off at $1 an hour the summer before our senior year. The farms were just short of three miles from my home. During the summer before our senior season Jack and I took turns picking each other up and driving to and from work in our own cars.

We usually spent eight hours a day doing physical work, hoeing row after row of various grains and sometimes acres of potato plants. Some days we spent using a Gravely mower to cut wheat that we would bring back to the central farm building to be threshed in a small desktop machine. The resulting few ounces of wheat kernels would then be bagged and the weight of each sample recorded in a research logbook. On other days we learned how to balance ourselves atop a flat-bottom wagon pulled by a 1940-vintage Ferguson tractor and use pitchforks to gather and spread the wheat stalks spewing from the thresher that led the wagon. We worked shirtless and by mid-July we sported bronze tans, rendering ourselves vulnerable to basal cell and squamous cell skin cancers, of course. But what did we know then?

John Shower was our boss and he was not an academic but a real farmer. He taught us to look at a field of barley or oats or wheat and know what varieties were more resistant to lodging after heavy wind storms or what the best yields of grain were in those days (nearly 52 bushels of wheat per acre)—things we never would have learned in our high school classrooms.

Some other young men working with us were also real farmers. One of them, Larry Babbitt, held our East Lansing High crew in special disdain: we were "city folk." And we certainly didn't understand country music. But then I don't think Larry and his friends liked our taste for rock and roll, either. When we were in the central farm building listening to our favorite music we tried not to work together.

The day's work was dirty, but it gave us an appreciation of the lives of people who eked out a living from the soil. At closing hour we would fill out our time cards and go right to Jenison Field House on campus, where we would shower up and swim in the college pool for a half hour before going home to dinner. Coach Carillot was one of the men who supervised the pool and I'm sure Jack and I thought we were getting a leg up with him by conspicuously keeping fit. Maybe so, but it wouldn't last. We were in great shape, but so were two new guys who transferred to East Lansing High that fall.

A Difficult Lesson

All of us at East Lansing High had bought into a culture of winning—an expectation of success. When you're winning, nothing seems to get in your way. You become convinced of your own importance—be it at football, a political contest, or a difficult job. That I was not so important was a lesson perhaps best learned at 17, rather than later. I believed I would be the starting guard when we played the first game of my senior year. That this was by no means certain became obvious a week before the season began.

The week before workouts started, a group of us went swimming at Paul Earl's family's cottage on Crystal Lake. Paul was Jack Moynihan's older sister's fiancé. We were enjoying the sun and water, playing King of the Mountain on a float made of 1 x 2 inch pine boards laid on top of 55-gallon oil barrels. It was our last breather before the two-a-day practices started and we were all testing our macho selves, shoving each other into the water. My right fifth toe got caught in the space between the wood slats as I was pushed off the float. It felt as if I had stubbed it. Later in the day, however, it looked a little swollen and the top of the toe was black and blue. It didn't bother me when I was running, but it was

The 1954 Varsity football team at East Lansing High School with a 6 win, 2 lost record as Vince Carillot debuted as the new Head Coach. I was number 61.

The 1955 Varsity football team at East Lansing High School with a 7 win, 1 loss record giving us a share of the Twin Valley Conference championship. We had been ranked as the top Class B team until our loss to Battle Creek Lakeview in the season's last game.

Friday night gametime was when it counted: Coach Carillot on the sidelines had the respect of the players, including those on the opposition.

My senior photo...
Perhaps looking better in print than I played as a pulling guard...
But, I embraced the competition.

uncomfortable when I stood still for more than a minute or so. No time, however, for minor aches and pains.

Practice began a week later on Monday after an hour-long meeting with Coach Carillot. His assistant, Jim Mulendyke, who was the backfield coach and had played football at Northwestern, paced the room that morning. He and the rest of us were anxious to get started. As we went over the schedule and pages of plays, the tension rose. We knew the drill.

The first five days went well, except that every time I'd pull up after a run, my toe would throb. And it got worse. After practice on Friday, I stopped at Dr. Pletcher's office downtown. He was the new team doc, and after an x-ray revealed a fracture of my little toe's middle bone, he said I should have it splinted for a few weeks. My first thought was simple: to the heck with that. You can't get your shoe on with part of a tongue blade taped to your foot. When he said it could get worse if it were not splinted, I agreed to consider returning after our Saturday scrimmage and have it treated. I guess he thought I might develop a pseudoarthosis—a false joint. But my real thoughts were: big deal. How much does your little toe count for anyway? My parents were none too happy that I wanted to ignore the doctor's advice, and I reluctantly agreed to tell coach about it.

Saturday's intra-team scrimmage went well, but beforehand, I had trouble getting my swollen toe and foot into my shoe. The pain had gotten worse. As everyone left the field after wind sprints, I approached Coach Carillot.

He stood there, absolutely still in his white jersey and grey sweats, his silver whistle hanging from a black cord around his neck. His presence that morning was no different than when he stood on the blocking sled during practice. When you moved it—and him—15 or so yards and had no strength left to move another yard, he wanted more. His authority was nothing short of formidable. I apologetically told him what Dr. Pletcher said about not suiting up for a few weeks.

My words were skewered in midair by his crisp response:

"Nobody's irreplaceable."

Nothing more: he simply walked away, leaving me alone in the middle of the field. I was silent, I think—at least, I can't recall responding. I had not considered what his reply might be and I was dumbfounded.

Maybe I wasn't as important to the team as I had thought. But this was the late summer of 1955 and in our town, if you could walk, you played football. While I was unlikely to start, there was no way I was going to be locked on the bench with a wooden splint keeping me from putting my shoe on and playing. So instead of wearing a splint, I taped my broken fifth toe to my fourth toe—and that was the end of it. I didn't miss a practice. I desperately wanted a chance to show my stuff, and staying in the game was more important than a little pain.

Only 10 from my class had made it onto the varsity squad our senior year, including eight of the 27 members of our freshman team. The two senior newcomers were Don Eaton and Dick Montgomery. They changed the landscape for Jack Moynihan and me, offering serious competition for the starting guard positions.

As the fall season progressed, Dick beat me out for my starting guard position, while Don took over Jack Moynihan's slot. I had to recognize that I was replaceable. That I had been supplanted by a much better player didn't help. But I never lost my competitiveness, even as I found myself vanquished to the bench more than I wanted to be. Indeed, I was stronger for knowing I would not quit.

1955 Varsity

Our senior-year season was football near its best. Nothing was overlooked. We were even issued face masks just before the first game. They were new additions to the high school scene. Mouth guards alone had been the standard protection against injuries to the face, but they were not always sufficient in the trenches; too many fists and knees caused too many broken teeth, bloody noses, and cut lips. Few high school teams had face masks for linemen in those days, and being one of the first to get them gave us a psychological advantage.

Practices were longer than the year before, with lots of sweat and exhausting efforts at conditioning before the first game. Salt pills and water on the field helped but usually didn't fully replace our fluid losses. Two-a-days were hard work, but a sense of satisfaction followed. The greatest pleasure was to finish those preseason drills, go straight to the A&W Root Beer stand, and chug a quart or so of root beer in a matter of minutes.

We had some exceptionally good players that year, most notably Jim Sorber, who had been a friend since grade school. Jim was an athletic prodigy and a phenomenal kicker. His punts averaged 44 yards, equaling the state high school record and earning him an athletic scholarship to the University of Miami in Florida. Also new to varsity that year was an exceptional sophomore, Art Branstatter, Jr. He was the oldest of five boys. His father, Arthur Sr., had been an All American football player at Michigan State in 1936 and was chair of its Department of Police Administration when I was in high school. As a senior, Art Jr. led East Lansing to a Class B Basketball Championship, defeating the perennial favorite, River Rouge High School, 62–51. He subsequently became an exceptionally talented end at Michigan State, receiving all Big Ten team honors.

When the season began, we were ready to improve over the last year's record. We found ourselves in competition with some of the state's better Class B schools. We opened with a nonconference win over Mt. Pleasant, who had defeated us the year before. We then annihilated our Twin Valley opponents in succession, walking all over Adrian, Marshall, Three Rivers, Albion, Sturgis, and Coldwater.

Our final game during the first week of November was against Battle Creek Lakeview, on their home field. We went in ranked by the *Detroit Free Press* as the top Class B team in the State of Michigan. We knew we were good.

The halftime score was 7-7 and we thought we were going to win. But when the game clock expired it was 21-7 and Lakeview was on top. Their star player, Walt McNally, did a trip on us and we were simply outplayed. We shared the Twin Valley Conference title with Battle Creek Lakeview because they had lost an earlier game, but they had the better of us and we knew it.

Something else painful happened that night. Halfway through the season I had fractured a rib during practice when I threw a downfield body block on someone who had 70 pounds on me. He was moving fast to catch the ball carrier a few feet behind me. He didn't get the tackle, but he creamed me. The rib felt good with taping and I wore rib pads for the last three games of the season. In the shower after that last game with Lakeview, I asked a teammate to pull off the tape. He did more than that: he pulled off about five inches of skin. Instantly, I forgot the original fracture as the pain of an open hunk of raw chest sunk in.

But the pain of the loss to Lakeview was worse still. The bus ride home felt indeterminately long—much longer than the 43 miles we had traveled to the game. Our 7-1 won-loss record was painful. It was only Coach Carillot's second season at East Lansing High, however, and he instantly began planning for an undefeated season the next year—the first of what would be two Class B State Championships. East Lansing beat Battle Creek Lakeview the next year, 34 to 6. But I wasn't there.

Why There?

East Lansing High School was an astonishing place for student athletes and their coaches. The football program in that era built student-athletes who valued scholarship, recognized the value of teamwork, and were willing to work hard to improve themselves both mentally and physically. Football also benefited a remarkable group of talented coaches.

Pat Peppler was my gym teacher in junior high, and was the head football coach at East Lansing High before Vince Carillot. Peppler had played football at Michigan State College and he too had brought a Class B Championship to our school. In the fall of 1954, as my team prepared to play football, Peppler became an assistant coach at North Carolina State University. Nine years later he began an illustrious career in the pros, first as player personnel director of the Green Bay Packers, coached by Vince Lombardi, then director of scouting for Don Shula's Miami Dolphins. He left those two teams with four Super Bowl rings and retired in 1985 after spending time with the Houston Oilers, New Orleans Saints, and lastly the Atlanta Falcons, where he was interim head coach for a nine-game stretch after his predecessor was fired. But he first made his mark at East Lansing High.

Roy Kramer followed Vince Carillot as head coach, from 1960 to 1964. He too was exceptional. His team won the Class A State Championship in his last year, after which he joined the coaching staff of Central Michigan University as an assistant, becoming head coach two years later and leading his team to a NCAA Division II Championship before accepting the athletic directorship at Vanderbilt University. He served as commissioner of the Southeastern Conference from 1990 to 2002, during which time he spearheaded the Bowl Championship Series which determined the national championship for a little more than a decade. He, too, knew football, and people in East Lansing still talk about his legacy.

Both Pat Peppler and Roy Kramer had won State Championships at smaller high schools before being recruited to East Lansing High—Peppler at Grant High and Kramer at Hudson High. Why did they come to my hometown? Perhaps because it was a small, enthusiastic college town that embraced intelligent kids who were receptive to being coached and a school system that would provide them support in developing a winning team.

What really made East Lansing that kind of place? To that I have no clear answer. But it was a different era. Football instilled discipline and student athletes and coaches became leaders. The spectacle of a legion of uninhibited fans cheering on a group of young players on Friday nights and Saturday afternoons may look different today to people who have followed the sport's astonishing transformation over the succeeding half-century, but back then, most of us considered a great team to be a sign of a community's well-being. Our teams were producing well-rounded young men with a drive to be the best and the capacity to be leaders in society.

15
But for the Grace of God

My insight into the fragility of the human body and the importance of even the smallest occurrences began early in life when tragedies ended the lives of two individuals I knew. It's unlikely that either would have happened today, but these events left an indelible impression on me: first, it's axiomatic that when anything can happen, everything becomes relevant; second, crummy things can happen to good people.

A Terrible Virus

Futility and terror permeated entire communities during the summer polio epidemics of the early 1950s. Today it's hard to fathom the darkness and gloom that cast a shadow on so many people, especially during the sunny days of summer. But I was there and it was scary. It was as if a solar eclipse had cast a shadow across the entire outdoors. At midday, when children's laughter would normally have been common in our backyards, there was silence. Those days were hot and humid, and the only sounds to break the thick air were the waxing and waning, shrill voices of the cicadas, calling to each other in unison. Humankind was indoors.

Then it got worse. By the end of the summer of 1953 there were more than 2,000 new cases of polio nationwide. After the first few reported cases, people stayed inside, afraid of contact with neighbors who might be contagious. My schoolmates and I were kept away from public gathering places, especially swimming pools and drinking fountains. It was early to bed every night, often hours before dusk turned to darkness. I wasn't always ready to go to sleep, and it wasn't easy. I felt alone and I feared something I couldn't see or feel.

The polio virus was small, a simple strand of RNA with a coat of protein. And it was much more prevalent than most of us knew. The usual manifestations of infection ranged from nothing to a fever with an associated headache, vomiting, and discomfort in the limbs and neck. Among the infected, only one in 200 developed an irreversible paralysis, and of those, 5% to 10% died when their breathing muscles failed. Progression of the illness was unpredictable—a crapshoot.

If you were a severely affected victim but you didn't succumb immediately, you were placed in an iron lung, a steel cylinder with your head out one end on a padded rest with mirrors so you could see those about your area of confinement. Being helpless with someone feeding you and wiping your bottom may have seemed an indignity, but it paled in comparison to the anxiety over the potential failure of the iron lung's motor.

No one inhabiting an iron lung wanted its "click-swoosh-click" to stop. That noise accompanied the mechanical device that substituted for their failing muscles and was responsible for every breath, without which they would suffocate and die—that is, unless someone was there with the physical dexterity to pump the emergency lever at the side of the cylinder.

In 1952, in the midst of the polio epidemic, Skip Carl, a classmate, came home one day to find his mother stricken with the disease. She died and left the six Carl children and her husband at a loss to understand something they had not asked for. It was recognized that if one person in a household had clinical evidence of the infection, more than 90% of the others harbored the virus as well. The rest of the Carl family escaped the ravages of polio. One might say they were lucky, but they didn't feel that way.

Polio spreads from human to human, usually entering through the mouth and upper respiratory passages, from whence it travels into the intestinal tract. There it multiplies, before being passed on to others

There were no medicines to take after you contracted the disease, then or now. The same year Mrs. Carl died, Jonas Salk developed a vaccine with an inactivated polio virus that showed promise. Three years later, on April 12, 1955, Thomas Francis, Jr., at the University of Michigan's School of Public Health, announced the results of a nationwide study revealing that the vaccine was effective in eliminating polio. The oral vaccine developed by Albert Sabin in 1957 was released in 1962 and has eradicated the disease from developed nations.

Before immunizations, many felt the deep pessimism and desperation that comes with the knowledge that the polio virus occurred with no obvious boundaries and avoiding it might not be possible no matter how carefully you tried. Family, friends, and the entire community were at risk. A chance encounter with the polio virus was not Mrs. Carl's choice; it simply was an unpredictable event, with a sad ending.

Unforgiving Bacteria

Diane Rinkes, a classmate who lived a block from my house, was another person who had a fatal encounter with what for most was a relatively common infectious agent. She and I had been inseparable buddies in 1st grade—at times, humorously so. One winter day we mixed up our near-identical grey-tweed coats. It took a month for us to realize that the coat she picked up had the buttons on the right side, and the one I was wearing had its buttons on the left—the basic difference between girls' and boys' coats to this day. Our mistaken swap went unnoticed until my mother recognized that the coat I was wearing was a girl's. We laughed about this as we grew older, realizing that gender differences were about more than coat buttons.

Diane was very slight as a child, and as she entered her teenage years and grew taller, she acquired something of a "skin and bones" appearance. Her hair was full but very fine and her steel-blue eyes and pale complexion made her seem a little more serious than the rest of us. Her legs were long and thin and my guess is that her extremities didn't have a bit of extra fat or muscle on them. That she refused to succumb to self-pity may have been the reason she extended herself to become an East Lansing High School cheerleader. But that may have been too risky of a boundary for her to have crossed. She didn't laugh as much as the rest of us and her joy seemed limited. Her fragile optimism seemed to mask the fact that simple tasks consumed a lot of her energy.

Diane's energy ran out on September 24, 1953. It was a Thursday night at the beginning of our sophomore year and my reserve football team had just lost an away game under the lights with Lansing Eastern. Our spirits were not very high as we filed onto the team bus to head back to East Lansing. Our coach, Gus Ganakas, had just sat down in front when a red glow from outside became the oscillating red beacon of an ambulance heading straight onto the football field. The bus didn't move and Gus was summoned outside. We sat there with no idea what had happened; perhaps a fan or a parent had fallen on the bleacher steps and broken an ankle. The stands alongside football fields in those days were pretty rickety.

Minutes became an hour. The driver, Ed Lyons, told us we were not to leave the bus when a few of us tried to get off to see what was happening. Then Gus jogged briskly back to the parking lot. He walked quietly up the stairwell of the bus and we were stone silent as he addressed us.

> "Guys, I'm very sorry to tell you that Diane Rinkes collapsed running off the field with her dad and the other cheerleaders. We don't know what happened. They tried to help her but it didn't work and she died. We will talk about it later. But we really need to go home now."

She was 15, five months older than me. I am not sure if any of us who attended her funeral grasped the finality of death at the time, but it became a reality in the weeks to follow as her empty chair in class reminded us of her absence.

No one ever spoke to us about what caused Diane's death, but in all probability, it was the streptococcus bacteria.

Streptococcus is a round or ovoid bacteria, much bigger than a virus and best known for causing strep throat in children and young adults. The beta-hemolytic streptococcus has many different types and immunity to one does not afford protection against the rest. We are all likely to be infected with one of these germs at some time in our lives. If all we have to deal with is a fever and pain from an inflamed throat when swallowing, it's just a few days' inconvenience, like the common cold caused by a self-limiting adenovirus.

But streptococcal infections can be followed by threats to other organs very distant from your throat—your kidneys and heart, or even your body in general. Rheumatic fever with a skin rash, fever, and muscle aches is a well-recognized complication affecting 3% of those who are not treated initially with antibiotics. The kidneys may also be a target causing renal failure due to glomerulonephritis, a nonspecific inflammation affecting the kidney's tissues.

If your heart takes the hit from this infection, known as rheumatic heart disease, you may be in store for a lot of problems, including a failure to pump blood efficiently from a direct injury to the heart muscle, damage to the valves in the heart, or abnormal heart rhythms. All of these can be fatal. In the 1940s, during my childhood, we didn't have ready access to quick diagnoses and effective treatment of strep infections.

Diane most likely had rheumatic heart disease that carried a death sentence. Her sudden passing was probably due to an electrical derangement or arrhythmia that prevented her heart from beating normally. Although rheumatic heart disease in the young is rare today, these electrical failures still occur on athletic fields; most often, in conditioned competitors, with a thickened heart muscle that underlies their arrhythmia. But that's not what afflicted Diane. Her problem started with a simple infection.

More than a half-century later, Diane's fate might have been averted with a defibrillator, now available at many high school athletic events, to shock her heart back to a normal beat. Rheumatic heart disease is very uncommon today—thank heaven for quick throat swabs and effective antibiotics. It was a chance occurrence that the streptococcus bacteria Diane must have encountered as a child exacted its price years later.

16

Bad Choices

Every once in a while bad things happened to my friends when they did something dumb. It often seemed unfair; after all, we were young. Nevertheless we all need to be awakened once in a while so we don't make foolish mistakes. At times the awakening is unbearably harsh.

Just Another Game of Chicken

As teenagers growing up in the 1950s, death was a stranger to most of us. But we also had fun challenging fate by playing "I dare you" games. Whether it was "I dare you to jump" from the branch of a tree you were climbing, or from the bank of a river where you were swimming, it always carried a risk—and an award of admiration if you successfully made the jump and landed with little more than a few bruises or a bit of water up your nose. Not surprisingly, the risks increased as we grew older, and the penalty for losing started to take the form of an irretrievable expense: loss of life.

Donn Hunt was a neighbor, living two blocks from my home. Four years older than me, he was the archetypical rebellious stud as portrayed in many movies of the decade. He loved speed—on foot, on a bicycle, and of course in a car.

Donn grew up in comfort and had one of the coolest cars in town, a 1951 Ford coupe with a hopped-up engine, dual carbs, fancy wheel covers, and a radio that would blast you off the planet when cranked up to full volume. He was the casual guy cruising around town with his steady girlfriend in the seat next to him. Many upperclassmen were envious. The underclassmen watched and waited. Donn had a large following and many younger guys hoped they would grow up to be just like him. I was among them. But somewhere along the way he failed to learn how to negotiate the perils that a combination of adolescence and demonic speed can produce.

On the night of December 9, 1951, Donn made a choice. He was in an illegal drag race. These races occurred frequently, often involving young boys and their hot-rods from the "Genovesse Gear Grinders" from Flint and the "Lansing Pan Draggers." That night was no different. Donn challenged another boy to race. They were on the outskirts of East Lansing on State Road, near Farm Lane, an isolated road. It was simple: two cars would race side by side from one end of the strip to the other end.

Donn and the other driver finished one run and turned around to race back. What they didn't see, until they reached the peak of a rise in the road, was that other cars were coming their way. There were no boundaries to protect him. Donn had no place to pull off. There was a horrendous head-on crash. In a split second he lay mortally injured, tangled in a web of twisted steel. Donn had a propensity for showmanship and before he died he asked a friend to give the racing gloves he had worn that night to his girlfriend. In that vein he went out in style.

But the grotesque wreckage of the car he was driving was a testament to the momentary value of material things. Donn's still body made brutally clear how quickly a blithe spirit can be silenced. He was just a month past his 17th birthday. Movie buffs will note a similarity with the movie *Rebel Without a Cause*, starring James Dean and Natalie Wood. The protagonists in the movie were racing to the edge of a cliff. Donn and the cars with which he unexpectedly collided were driving toward each other. James Dean's real-life death in a car accident not long afterward was portrayed as the romantic loss of a hero. Some spoke of Donn Hunt's violent death as a romantic tragedy. That was certainly not how his parents or his girlfriend saw it. The reality was that his death was just plain dumb.

As I say, most of us thought little of death, especially if we could view it as a consequence of some other person's ill-advised behavior. But I distinctly recall walking home from school in silence after Donn's accident, wondering for the first time how death would visit me. I was only 13.

Booze

In the 1950s, when we wanted to leave our inhibitions behind and replace common sense with unbridled laughter, the easiest way was to consume alcoholic beverages. Booze was the most available mind-bender of the day. Recreational drugs were inaccessible and marijuana unobtainable in our town. Rebellion in those days was a game, perhaps a revolt against adult values. Unfortunately, some of us were not well anchored.

Drinking a few beers with friends on a hillside near the outskirts of town was how it began. We were juniors in high school. A year later we would gather on weekends at classmates' homes when their parents were out of town and break into the hard liquor. A few of our classmates seemed to revel in getting unceremoniously plastered. More often than not, we laughed at these poor souls who couldn't hold their drink.

Most of us survived being liberated with a little booze when we were young. In others, alcohol unleashed an uncontrolled need that could only be squelched with more booze until death interceded.

The legal age to buy alcoholic beverages in Michigan when I was in high school was 21. Some of us had false identification with altered birthdates on our newly acquired drivers' licenses. A license then was a simple photocopy, unlike today's tamper-proof cards with their embedded, indelible identifiers. It was easy in the 1950s to scratch out your real birthdate and change it so that it appeared you were old enough to imbibe.

We could get into Coral Gables, the darkened college hangout just outside the border of dry East Lansing, with our new I.D., but we rarely dared use it in a store to buy beer: the lights were too good. Only one of my classmates was ever caught with false identification, and his name was published in the *Lansing State Journal*. That was a problem for Gary Gross, whose father owned and managed the local radio and TV stations. Neither he nor his father needed the notoriety.

But there were easier and less risky ways to acquire booze. The modus operandi was to drive to the poorest section of Lansing and wait until we saw some down-and-out person about to enter a package-liquor store. Invariably, when offered a few dollars, this person would agree to buy some hooch for us: a little extra money for one's own libations was too good to turn down. Of course, they were illegally purchasing alcoholic beverages for minors, and we were clearly outside the law once it was in our possession. Boys will be boys—so we rationalized. But the little alcohol-induced buzz that seemed like fun as a teenager became pernicious and turned into full-blown alcoholism and caused the senseless deaths of two of my classmates, David Sackrider and Ron Lindell.

Booze never let go of David Sackrider. He was a reasonable jock, less of a student, and his popularity was rooted in his social behavior. He could drink a sailor under the table by the time he was old enough to legally buy beer. I don't know what the allure was for him, but it must have been exceedingly strong—like the bright flame that attracts moths at nighttime, until they perish in its heat.

David knew the dangers. In and out of rehabilitation as a young adult, he was prone to falling off the wagon until the day it all stopped. He was driving, half-inebriated, and reached into the backseat for another beer—a mistake cut short as he lost control of his car. He had a horrendous accident. Hospitalized with massive injuries, he died days later. He was 46 years old. David had a heart of gold and would do anything for others; he just couldn't help himself.

Ron Lindell, who became an alcoholic in early adulthood, suffered an even more tragic demise. He grew up in a very affluent family. His father owned Lindell Drop Forge, a major supplier to the booming automotive industry. Ron was spoiled, and he received a new Buick Roadmaster as a junior at East Lansing High. He also had the beginning of a drinking problem.

Ron and I had a long talk at our 25th high school class reunion in 1981. He sounded nihilistic and unrepentant as we chatted at the hotel bar where he had spent a sordid evening, while our classmates ate dinner at nearby tables. He was pouring the liquor down almost as fast as it could be served. Any insight into his drinking seemed to be masked by loathing for everything in his life that had gone wrong—and that provided an excuse for his unchecked alcoholism. Ron had been evaluated earlier that year at the University of Michigan Hospital by one of my colleagues for his evolving liver cirrhosis. He got good advice but didn't accept it. Ignorance was clearly as dynamic as intelligence.

Ron, like Dave Sackrider, attended more than one rehabilitation program until the end, when he had a minor mishap while driving home drunk. It was a year after Dave's accident and Ron had been out of rehab for less than three days when he took to drink again. When he left a bar to go home, he drove off a snow-slick road into a ditch. His car was stuck in the snow and mud and he couldn't get it to move. He decided to walk home, which wasn't far.

No one really knows what happened in the next few hours—he may have fallen or decided to sit and rest for a few minutes. Ron was found alone the next day, frozen to death in a snow-covered field. Like Dave, he was only 46.

When someone else experiences a terrible loss, I try not to forget that it could have happened to me. Fate and boundaries set by teachers, coaches, and parents helped me stay clear of many traps and have kept me intact to this day. It might have been different.

17
Pain: The Absence of Choice

Some people don't have choices. Their options in life have been limited by others who hold preconceived opinions about them and subsequently create boundaries that narrow or eliminate their choices. This huge social issue rarely affected me as I grew up, but when it did, it was painful. I did not always do well on those occasions.

Bias

There was no overt caste system in East Lansing in the mid-1950s, but I am sure that prejudice was widespread. That it was not more apparent was mainly due to the fact that no families with roots in Africa or Asia lived in our town, aside from a very small number of college students of color. But if bias is the embodiment of inequality, then there was plenty of minor inequality to feed the small-minded of East Lansing.

Genteel WASPs predominated; I could easily count the Catholic and Jewish students in my class on my fingers and toes. East Lansing folks were comfortable, and no doubt inertia and ignorance sustained their silent biases, more so than any ingrained deep prejudice.

Much of the town's social talk did little more than feed the community's sense of self-importance. I, too, contributed to this pattern until I found myself being unfairly judged for something over which I had no choice: who my parents were. For the first time I understood, painfully, what people who didn't look like me had felt for generations. In my case it had to do with wealth. Three events have remained with me as reminders of the problems caused by differences.

A Garden or a Cottage

Some people always see themselves as the victims of social bias, even if such is not the case. Wallace B. Moffett was an example of such a person. He lived on Collingwood Drive, across the vacant lot on the block in front of our home, where he resided in a quiet and well-kept, red-brick Tudor-style home built on two residential lots.

Moffett's yard was immaculate. It was completely surrounded by a low lying hedge, about three feet high and always meticulously manicured. Enclosed was a beautiful garden in full bloom every year from May to October. His trellised roses stood behind beds of hundreds of annuals and perennials that created a picture like an old master's painting. The flower beds were at least 10 feet deep, with carefully placed stepping stones hidden among the lower lying foliage. Mr. Moffett could be seen nearly every afternoon, even on weekdays, tending his flowers. If ever East Lansing offered an award for the most attractive garden, his would have been in the running. The only problem is that he would then have been interviewed—and he would have come off as a most unlikable individual.

Mr. Moffett was consumed with a burning dislike for his next-door neighbor, Todd Leavitt. Dr. Leavitt was a very successful dentist with three children. His yard ran right up to Mr. Moffett's, but he was rather casual about its upkeep, especially during the summertime, when he spent weekends at his cottage on Duck Lake, a few hours away. The Leavitts' cottage, a log cabin-type on the water's edge, was where his family water skied and swam from a float offshore, and where he could unload the intensity of his busy hours in the office. His East Lansing home was ill-attended while the Leavitts were away—and that was when Mr. Moffett's garden next door was at its best.

Wally Moffett, as he took note of his yard and his neighbor's, was not a happy man. Here he was, working so diligently to maintain his garden, while the wealthy Dr. Leavitt simply packed up and took a vacation every weekend. There was more. Mr. Moffett owned an old car in constant disrepair, and the Leavitts had two cars—new ones every few

Pain: The Absence of Choice 161

years, often seen with one of their boats trailing behind. The differences in values and priorities were palpable.

Mr. Moffett was a bit like Miniver Cheevy in Edward Arlington Robinson's 1910 poem, who:

Grew lean while he assailed the seasons;
He wept that he was born. And he had reasons.
Miniver scorned the gold he sought, But sure annoyed was he without it;
Miniver thought, and thought, and thought, And thought about it.

That was Mr. Moffett's predicament. He was inconsolable about Leavitt's greater wealth and lack of interest in having a perfectly attended yard.

One day when I was walking around the block with my father, we stopped to say Hi to Mr. Moffett. Dad offered a simple salutation:

"How are things going?"

That's all it took. Wally let out his anger.

"It's unfair. Leavitt has all that money, cars, and a cottage."

My father's response, as logical as it was, stopped the conversation.

"Look at all the years it took him to be a dentist. He has no time to have a beautiful garden like you. Look at his yard. You're better off."

Mr. Moffett's response was short. He was adamant and bitter, no matter the obvious fact that my father saw.

"Maybe."

Wallace Moffett was an excellent English professor at Michigan State College, a fine Homeric scholar, and a truly expert gardener. Todd Leavitt was an exceptional dentist. Somewhere along the line both had made a choice to be what they wanted and both had succeeded. The difference was that Mr. Moffatt was sadly uncomfortable with his choice. Maybe accepting our choices is what matters, before they become onerous boundaries to our peace of mind. And we should stop wasting energy comparing our choices to others'.

Dad and I quickly walked away, and when we were out of earshot, my father told me that Mr. Moffett was too angry to spend much time with. Witnessing this as a child was painful. I wondered what place Mr. Moffett assigned my family in his scheme of things.

The Doctor's Son

The worm turned when I entered 7th grade and had a chance to see the world a bit like Mr. Moffett. For the first time I, like the other boys in my class, was becoming clothes conscious—especially during the first week of school. We would try to wear a different outfit every day, just to impress our friends. That year the best dressed guys wore grey flannel pants with pastel button-down shirts or corduroy pants and Pendleton plaid shirts. I got both outfits at Lansing's classiest men's clothing store, Kosticheks. I was proud of my new look. No more the brown gabardine pants or wool knickers and long socks of earlier years. I was more mature, after all. I was 12 years old.

My friends and I from Bailey School found ourselves mingling with kids from Central School when we entered freshman class at East Lansing High. Fred Tamblyn was a Central School guy. He was an exceptional athlete, very self-confident, and a leader among his friends. He was disarmingly good looking, with dark red wavy hair and a square jaw. Most kids stayed at his side and did not try to one-up him. He was also a blowhard and a bit arrogant. Fred's father, F.W. Tamblyn, was a highly regarded obstetrician and gynecologist, but he must have provided little guidance to Fred, who was often on the loose. Fred was a bully.

One day after school let out, Fred knocked my books from my arms on the way out the door. When I bent over to pick them up, he knocked me to the ground by grabbing the side pocket of my new corduroy pants. The seam split down to my knee. Fred must have thought it was funny, for he proceeded to pull harder until my pants were ripped open all the way down to the ankle. So much for the first week of junior high and my newfound friends. I was in no position to counter Fred's behavior—I was too small. Whatever pride I possessed was destroyed and I ran home as fast as I could. I wanted to change my pants and be left alone.

My mother was predictably upset and my father infuriated by the day's event. After dinner he called Dr. Tamblyn and suggested he needed to have better control of his son. My father's face soon glowed red and he abruptly hung up the phone. Fred's father had suggested that if my family couldn't afford to buy me a new pair of pants he would be happy to help out. My dad was furious at the implication that he couldn't afford to buy me a new pair of pants and I was even more upset.

We weren't poor, and I didn't like being made to feel that I was. But maybe we were. We certainly weren't as wealthy as the Tamblyns. And what was going to happen the next day, if Fred got wind of my father's call? It seemed like a no-win for me. I hadn't done anything to deserve to feel bad. But I did feel bad. It was pervasive, and I couldn't escape a sense of not being able to defend myself because of my small size and, perhaps, my family's less prominent standing in the community. The very idea that someone could buy their way out of responsibility for their bad behavior because they had a lot of money like Dr. Tamblyn rankled me. Abruptly, I had learned that being wealthy doesn't guarantee common decency.

I never forgot that day, even though I got a new pair of pants and Fred was civil to me the rest of the school year. Decades later it all came back to me in spades. I was in my surgical residency, rotating at Wayne County General Hospital, when my wife had me paged—a rare event. When I answered her call I was worried that something bad had happened: a broken bone, a car accident, something not good. As it turned out, our first born, Tim, who was four years old, had gotten into trouble in preschool. Nancy had been asked to come to the school and take him home: Tim had bitten the teacher. My first thoughts were almost unbearable. I didn't want Tim to be like Fred, and I didn't want to be the doctor whose son was always out of control because I was too busy to be a good father.

What had happened, it turned out, was not so terrible. The teacher had assigned each student a role as one of the jungle animals. Tim was told he was a lion. When I quizzed Tim, he explained that he had seen a book on lions and they were always "biting": eating lots of meat, then taking long naps. Leave it to a child to let his imagination tell him how to really act like a lion. He was forgiven, but I found myself asking:

"How can I ever be sure that my children, the doctor's kids, always respect other people?"

In retrospect, my wife and I must have done a good job, for our three offspring have never failed us by treating others unfairly.

Country Club and Church: The Businessman

I found myself on the short side of a third and more subtle form of bias later in high school—or so I rationalized. For more than three years a classmate and I were "steadies," often studying at her home on weeknights, and on weekends hanging out with the gang, going to movies, swimming at the Lansing Country Club in the summer, and always in church with her parents on Sundays. I cared a lot for Annette McDonald.

Our first date was the Sophomore Prom, after which we went to Mary Lou Cole's home. We sat in the living room, talking with Mary Lou and her date, Daryl Olsen, until someone turned down the lights. On opposite sides of the room we necked for an hour before leaving at 1 a.m. That was the first time I'd made out with a girl—something I hadn't prepared for. As I walked home, everything seemed so quiet. In the solitude of the nighttime, I realized I wanted to spend as much time as I could with Annette. It was a very different feeling, and it would take some getting used to, but I wasn't confused. Later, during a walk home from school, she let me know that she shared the same feelings. The seeds of love were there.

We were serious about each other—a first for both of us. But we must have been together too much, too soon, and too visibly for her parents,

Dewey and Grace McDonald. Her father was by any measure a successful man. Born in Iowa, he attended college there before transferring to the University of Colorado, where he obtained a law degree. He then entered the dairy business. At the time I was dating his daughter, he headed up Heatherwood Farms, the major dairy in the Lansing environs. He carried the message that all dairy products were healthy: milk, butter, ice cream. I remember his reaction to the opening of the town's first Dairy Queen, and his dismay that they were using soy in their products. What we didn't know about healthy foods in those days!

Mr. McDonald was very active in the local business community, and a frequent presence at the Lansing Country Club. But he was not a "slap you on the back" type: in fact, he was very thoughtful and serious. That sincerity may have explained his close involvement with the First Presbyterian Church, a stone's throw from the Capitol in Lansing. I had left Peoples Church in East Lansing to join the McDonalds' flock, and it was different from the community I had grown up in—more businesslike, with less time for thinking and praying. Annette and I used to sit with her father in the balcony on Sundays, and he had an unusual habit that was somehow consistent with my impressions of my new church. Every Sunday Mr. McDonald would time the sermon, and tell the minister its exact duration as he bid farewell at the church's front door

Mr. McDonald was always polite in his discourse with me, but in-depth conversations about school, sports, politics, or his daughter were rare. He may have already concluded that I wasn't his or his daughter's type. If such was the case, I hadn't a clue. Grace McDonald was different. I truly liked her, and we often spent time talking about important aspects of our lives. She too was very successful. She headed up the nursing services at E.W. Sparrow Hospital in Lansing. And it was she, at 11 p.m., who would turn the hallway light on and off from upstairs, signaling that it was time for Annette and me to break it up and for me to be on my way home.

Later in life I received an A in an undergraduate psychology course and an A+ in my medical school psychiatry class, but my understanding as a teenager of the dynamics and emotional biology of myself and the McDonald family fell short. Perhaps Annette's parents simply thought we were too young to be so serious, and maybe Annette wanted some space, but I had a sense that Grace and Dewey wished better for their daughter. That was painful. My parents thought the world of Annette and gave me great freedom in spending time with her. Perhaps I should have been more analytical about where I was going and where I had come from. I never would have guessed that I might be on the losing end of someone's bias. But it seemed that I was.

My parents didn't belong to the country club, my father never attended college, and he was not in Rotary. I wanted to be an engineer—perhaps working for someone else, rather than owning my own business or setting out as a self-employed professional. There were other differences. Annette received a brand new 1954 Chevrolet convertible in her junior year of high school. Such a gift would have been unheard of for my brother or me. Annette's parents traveled widely, including to Europe. My parents vacationed in the National Parks, getting there by car and sleeping in their canvas umbrella tent.

Perhaps most notably different were the neighborhoods where we resided. The McDonalds lived in the northeast sector of the city, with most of the town's doctors, dentists, and independent businesspeople. My parents lived in the southeast sector, with university professors, school teachers, and employees of the town's businesses. East Lansing was not a large place, but some neighborhoods were unquestionably more affluent than others. These differences may have been much more visible to Annette's parents than to my parents or me. I probably missed the nuances—the early signs of my not being part of their world.

Different socioeconomic families, of course; different children, not really. Annette had a bunny nose and strawberry blond hair, and willowy arms and legs. Her blue eyes sparkled when she laughed and when she was studying she always looked intense. She and I shared a lot in common, especially in our values of life and family. We cared deeply for each other and talked of marriage and growing old together. But there must have been something missing.

Our dating took a turn south in the late spring of our senior year in high school and the following fall, when I found myself going to the University of Michigan and Annette to Ohio Wesleyan. Her choice of this highly regarded, small liberal arts school floored me—I never knew if it was her choice or the place her parents thought best. We had always talked of going to the University of Michigan together. But there we were—me in one place, she in another.

Separation may make some hearts grow fonder. I tried: letters between Delaware, Ohio, and Ann Arbor, Michigan, three or four times a week, lots of phone calls, and trips to each other's campus. But as the summer break arrived between our freshman and sophomore years, something occurred that cooled things even further. It wasn't my doing. Annette took a job as a nurse's aide at Ingham Chest Hospital, a longtime center for care and treatment of tuberculosis. The most senior surgeon there was C.J. Stringer, a close friend of Annette's parents. That summer they mandated that she be home and in her room very early every night—all under the guise that she was working near tuberculosis patients and needed lots of rest to keep up her immunity. It was a subtle means to an end: no movies or snuggling in each other's arms those nights. But Annette seemed comfortable with the arrangement.

Not me: I experienced a bottomless sadness as I began my sophomore year at Michigan. For months I felt a daily, gut-wrenching discomfort. I've often wondered what biochemical events, beginning in the brain and ending in the abdomen, make you ache like that. It was not easy for me to get through those days, and it took me a long time to accept that my life had changed, but I slowly reset my sails, hoping for better days. For Annette, life may have been better for a while—But I'm not so sure. She transferred to Michigan after her sophomore year at Ohio Wesleyan. We had a few evenings together and we tried to be close. But it wasn't the same. Perhaps both of us felt burned. There would be no rekindling of our relationship.

Her father died in May of our senior year in college. It was a tragedy of sorts: He had experienced what everyone thought was a kidney stone on a winter train trip to the west coast. It turned out to be cancer of a kidney, and after a nephrectomy he developed a metastasis to his lung that had to be removed, but it was too late. He died a shadow of himself, and his passing was very hard on his wife, on Annette, and her older sister, Nancy. Whether in his waning days he had less influence over his daughter is unknown to me, and we never talked about it when I saw her on campus. But by then, my own life had changed. I had fallen in love with Nancy Norville.

Nancy and I were married shortly after her graduation from the University of Michigan and after I had completed my first year of medical school. Our wedding took place in south Chicago. Lots of my East Lansing friends were there, including Barry McDowell, who had been my roommate our freshman year in college and who was an usher. My best man, Phil Warren, drove Barry and me to the church. All three of us had been staying at the South Shore Country Club. A few blocks into the drive, Barry asked if we could stop by a hotel and pick up someone who had accompanied him to Chicago: Annette.

Awkward, yes. Strange, even more so. I sat in the front seat with Phil, and Barry and Annette in the back, and I asked her if she ever thought she would be riding in the car taking me to the church where I was going to get married.

Her reply was a poignant and almost inaudible.

"No."

I didn't turn around to see her face. We both understood.

I didn't see or hear from Annette again until a high school reunion two decades later. Jack Moynihan, Nancy, and I were talking at an informal reception the first night. When Nancy walked away, Jack asked me if Annette was there. I motioned toward her across the room. His spontaneous reply sort of set me back:

"You made the right choice."

I'm not sure it wasn't Dewey and Grace who made that choice, years earlier.

Since those few wrenching days of my adolescence I have abhorred well intended people who carry even a hint of an ill-founded bias. My pain in the absence of choice was transient, but it hurt enough that I have never judged others by the things they could not change. No more than I could change my own parents.

18

Speaking Aloud

As a child I looked at the cartoons and read the limericks in the *Saturday Evening Post* every week. To paraphrase one poem I have often repeated: *"You can say it with flowers, or candy, or anything you think. Just be careful before you say it in ink."* I learned to speak decades before I learned to write intelligently. And as adolescence passed I clearly favored the spoken word over the written word. I may have learned too much about orations for my own good as a future writer.

Content versus Grammar

Even well-crafted words can send a confusing message. "Look out" may mean to put your head out the window and see what's going on—or, on another occasion, it could mean to duck your head before a passing object hits it. An exclamation mark versus a simple period might help make the import clearer. In the 1950s, the rationale for learning proper grammar in every high school English class was that it would narrow the number of interpretations that could be placed on our words. A great idea buried in a grammatical cesspool is likely to be overlooked, after all.

I was a poor speller and at times an even worse grammarian. Perhaps I should have recognized my weakness, since clear, correct, and concise communication was the rule in most of the printed media of those days. The first sentence of the first paragraph of a story in the morning's paper often said it all. Everything that followed expanded on that first paragraph's principal subject. Freedom from grammatical rules was the exception, usually found in the work of creative writers outside the mainstream.

English teachers in my day idolized the writers who adhered to the rules. One of my teachers liked to point out to us that Ernest Hemingway would retreat to his hotel room in Paris during his most productive years, where he would spend hours writing one perfect sentence—clearly, the kind of commitment she expected from us. Sure—but Hemingway's writing was more than grammar-perfect sentences. Content carried his prose, and it was for content that writing engaged me.

I loved words and their subtle meanings and I often played a game of trying to find the one ideal word that would capture what I was writing about. Serene, chaotic, dilatory, frigid—depending on the context, any one of these could make all the difference in giving a sentence its emotional impact. My interests were about content, not grammar. Perhaps as a result, speaking, more than writing, became my strength.

Storytelling

My belief in the primacy of content was confirmed in my sophomore high school English class, taught by Patrick D. Hazard, who was a media guy. Mr. Hazard left East Lansing shortly after I took his class, when he received a Ford Fellowship in New York City. There he became the TV editor for Scholastic Teacher, an important periodical for educators. He then received a PhD in American Studies in 1957 from Western Reserve University and proceeded to do postdoctoral work at the University of Pennsylvania, where he wrote the first curriculum for the Annenberg School of Communication. His success may have begun when he convinced our sophomore class to take some of our free time to watch and analyze the content of the movie *Macbeth* at a local theater or an original Paddy Chayefsky play on TV at home.

In Mr. Hazard's class we dissected popular TV shows like *Dragnet*, famous for Sgt. Joe Friday's admonition, "Just the facts, ma'am, that's all, just the facts," or Shakespeare's *Hamlet* on Sunday's Hallmark Hall of Fame. He was fascinated by the power of television. The year was 1953.

Eventually Mr. Hazard took a small group of us to the new WKAR-TV studios at Michigan State, where he produced a 30-minute show called "Rec Room." In my year, Sue Hodge and I were the hosts. No scripts, just notes, and we freelanced the presentations very successfully. It was a great way to build our confidence at communicating content. Cuss words and cheap slang were out of bounds. But the rules of grammar were not part of the show. We learned the sleight-of-hand techniques for wrapping up or prolonging our discourse while on camera, without losing the meaning we wanted to convey. Unfortunately, our television performance could not substitute for the conventional knowledge of grammar we gained through writing in our other English classes. But I wasn't worried about that at the time.

Mr. Hazard considered the media an important educational tool. Marshall McLuhan, a popular but controversial academic and literary critic in those days, likely influenced him. More than a half-century later, McLuhan's famous pronouncement, "The medium is the message," rings even truer. The medium has become the master, displayed en force on the screen of one's wrist watch, smartphone, iPad, or computer. The attraction is so strong as to command our attention to the exclusion, at times, of anyone else wanting a few minutes conversation with us. McLuhan must be resting in peace.

Addressing the Class of 1956

My self-esteem as a communicator rose to an even higher level two years later, when I became one of the class speakers at our graduation ceremony. We were the last class to attend the "old" East Lansing High School, and there was a buzz that we might be up to some pranks during the ceremony. This may have been partly the result of the school administrators' frustration surrounding an event that had occurred two weeks earlier.

A few of the guys, including myself, thought we should leave a memento as the last class to leave the old building. On night around 10 p.m., we carefully cut the class numerals, 56, out of the grass on the knoll near the school's front entrance, each number about two and a half feet tall. We removed the dirt below the cut-out grass to a depth of eight or so inches and poured in 25 pounds of phosphate fertilizer taken from Jack Moynihan's garage, then covered it with the dirt and the grass sod.

The Class of 1956 as we assembled on Britton Field bleachers the day of our graduation, June 14th.

You couldn't tell anything had happened the next morning, but a week later, the 56 was a blazing yellow of dead grass.

The administration replaced the grass a few days later, thinking someone had simply poured a toxic chemical on top, but within a day or so the new grass died too. It was a week before graduation. I was not a suspect, but nevertheless Mr. Kinney, the principal, asked to hear my talk ahead of time in the outdoor area where graduation was to take place. The request came under the guise that he wanted to be sure the public address system had enough volume for me to be heard. I had the distinct sense that he didn't trust any of us. All he heard from me was the first sentence of my address, over and over again. It was too late to do anything other than trust me.

Our class motto was "Today We Follow, Tomorrow We Lead." The faculty had picked two of us to be the class speakers. Diane Dennington, a good friend and an excellent speaker, offered our thanks to the teachers, church leaders, parents, and friends we had followed as students. Then I spoke.

Standing before my class, surrounded by nearly 800 family, friends, teachers, and townsfolk and speaking to them from an outdoor podium just before dusk, was a heady experience. I kept my original script and what follows is what I said, verbatim. If nothing else I spoke with style—grammar be damned.

Commencement, June 1956

If one were able to examine the complex and rather complicated path a person's life follows, you would notice a period of transition, a time in which the being ceases to be dependent and becomes a leader with one's own ideas and convictions. We seniors are approaching that transition. America's future and the world's fate will depend largely upon the decisions of today's youth, who will be tomorrow's leaders. We, East Lansing's graduating class of '56, will undoubtedly make some of these decisions—decisions which can make or break society.

The opportunities which unfold to us outnumber by far those of preceding generations, but the problems of society have increased too—problems which, if solved, could lead to a world united, a world whose nations wouldn't attempt to annihilate one another but would work in harmony for all of mankind.

Our paths are likely to divide after today, as we enter the real world. Each of us may find an opportunity to contribute to the betterment of society. The paths in which we may walk are very different. If they had signposts, they would likely include religion, education, medicine, industrial sciences, and the social sciences. If we could make a difference in any of these arenas, we could certainly say that we have done justice to the human condition. Let us briefly glance down these paths.

It can truthfully be said that a nation can be judged by its faith, and a nation without religious citizens will not survive. America began because of a want for religious freedom, and if today there be any single solution to the world's ills, faith in something more important than ourselves may provide an answer. Those walking this path will not only have peace of mind, but they will be a blessing to mankind.

The second path has lots of room to make a difference. This is the path of education. With the increasing population and the need for learning,

> there is a demand for instructors of excellence—teachers who will bring forth the very best in their students. We have been fortunate to have many of such teachers at East Lansing High School. Some of you will honor them by following their footsteps.
>
> A third path less traveled is that of medicine. Although advances in health care have at time appeared miraculous, it is obvious that many victories are yet to be won. The fact that one life can be saved, or one hour of misery avoided, makes this path very valuable. Walking this path is for those who can give unselfish devotion to others, the real reward being the recognition that one has helped a fellow human in need.
>
> The fourth path is that of the industrial sciences. At no time in history has there been a greater need for creative individuals to walk this path. Today, there is an unending plea for physicists, chemists, and engineers to build the future tools to meet society's needs. Industry reflects the progress and stability of a nation. In the future, America must excel in the industrial sciences if we are to maintain our world leadership. No doubt some of you will make her that way.
>
> Perhaps the path where leadership is a primary requirement is that of the social sciences, and of those, political science may be the most relevant. Our world can never have enough qualified leaders to guide society in its governance. Good statesmen can quickly make war and many other failures of people obsolete.
>
> Now, Class of '56, it's up to us to find and accept society's challenges and become the leaders of tomorrow!

My classmates did well over the ensuing years. Eight of us received doctoral degrees of one sort or another. Only one obtained a PhD in a hard science: Tom McIlrath earned two degrees from Michigan State University before obtaining a PhD in physics from Princeton. Tom became a professor at the University of Maryland's Institute of Physical Science and Technology and was an associate dean for research and graduate studies there. It took a brainy sort to keep up with him during our days in class together, and it was a smart student who listened to him. Tom knew the right answers.

Bruce Erickson received three degrees from Michigan State, including a PhD in economics. He retired from the Carlson School of Strategic Management and Organization at the University of Minnesota, where he was departmental chair and received the Teacher of the Year award five times.

Bruce was a legend in my neighborhood. He lived just around the corner, about six houses away. To say he was disadvantaged because of poor eyesight would be an understatement: Bruce had extremely poor vision and wore lens at least a quarter-inch thick. His distance vision was nil. I remember riding our bikes on the sidewalk in front of his house in 3rd or 4th grade, when he rode into a tree. It was scary. But his close-up vision was fine, and he read circles around the rest of us. Bruce's father was a professor and dean of Michigan State College's School of Education. Their home was like a library and newsstand combined. When the rest of us were reading Dell comic books, Bruce was reading the *Saturday Review*. He applied his intellect better than others to real matters of importance, and he was successful.

Ed Reuling obtained his PhD in educational administration from Michigan State; he retired as vice president for student affairs at California State University, Hayward in 2000. Susan Nelson received two nursing degrees and then a PhD in human development, and was a faculty member at a number of institutions, including the University of Florida and Georgetown University.

Three of our class received MDs—Mary Ann Tinker, Steve Wilensky, and myself—while Greg Montgomery received a DDS. All four of us received our doctoral degrees from the University of Michigan.

Many of my classmates made their mark in the nonacademic world. Tom Grimes became president of Montgomery Ward, one of the iconic retailers of the last century. Wynefred Halpin became a pharmacist and retired as an assistant dean of student affairs at Wayne State University. Barry McDowell, John Kerry, and Doug Smith became successful engineers. Gary Gross developed a highly acclaimed restaurant business,

My dad, brother, Bob, and I, as my student days were waning and I was preparing to give a speech at my high school graduation. My brother had graduated from East Lansing High a decade earlier, almost to the day.

including 12 in Houston, Texas. Scott Herrick sang his way to fame as one of the founding members of The Arbors quartet, recording popular songs but remembered more often for the tunes accompanying advertisements for United Airlines ("Fly the friendly skies of United") or a brand of frozen vegetables ("In the valley of the—Ho, Ho, Ho—Jolly Green Giant"). Emily Derr sang with the New York City Opera. Interestingly, only one classmate, David Hull, became a lawyer, receiving his law degree many years after our high school graduation. The Class of '56 had many other successes in the areas of business, education, and health care.

When I reread my address to my classmates at our 50th reunion in 2006, it made me realize how little we and our society had changed. I still liked my speech and its message, but there was something missing—it related to the relationship between the hard sciences and everything else.

C.P. Snow, the English physicist and novelist, spoke of this in a book he published three years after my graduation talk, based on a 1959 lecture he had given at Cambridge entitled "The Two Cultures and the Scientific Revolution." His message was that two cultures were evolving—one of science, the other of the liberal disciplines—and that this was going to cause a polarization of those guiding the path of society. Nothing seems to have changed in the half-century since his lecture and my speech. Leaders having experience in both arenas are few and far between and this hampers many decisions affecting all of us. We need those who can work within the boundaries of both cultures.

Certainly, science has improved the standard of postwar living in the western societies and even many of the developing countries—but it has also brought us the beginnings of global warming and the ability to annihilate all life with nuclear warfare. Some tradeoff—especially for my generation, who at our age in the 1950s had no way of anticipating the mighty conflicts of the coming decades. My somewhat naïve graduation address recognized the importance of the social sciences, even though I favored the hard sciences and the promise of modernization they held out. Perhaps I should have been more forceful in supporting the non-sciences.

19
Failure

It would be an understatement that I was pretty cocky after high school graduation, confident that my work ethic and brains would shepherd me to great success at the University of Michigan. I was convinced that my ability to communicate was going to be a major asset. What I didn't realize was that writing would be more important than speaking.

First Days of College

Engineering classes at the university during my first semester started off fast. I signed up for 18 credit hours, including five hours of Advanced Chemistry, six hours of Mathematics, three hours of Mechanical Drawing, one hour of Oral Exposition, and three hours of English—all capped off by a mandatory Physical Education course, which for me was swimming taught by Gus Stager, the varsity swim team coach. Our progress in class was tightly monitored by the College of Engineering. At the fifth and tenth weeks of the 15-week semester, we received interval grades.

All entering freshmen, regardless of their major, were required to live in university student housing their first year. I shared a room with my high school classmate, Barry McDowell, in the South Quadrangle, a few blocks from my engineering classes. Barry had had the highest grade-point average in our high school class, and he was a good influence when studying grew burdensome for me that first year. I thrived in the newfound freedom of living on my own and I enjoyed all my classes, but I was about to be leveled by one learning experience that I was unprepared for.

Engineering English

Ralph Loomis, 15 years my senior, was my professor for English 11. He was an imposing and demanding instructor, determined to teach a brash group of freshman engineering students how to write. Tall and robust, he wore round glasses and combed his thinning dark hair neatly back, towered over most of us, and didn't miss a thing. In the early sessions of his class, which met three times a week, we discussed various assigned readings and a few of the students read the weekly essays Professor Loomis required from each of us.

I don't recall the theme of my first two essays—perhaps because of the emotional wallop I received when both were returned to me with a grade of F. Only one of them came back with a comment:

"Spelling and grammar need improvement."

I had no excuse and I didn't have a clue what to do next. Mr. Loomis must have regarded my writing as the gibberish of some lowly ignoramus. Certainly, my overrated skills as a communicator had gotten me nowhere. My sense was that I had been exiled to a hostile country where I didn't speak the language. I was ashamed of myself and I was clearly lost.

The third week, I walked into class concentrating on the floor, not wanting to reveal my anxiety or sense of defeat. Things improved a bit: Mr. Loomis asked me to read my third essays to the class. In retrospect, he must have appreciated something in its content. But I was still far from being an acceptable writer.

I can't recall the topic of my essay, but to this day I can remember finishing reading my essay with some pride, only to find my wind being sucked away when I turned the last page of my blue book to read:

"Keep working. You'll soon be out of the woods. D+."

Not exactly what I had hoped for.

Mr. Loomis asked me to stay after class to speak with him. I thought he would pat me on the back and offer some encouragement. Wrong again. In a very brusque tone, he asked if someone had helped me to write my essay. To be asked such a question was a more serious matter than it might seem.

The Engineering College had an honor code. At the end of each exam, we signed a statement that "I have neither received nor given aid during this examination." A similar statement accompanied written class assignments. This was a big deal for engineering students, underscoring the higher professional standards of conduct expected of them. By contrast, proctors patrolled the aisles during exams in non-engineering classes to keep the students honest.

I had not cheated. But I had tried hard to do better, and now my honesty was being challenged. I was humiliated and as the blood rushed to my face, I replied simply:

"Mr. Loomis, if I had help on my paper I wouldn't have gotten a D+."

I knew my essay was devoid of egregious misspellings—that I had dealt with. So that left poor grammar as the culprit. I couldn't seem to get it right and by all measures I was becoming the class flunky. That I was a good flunky and got to read my essay to my peers was not going to do it.

Forget the gentleman's Cs my father had warned me against. The rule of the day was that any interval grade of a D or F after the fifth or tenth week of the semester would be reported to the student's parents and academic counselor. When my father got the fifth week notice I was in hot water. I also was summoned to see my counselor, whose name I've forgotten. In a very slow southern drawl, he tried to allay my anxiety. I can still hear the twang in his voice:

"Why, Mr. Stanley, with your other grades being all As, anyone looking at your transcript will think that English teacher must have had a problem."

I was the one with a problem, not Mr. Loomis.

That D+ in the third week was the last bad grade I received in his class. No Pulitzer Prize for my remaining work, but I did write simple, complete sentences from then on. Mr. Loomis's remaining notations on my essays were constructive and helped me think before putting my thoughts down on paper. I actually received a B on the final exam. Some success, but the failures of those first few essays are indelible memories etched into my persona.

Given my father's rules of engagement, it would be entirely reasonable to assume I was in deep dung—but that was not the case. In spite of my failings in English 11, the first semester of my freshman year was an academic success. After completing my first 15 weeks of college, my performance put me in the top 10% of my Engineering College class. I received the Oreon E. Scott Prize for that accomplishment, which also included the gift of a book of my choice. Ralph Loomis never knew it, but I chose *A Treasury of the Theater (From Henrik Ibsen to Arthur Miller)*, a 1,120-page book edited by John Gassner. Needless to say, I chose it because of the stories and content, not the grammar.

The next semester I received an A in English 12, and at times I thought I might have been misunderstood or mistreated in that earlier class. There even were moments when I felt bitter. With a little hindsight, however, I suspect my success that second semester and in subsequent writing was a reflection of Mr. Loomis's stern influence.

Perhaps today's students will never feel the burden of writing by the rules as much as those of my era. The acceptance of slang, along with the easy correction of disjointed sentence constructs and spelling errors by preprogrammed aids on the computer, have changed the way writing is taught and practiced—perhaps for the better in most cases, and certainly with less sweat than I experienced in the fall of 1956.

A Career Writer

Writing scientific papers has been an important part of my professional life for nearly 40 years. It is also a joy, and ranks as one of the most satisfying aspects of my career as an academic surgeon.

Most of my contributions to the literature have been linear constructs: tightly edited laboratory or clinical reports that conform to a very rigid style. Everyone in medicine is aware of the ritual: objectives-hypothesis, materials-methods, results, conclusions. Not always easy to put together, but I found it more comforting to write by these rules than in the more creative fashion that Mr. Loomis expected. My first senior authored paper was published in 1970, when I was a third-year surgical resident. I was 34 years old. By the time I turned 70 I had published 321 peer-reviewed articles, 178 chapters in medical textbooks, and edited or co-edited eight major texts on cardiovascular diseases. That's one publication every 27 days for 38 continuous years.

I'm proud of my publications. However, I suspect that only one of them would pass muster with the most critical English teacher. I wrote it in 1972 with Calvin Ernst, a faculty member in the University of Michigan's Department of Surgery, and when it was published it was only two and a half pages in length. We argued and negotiated our way through each sentence—not quite like Hemingway, because we had no wine or absinthe to keep things mellow. But the end product was clean, and it would have been suitable for the *New York Times*. It neared perfection—but it was the only one.

In the past few decades I have arguably become something of a Ralph Loomis in my own shop, and I have rather enjoyed it. Some of my proudest achievements as a teacher have been tied to my trainees' writing successes. By 2004, after serving as head of the University of Michigan Vascular Surgery Service for more than a quarter of a century, I had taught one out of every eight directors of vascular surgery training programs in the country. I had published with each of them during their training. They all could write, and write well.

Only a few times have I come close to escaping the rigid structure of scientific writing. In 1980, I wrote a paper about the value of biomedical research; in another paper, in 1997, I touted the importance of specialization in the surgical disciplines, particularly in vascular surgery. In two other papers I wrote about the historical aspects of the operative reconstruction of the arteries to the kidneys. I also contributed two chapters that avoided linear science—one, a history of vascular surgery, and the other, a biography, following a long series of interviews, of one of the founders of my specialty, D. Emerick Szilagyi. That comes to six relatively creative pieces—barely exceeding 1% of my total output. Not much, but it was a start toward developing a different way of communicating on paper.

In 2006 I decided to take it a step farther. Like many others who have lived in the academic arena, I wanted to sum up my life for my family and colleagues. That meant learning to write about intentions and emotions rather than hypotheses and facts.

Saturday

In 2007 and 2008 I was a student in two memoir-writing courses, each lasting a little more than a week. I found my writing moving in more fluid and descriptive directions than it ever had before. I liked it, and it got me started on the work you are now reading. Along the way I published my first really creative piece. If, perchance, you have read any of my earlier papers, you will know that my writing has changed—and so have I.

It was a little essay entitled "Saturday," published in 2008 in *JAMA*, the Journal of the American Medical Association, less than eight weeks after I submitted it. I had composed it as part of a writing course taught by Patricia Foster, a professor of English at the Writers' Workshop at the University of Iowa. She had asked the class to write about something we wished we had done, but hadn't done.

Roxanne Young, an associate editor of *JAMA*, sent me a prepublication typescript of the accepted paper for my review. I made a few minor suggestions and returned the finished manuscript to her. But Ralph Loomis was right: my grammar was not there. Her response on my 70th birthday hit home:

> *"Dr. Stanley, I have incorporated all of your suggestions. I have only one small quibble, and that is with the punctuation of the last two sentences. You indicated a comma between them, yet they are independent clauses, which would call for a semicolon or a period."*

I could hardly believe it: More than half a century after my first col-

> # Saturday
>
> I wish I had operated on Saturday, not the next Tuesday.
>
> He was only 3 months old, with an aortic aneurysm and failing kidneys. He didn't look sick: fat rosy cheeks, bright sparkling eyes, a tuft of brown hair, and two chubby hands that would hold your fingers tightly, wanting you to play with him. But his breathing was shallow and labored, his lungs were overloaded with fluid, and his smiles were often cut short, by things he certainly didn't understand.
>
> Surgeons often have to judge the benefits of waiting, to prepare a patient for an operation: "Lose weight, Stop smoking, Let's get your blood pressure under better control" are common preoperative utterances, but not so in his case. He simply was retaining a little too much water, not much, perhaps a few hundred milliliters ... a teacup full ... but then again he weighed only 11 pounds.
>
> We had carried many young children through operations for rare diseases of the abdominal aorta and its branches, never having lost a child. That is why he came to us. Most often we made the right choices. We thought we knew what was best.
>
> So we tried to polish things up and the operation was delayed. Three days of temporary dialysis ... or so we thought. It got the fluid off, but at an unexpected price. His kidneys with their blocked arteries shut down, his lungs retained more fluid, and his liver stopped making clotting factors to prevent bleeding. But his need for surgery did not stop.
>
> On Tuesday the operation was a technical success. The aneurysm was resected, the aorta was replaced, and the renal arteries to one kidney were reconstructed. The other nonfunctioning kidney was removed ... but the magnitude of it all was too much.
>
> His dialysis continued and a few days later he was placed on extracorporeal membrane oxygenation for his failing lungs, and the bleeding required more operations. The pediatricians and nurses were constantly at his crib side. They tried so hard, caring for him and his parents ... and, without realizing it, caring for me, the surgeon, who had been so optimistic at the start. Every tiny failing of this little child hurt. We had such high expectations.
>
> He held on for nearly 4 weeks, with his two young parents, barely beyond their teenaged years, hoping for a change at the bedside vigil of their only son, watching his precarious life at arm's length, until the last day, when, for the first time since surgery, they held him in their arms, until the life-support machines were turned off ... and the only thing left in the room was silence.
>
> They took him home, some 700 miles away, to where his older sister was staying with family ... and to his final resting place.
>
> It might have been different; I wish I had operated on Saturday.
>
> James C. Stanley, MD
> Ann Arbor, Michigan
>
> A Piece of My Mind Section Editor: Roxanne K. Young, Associate Editor.

My first venture into creative writing: An essay published in JAMA entitled Saturday, reprinted with permission of the Jounal of the American Medical Association, 300 (14): 169. Copyright © 2008 American Medical Association. All rights reserved.

lege English course and I still couldn't properly punctuate a simple essay. My response within minutes of receiving her note on my computer was:

> "Ms. Young, many thanks. You are absolutely correct. Let's go with the semicolon. Thanks again."

That day it occurred to me I had completed a loop—back to my initial failure as a writer in 1956. But I was older, and the words of the Irish playwright and novelist, Samuel Beckett, who received the 1969 Nobel Prize for Literature, rang true:

"Try Again. Fail again. Fail Better."

Perhaps I should have felt bad, but I was unabashedly happy that I failed better. After all, I was going to publish a piece of my own creative writing. I was absolutely flabbergasted by a related event that occurred later that night.

Closure after Five Decades

Nancy had planned a wonderful family affair to celebrate my 70th birthday; all three of our children, our two daughters-in-law, and our four grandkids all came home for the festivities. The day ended with a dinner in the private dining room of our favorite Ann Arbor restaurant, The Earle.

I had always thought I was half English (for my civil behavior), a quarter German (for my scientific aptitude), and a quarter Irish (for the dickens that imparted my sense of humor and the shenanigans I usually got away with). All of our children were part Irish, and we gave them great license to feel good about being so when they laughed and had a good time, even if their behavior could be a little bit out of bounds.

Given that background, then, it may not be surprising that my youngest son, Jeff, had contacted Ralph Loomis, who had retired from teaching but still lived in town. Jeff told Mr. Loomis that he had been an important figure in my career and asked him if he might autograph one of the books I had published and write "A+" inside the cover, as a birthday surprise. Consistent with his well-known thoroughness, it's likely that Mr. Loomis looked up my academic publications on the internet before he agreed to put pen to paper. He also told Jeff he had purged his old records and didn't know what grade he had given me. Jeff knew that Mr. Loomis had given me a rough time, but he didn't know the details about the failing grades—thankfully.

At the end of the day, Ralph Loomis did better. He sent a letter that my family had framed and gave to me that night. It was very complementary and reading it brought my relationship with him full circle—in a wonderful way.

> To James Stanley --
>
> It was wonderful to hear from your son Jeffrey that a course you took with me in 1956-7 turned out to mean a great deal to you, that you credit it in a major way with helping you learn to write well. When we teach, we generally cannot know if what we say falls on stony or fertile ground. We hope the results are good; we are thrilled when the results are great. This has happened in your case. I salute you on your 70th birthday for your fine career, including your outstanding publication record.
>
> *Ralph Loomis*
> Ralph Loomis
> Emeritus Professor Of English
> College of Engineering   September 18, 2008
> University of Michigan, Ann Arbor
> (Just turned 85)

An unexpected letter more than a half-century later from my Freshman English professor, Ralph Loomis, at the University of Michigan.

We all should be so fortunate as to have teachers who are willing to put in long hours molding us when we are young. Ralph Loomis helped me learn a skill that's been an enormous part of my life in the years since. He helped me become better. His framed letter, on display in my study, is a prized possession.

20

A New Mistress

Science had been in my blood during high school, and I was committed to becoming an engineer and contribute to building something that would benefit society. It was not until several years later that I realized that building something was different from helping someone. That new awareness changed everything.

The United States of America Needs You

The mood of American youth—the way we thought about our future and our country's place in our system of values—was so different in the early 1950s as to require some explanation. Less than a decade had passed since the end of World War II. VJ and VE days had supposedly signaled the end of all wars, only to be followed by the Korean conflict, which ended not in a real peace, but only an armistice, and with it, the heightening of the Cold War. The threat of aggression by communist demigods seemed ever-present, to the point of a national paranoia. Basement bomb shelters and a deep distrust of those who didn't support the mainstream political system were commonplace.

The country's need to protect itself seemed most urgent as I entered college. Bright young minds were needed to build a secure nation. It seemed that the country needed us more than we needed to follow our own leanings. Far from feeling that our leaders were exploiting us, we believed we were being challenged to protect the next generation. A genuine idealism drove us.

It was under these circumstances that I hooked up with my first mistress: I was going to be a mechanical engineer, learning my skills at the

University of Michigan, where theoretic issues were topics of the day and gave students the tools to be more creative than might be the case with a more pragmatic education. Next, I planned to pursue graduate studies in metallurgical engineering at the Massachusetts Institute of Technology, which would be invaluable to me as I entered industry.

I really wanted to build something that made a difference. If it were not to be cars it would be something else. After all, my backdoor neighbor, Don Burnham, had switched from automotive engineering to overseeing the Nautilus submarine project for the nation's defense. If he could do it, so could I. I didn't believe the path I had chosen would close any career options.

It received a bit of a challenge during the first week of my freshman year, however, when the entire engineering class assembled to hear the Engineering College's dean, George G. Brown, welcome us. His closing remarks included something I hadn't considered:

"Take a good look at the person on either side of you; at the end of your senior year only one of you will be here."

What a bunch of poppycock that seemed at the time: the odds couldn't be stacked against us to such a degree. But his words were a curiously prophetic preamble to my own future.

The road to the College of Engineering was a singularly straight line for me. East Lansing High provided a broad and reasonably rigorous education, although it didn't rank with the country's best public schools, such Mt. Lebanon outside Pittsburgh or New Trier in Winnetka, outside Chicago. But my high school classmate, Barry McDowell, and I never wavered in our focus on becoming engineers. We were in the top echelons of our senior class and we were ready to compete with anyone from anyplace.

During our senior year, Barry and I were invited to visit Elliot M. Estes, better known as Pete Estes, in his office. He was, at the time, assistant chief engineer at the Oldsmobile plant in Lansing. A product of the General Motors Institute, Mr. Estes was also a neighbor, and his three children were my schoolmates. His oldest son, Tom, was a terrific athlete and was my teammate on the varsity football squad. Mr. Estes's pitch to Barry and me was that he had got his education at the institute at no major cost, as was true then of many senior executives at the world's largest automaker. He thought we should consider applying. His advice was well intended and was flattering. For Pete Estes, his own brand of education worked: in 1956, he became chief engineer at Pontiac, and shortly thereafter he assumed the role of the fifteenth president of General Motors. But Barry and I both wanted to attend the University of Michigan.

In the spring of our senior year the two of us were notified by mail that we had been accepted to the Engineering College. During the early summer Barry and I traveled to Ann Arbor for an orientation session and testing to see if we qualified for any advanced classes. On the way between meeting various staff and faculty, we carried our high school records and our new university files in large manila envelopes. Being the inquisitive sort, we both peeked at the contents. In the mid-1950s, the Scholastic Aptitude Tests were not yet universal for gauging literacy, numeracy, or writing skills. But there were IQ tests, and our IQ scores were there in bold print. Suffice it to say we were both above average. I've often wondered how much weight my IQ carried in deciding whether I would get into the university—and, at times, whether teachers and administrators also had their IQs tested before they were hired. A half-century later, I know the answer to that question!

Also inside the envelope was a record that we had paid the $125 in-state tuition for the fall semester at Michigan, and a copy of our high school grades. But in 1956 you needed more than money and grades to get into the College of Engineering.

First, you had to be 16 years old.

Second, you had to present evidence of good moral character. I got over that hurdle, but not without a measure of qualification from Miss Stophlet, the assistant principal at East Lansing High School. Her letter in my file was complementary for the most part, but she said I was "stubborn." Perhaps the admissions office viewed this as a positive element of my character—after all I was often determined to get things done even when the project was a tough one. I scoffed at the idea that I was truly a "bad" stubborn, and in any event, I heard no more about the matter from the university.

Like me, most of my engineering classmates wanted to make a difference in the world. Missing out on the terrors of war, we had only known the boom days of an expanding military-industrial complex that seemed to us a wonderful source of technological innovation.

After the USSR's Sputnik I became the first artificial satellite to orbit Earth in 1957, America's scientific community was challenged to produce something comparable. It would be three years before the nation's Echo I satellite could be observed passing in the night sky, carrying with it the thrilling sense that our engineering genius had risen to the call. Many of us wanted to be part of that effort. It may be hard to fathom that this was the way many of my generation looked at the world.

But even then, there was a subtle caution that the Cold War creed of progress at the expense of one's deeper yearnings didn't always ring true. Another way of thinking about it was that losing one's soul to the "company store," as Merle Travis called it, was a trap. I experienced a bit of this during the summer before I started college.

Knowing that mechanical drawing would be important to my career as an engineer, I thought I had landed in heaven the summer before going to college, when I started a job as an Engineering Aide B for the State of Michigan. I was assigned to a team of engineers and draftsmen who were working with the Highway Department. Gene Hamel was the team leader and boss. I had my own drawing table, T-square, triangles, drawing pens, and a quiet space on the fifth floor of the Stevens T. Mason State Office Building, just two blocks behind the State Capitol. The building was eight stories tall and only four years old when I started work there. It had a little swagger, too, in that it was named for Michigan's first governor, who had been elected when only 23 years old—the youngest person to ever be a state governor, a record that still stands today. To me, it was a pretty neat place.

My task was to transfer elevation numbers from surveyor worksheets to blue print-like paper, in thin inked lines representing a cross-section of the proposed road, with its crown, sloping sides, and limited shoulders. I had to do this for every 100 feet of the road. The exact elevation figure was placed above each sector of the road's cross-section, and I was proud of my careful inking and penmanship; Lynn Adams had taught me well in his drafting class at East Lansing High. In fact, my work and speed ranked me in the middle of the five adults on the team.

But there was a fly in the ointment. The building had a lot of employees and only two elevators. If everyone came to work and left work at the same time, many would have suffered a lot of frustration waiting for an elevator. So the different floors had different work hours, spaced 15 minutes apart. You came and went during your floor's allotted time. I came to work at 8:15 a.m. I was just finishing my second week of work, when I grabbed my triangle to finish one more line as the clock passed our usual quitting time of 5:15 p.m. No such thing! Mr. Hamel came over to my desk and abruptly pulled the canvas overlay from the top of the table to cover my work, preventing me from making another stroke. I found his admonition somewhat insulting:

> *"Jim, you just have to stop at quitting time. The others will think you're trying to get ahead if you keep on working."*

I was a summer employee without a college degree. There was no position I could advance to by being more productive than the others. I walked to my car that day thinking that the real reason may have been that the others either didn't care as much about their work as I did or they simply didn't want to work very hard. It was disheartening, but I was convinced that whatever I might do in the future, being a civil servant and accepting that mentality was not for me. I didn't want to be someone else's helpless pawn. This began to sink in a bit deeper the next year.

People Need You

During the first week of my sophomore year at Michigan I took inventory of my short life. I recalled a conversation with my high school girlfriend, who had asked me rather bluntly if my life was going to be measured by

"Building the very best of brakes for cars?"

That conversation, while driving to downtown Lansing, struck a possible hitch in my quest to be relevant. Her words, when recalled, unmasked a number of suppressed feelings I had about being an engineer and the price I was willing to pay as an engineering student. I didn't expect to spend my life building brakes—or, heaven forbid, producing drawings of highway cross-sections. But there were times when I was haunted by a waking nightmare that I was sitting at a drafting table in a large coliseum, surrounded by hundreds of other engineers at their own tables, all of us working in silence. I was one of an anonymous crowd, my work indistinguishable, perhaps, from any of the others', and I was not making a difference. It was an uncomfortable thought.

Taking four or five different engineering classes at a time was like taking four or five foreign languages. There was no slacking off; everything was cumulative learning, and cramming a lot of disparate facts into my mind the day before an exam wouldn't work. The relentless classroom assignments that filled each week meant that a lot of students needed to spread out their class loads, resulting in their taking four and a half years to finish their undergraduate engineering degrees, instead of the four years most other programs required. Some left engineering school for other majors. Dean Brown's prediction that first week of freshman year appeared to be on target.

It seemed I was doing a lot of what others expected of me, and not always listening to myself. The archetypical image of the lonely engineering student with a slide rule in hand and bags under the eyes was close. If you weren't a nerd going in, you were likely to be a nerd on the way out. Humanity, both in my studies and my personal life, was sparse. Facts, not people, dominated my existence.

A simple question confronted me:

"Could there be something else, where my everyday efforts would have an immediate impact for good on another being? Or was I helping a company that didn't belong to me to create something that in the end would be valuable to many, but might take years to accomplish?"

It was a complex issue for someone in his last year of being a teenager. My life was not in crisis at the time, but this question about the future was frequently a topic of late night bull sessions with my friends. Devoting my life solely to advancing America's needs seemed like a sell-out. The answer I was looking for came, indirectly, from someone in the public eye, who asked Americans to think of other people first.

Dooley's Influence

Many Sunday evenings, my fraternity brothers and I would gather around the television set and watch the latest cowboy or mystery show, but every few months I found myself watching *That Free Men May Live*, a series of CBS network specials broadcast live by Thomas A. Dooley, M.D. He was a charismatic and evocative speaker who provided medical care to people in Southeast Asia. He wove compelling stories that underlined the importance of serving those who couldn't always help themselves.

Dooley was a talented pianist who had enrolled in the Julliard School of Music as a teen. He later attended Notre Dame, leaving without a degree to enter medical school at St. Louis University. He finished at the bottom of his class and had to repeat his senior year before starting his postgraduate training in the Navy. Tom Dooley's personal life was complex in that he was gay at a time when that was much more controversial than would be the case today. But nothing interfered with his humanitarian work.

Dooley was the principal reason that MEDICO, the organization he was associated with, became successful as a provider of medical aid to those in need overseas. MEDICO merged with CARE, a food distribution agency, in 1962. He was also a captivating author, and he published three remarkable books: *Deliver Us from Evil: The Story of Vietnam's Flight to Freedom* (1956), *The Edge of Tomorrow* (1958), and *The Night They Burned the Mountain* (1960). He was awarded many honors for his humanitarian work before he died of widespread melanoma in January 1961.

Dooley received a letter from Albert Schweitzer that bears rereading. In it, Schweitzer said,

"I do not know what your destiny will ever be, but this I do know, you will always have happiness if you seek and find how to serve."

Schweitzer also addressed the bigger issues facing humankind:

"It is good to be reminded now and then that even in a world struggling with the momentous issue of war and peace, the individual has problems."

How much closer to my thinking could he have come—in some respects, echoing the ideas I had expressed in my high school commencement speech.

I was one of the young people who were mesmerized by Tom Dooley's writings and television appearances. He was focused, bold, and absorbing. And he helped start me on a train of thought that would change my life. My decision to go into medicine, when I made it, came quickly and easily and I've never second-guessed it. But I knew the nitty-gritty of becoming a doctor would be work and more hard work, and that part of my life would never belong to me or my family. It was my new mistress.

No-Degree Kid

The first hurdle to my going to medical school was to convince my parents that my decision at age 19 was not a simple mood swing. Complicating the matter was the life that my brother, Bob, had chosen to lead without having a college degree in hand. It wasn't that he didn't have the talent or drive. It's possible that what happened to him right after high school made a difference. I don't know.

As long as I could remember, Bob had been a phenomenally talented artist. His hand-eye coordination made ink, watercolor paint, and oil paint take on life. His ability to draw and captivate an audience revealed itself in his painted murals that remained for decades at East Lansing High; when he was a senior in 1946, the school yearbook that he illustrated set a standard that has never been surpassed.

Like the majority of boys in his class, Bob's senior year was followed by armed forces duty, not college. It was only months after World War II had ended, and Bob was among those in the 27th Infantry who joined the occupational troops in Japan.

When I was only seven years old I found myself standing with my parents in the depths of Union Station in downtown Chicago as a steam locomotive, belching a cloud of smoke and water, pulled a long line of

My brother, Bob, emerged as a talented artist in High School and two years later he attended Parson's School of Design in New York City. Included were studies in Europe, evident in this scene with his portfolio under arm in Italy.

troop cars out of the darkened freight yard with my brother on board. It was like a somber black and white motion picture, and it depressed me. Bob, with all of his belongings in a duffel bag at his side, was on his way to the west coast. There he would board a ship and sail across the Pacific, where some of the bloodiest battles in history had taken place, to Japan where two atomic bombs had silenced the emperor's warlords and left the world with the continuing threat of nuclear war. My brother would see that place firsthand.

Two years later, Bob returned with an honorable discharge, a good conduct medal, an Expert Rifle badge, and an admission slip to Parsons School of Design in New York City. Bob was not going to be a starving artist: the GI Bill afforded a modest amount of financial support for his big city education.

Bob expanded his artistic skills after Parsons and became a very successful leader in the nation's advertising and design community. He went to work on Madison Avenue, first as a senior artist at Donald Deskey

Bob became an expert in graphic design long before computers took sway. He was a leader in corporate identity and marketing in the 1950s and 1960s, and was the Vice President of Lippincott and Margulies in New York City. His mark with the pentastar logo that he designed for the Chrysler Corporation still stands today.

Associates, where he was instrumental in their package design efforts—you may remember the geometric cardboard box for Pert Shampoo that Bob created, in the days before molded plastic containers changed commercial packaging. Bob subsequently became vice president of Lippincott & Margulies, an anchor agency then, where he oversaw a host of corporate identity programs, including those for Kraft Foods and U.S. Steel. Bob was the designer of the Chrysler Pentastar, bringing that company its first unifying logo.

Nevertheless, my father always ascribed my brother's success at least in part to good luck, and he kept wondering what might happen if Bob's luck ran out. Bob had completed his three years of art schooling with flying colors, but he had not taken any additional course work at NYU that would have given him a B.A. degree and the insurance it might have provided if his creativity and luck stopped. Whatever the reason for Bob not having a degree, its absence created a boundary for me.

It's possible that my dad, who never had gone to college and didn't have a degree himself, just wanted my brother to have something he never had. With this history in mind, there was little question that my switching to premed without a clear path to an undergraduate degree might not be well received by my father. Negotiating my new interest with my parents would take some careful planning.

Selling the New Mistress

I made a firm decision to pursue medicine a few weeks into my sophomore year. It was something of a high stakes gamble: I planned on taking premed courses for the next two and a half years with no intent on receiving an undergraduate degree, which would have required an additional semester of foreign language at the expense of more science credits. In the 1950s it was possible to enter medical school with no degree after only three years of college, so my thinking was not completely out of bounds.

A week after I made my decision, I invited my mother and father to Ann Arbor for a Michigan football game—I had obtained two tickets from one of my fraternity brothers, Jim Orwig, an offensive guard and captain of the 1957 team. Jim, an all-As student, was also an Angell Scholar and campus hero. After college he entered Medical School at the university, then completed a residency in orthopedics at the University Medical Center. Many of the athletes I knew then were students first. The Michigan football team that suited up for the game my parents attended included 14 of my fraternity brothers.

It was September 28, 1957, one of those sunny and warm early fall afternoons in a college town, and I had great seats for Mom and Dad. We won, beating the University of Southern California 16 to 6. The moment couldn't have been scripted any better. My parents drove me back to the fraternity house. There, away from the raucous stadium crowd, we sat quietly talking about how school was going. Then I broached a new topic:

"Dad, I think I want to be a doctor."

There was little comment other than a quiet and very helpful smile from my mother. Then my father said,

"Well I've always trusted your judgment. Think about it for a while before you make any change, and let us know what you've decided."

How much more could a son ask of his parents than for them to respect his choices when he was still a teenager? Down deep inside, I wasn't entirely sure I deserved that much trust, but I wasn't about to question it. I was prepared to forego my earlier ambitions and risk everything to be my own self. Maybe Miss Stophlet was right: I was stubborn, when I wanted to be.

Mom and Dad left for home, driving down Washtenaw Avenue in Ann Arbor. As the car turned out of sight, I jumped high in the air, both arms outstretched—what I would describe as a mix of an extended Michael Jordan leap and the high kick of the new car owner in a recent Honda commercial.

That they wouldn't stand in the way of my new ambition was one thing. What was perhaps more important, my parents were willing to invest in me, not in a program. Many of my friends' parents had pushed them to realize their parents' idea of the right program, perhaps foisting too high of an educational challenge on their children and setting them up for frustration and failure. That was not for me—I had made my own choice and was ready. By noon the following Tuesday I was out of the College of Engineering and a premedical student in the College of Literature, Science, and Arts.

My own children have heard me repeat this story to others as well as to them. It has two messages, I think: first, earn your parents' trust; second, if you do, you can make your own judgments with confidence they will support you. With my parents' support I had found a new mistress—one that serves people, not a company.

21

Premed Competition And Integrity

Often, we judge others according to whether they hew to the same boundaries we set for ourselves. When someone goes around us and misrepresents us to others, and that misrepresentation violates a principle we stand for, it's deeply hurtful. Something like this happened to me because of an effort my father made to help me as I was finishing my premedical studies. I found myself pushed beyond a boundary that I didn't want to cross; my integrity had been violated and I was very angry.

Getting to Medical School: A Contact Sport

I quickly learned as a premed student that all undergraduates who wanted to go to medical school were engaged in a competition—a contact sport. It was like an open-season event, only the stakes were higher. There were many more students applying than available freshman class openings at the country's 105 medical schools in 1960. My time in engineering classes left me with only two and a half years to establish my credentials for the medical school admissions committees, and that meant work, work, and more work. It meant burying myself indoors to study, surfacing occasionally to remind myself there was a human race out there and I was part of it.

In the late 1950s the courses that separated the successful from the unsuccessful candidates were organic chemistry and comparative anatomy.

Professor Peter Smith taught organic chemistry. His lectures generated pages and pages of formula after formula to be memorized. Study tables didn't exist at the University of Michigan in those days, but a few of us found a small group of classmates willing to share notes and test each other before we sat down for the real exams. I did much of my studying with Don Sam and Wing Chin, and we pushed each other to the limit when rehearsing for exams. Wing was a premed student and Don was a chemical engineering major who had been an All-State golfer. He had it all together. In the lab, he was light years ahead of the rest of us. He was constantly at the side of the teaching fellow, suggesting alternative experiments that might be more efficient.

The laboratory routine in organic chemistry was straightforward. Each student received a vial containing a specific amount of a given organic chemical; we were asked to use it to produce a second organic substance with free access to a number of common inorganic reagents. The precise amount you generated of that second organic substance determined your grade. The more you made, the better your grade.

The trick was to not squander any of the material through sloppy chemistry. You stuck to strict details of known reactions, at tightly proscribed temperatures, at a given pH, and for exact times. If you deviated from the rules, you didn't end up with as much of the final product and your grade suffered. What, you might ask, does this have to do with medicine? Other than learning to follow instructions, my answer, then and now, is—not much. But following instructions is essential in the practice of medicine.

Wing Chin and I did well in "organic." I received an A in the lab and A- in the class work. We became medical school classmates and many years later, his son rotated on my surgical service as a junior medical student. He was every bit as smart and nice as his dad. I wrote him letters of recommendation for his surgical residency, and upon graduation, he stopped by the office to give me a tie from his undergraduate school, Bowdoin College, which I still wear.

Organic chemistry was rekindled in my mind years later, when Peter Smith showed up in my clinic. It was 1998, some 40 years after I had been sitting in his class. He had developed a pregangrenous toe with severe vascular disease affecting his left lower extremity. Someone in the university's health service had referred him, and I just happened to be available that day. When I finished offering him an opinion as to what needed to be done to save his leg, I mentioned that I had been his student. He certainly didn't remember me. His response was as proper as his chemistry lectures had been:

"Well, with thousands of students, I can't remember them all."

I sure remembered him. The medical student who accompanied me that day remarked that perhaps it was "get-even time." Some misguided students didn't have much affection for organic chemistry. But I wasn't one of them. The course had been good for me, and I was going to be equally good to Professor Smith. My delayed payback to one of my most important teachers was a leg-saving bypass to restore blood flow to his extremity. He proved to be a very thoughtful and pleasant person who carried none of the rigid mannerisms attributed to those who taught courses that were either the ticket or road block to becoming a medical student. It just took getting to know him a little better to realize that.

Comparative Vertebrate Anatomy was the other separator for aspiring medical students. Professor Alfred H. Stockard was the sole teacher of this subject at the University of Michigan, and his class was austere by any standard. His lectures, fit for a paleontologist and linguist, were overwhelming when combined with his textbook, *Laboratory Manual of Comparative Anatomy of the Chordates*. The book was like a dictionary describing an ancient language—that is to say, it was almost too much.

In the lab, we explored the innards of all kinds of species, from fish to mammals. The course culminated with our dissection of a feline subject that had the arteries and veins injected with agents to differentiate them from other tissues. It was an awakening to see the organs that we knew we possessed as humans, in bold relief—much more dramatic than seeing drawings in a book. Most of the class was in awe of the body's complex organization after seeing the heart and lungs, the liver and gall bladder, the intestines, the aorta, and the ureters connecting the kidneys to the bladder. These and all the other organs seemed arranged in such an orderly fashion

What weren't orderly were Professor Stockard's examinations. On the first occasion, he gave us a 200-question multiple choice test, to be completed in two hours—an absolutely impossible task. It would have taken that much time to simply read and reread each question, forsaking any thinking about the correct answer. Most of us got scores in the 30s on that exam; based on a curve, that resulted in a B. One of our classmates, a girl, recognized the futility of completing the entire exam and simply marked every remaining question in the last few minutes with the same letter, B. She set the curve with a total score in the 70s, but she didn't really know much. She eventually got a C in the class and didn't make it into medical school. So much for playing guessing games with the system. Today, if you guess wrong on some multiple choice examinations, your incorrect responses may be subtracted from the correct ones—and you quickly learn not to guess. But my A- in comparative anatomy kept me in the running for medical school.

The Application

I asked for and received letters of recommendation to accompany my medical school application from three of my teachers. Henry Tan, David Bordua, and Max Hutt were my instructors in advanced inorganic chemistry, sociology, and psychology, respectively.

When I was a premed student and for many years afterward I thought Henry Tan was a professor. It turns out that he was a graduate student and teaching fellow. He supplied important ballast for me during the first semester of my freshman year in Engineering School. Chem 5e was a single semester of advanced inorganic chemistry for five hours of credit. I had placed myself in this class during orientation testing and thus avoided having to learn the same material usually taught in two back-to-back four-hour courses spread out over both semesters of freshman year. Each week, the course included three formal one-hour lectures by a senior chemistry faculty, accompanied by Mr. Tan overseeing two one-hour recitation classes and two two-hour periods in the laboratory. The whole course had the potential to be a killer, but our teaching fellow made it easy.

Henry Tan ranks among the most disciplined teachers I encountered in college. His lectures and laboratory instructions were highly organized, and he had a sixth sense as to when someone might be falling behind. Because of his teaching style, his class was actually easier than the alternative courses that most of our engineering class took. One major difference was that the content of his examinations came exactly from his lectures and laboratory exercises: no random new facts from a textbook that he hadn't covered with us. What he taught, he expected us to know, and it worked. I received an A. He wrote a wonderful letter supporting my Medical School application, which I am sure helped me regardless of his academic status. It was probably a rarity then for a teaching fellow to write such a letter: most admission committees knew that the majority of teaching fellows were only a few years older than the undergraduate applicants. Certainly, it would be unheard of today.

Mr. Tan never pursued his doctorate or a teaching career, instead going to work for DuPont Chemical Company, where, with his linguistic breadth, he became a lead contract negotiator for DuPont's business in the Far East. I believe he could have made a great academic, although the only paper he ever published while at the university was coauthored with my future organic chemistry professor, Peter Smith. Henry Tan died a little more than a decade ago, but he left Ann Arbor with a trail of students who thrived in his class, including me.

David Bordua was one of my premed advisors and strongly supported my medical ambition. I wrote a lengthy paper for his course, based on Ivan Belknap's book, *Human Problems of a State Mental Hospital*. It was a humbling experience to write about such a difficult subject—covering a large swath of humanity, from all economic and social strata, whose illnesses rendered them defenseless in the everyday world. Effective drugs to treat schizophrenia and manic-depressive psychoses were almost nonexistent in the 1950s. My assignment was also my professor's way of introducing me to some of the complex sociological issues that physicians tackle.

Professor Bordua was a consummate academic and one of the university's more popular undergraduate teachers. He gave me helpful advice as a premed student, and he almost had me convinced that the social sciences would be more fun and rewarding than medicine. He had received his PhD from Harvard in 1957, just a few years before I took his class. He was an associate professor at that time. The year I graduated from medical school, he joined the faculty of the University of Illinois as a professor of sociology. He had broadened my perspective of humankind and his letter of recommendation to the Medical School helped get me started. I was and remain in his debt.

My third letter came from Max L. Hutt, who taught a psychology course on abnormal and deviant behavior—a great topic for anxious and stressed premed students. I did well; in fact, I tied with several others to post the highest grade in his course. His exams required a regurgitation of "rat facts" directly from the textbook, *Patterns of Abnormal Behavior*, which Professor Hutt had published in 1957 with Robert G. Gibby. His lectures followed the chapters of the book and ranged from elementary Freudian concepts of id, ego, and superego to behavioral modification of personality disorders.

The day before the Christmas–New Year's break, Professor Hutt lectured to an auditorium with only a handful of students. He seemed perturbed. To those of us who hadn't had the temerity to cut class or the luck to get an early pass out of town, he gave a bonus. The final exam, he told us, would include a question asking us to define the issue of "sensibility." That word was not in the book and he had just made it up. He also made up the correct answer: "gobbledygook."

In those days, there were no class scribes who took notes that absent students could subscribe to for a modest fee. If you weren't in class you didn't get it. And sure enough, the question was there on the final. I'm sure those who were absent from class the day we got our freebie were utterly lost when they read it.

Professor Hutt's sense of humor was a little out of camp for the 1950s. One day, attempting to define passive-aggressive behavior, he gave the example of a New York City Fifth Avenue lady in a hurry to get to a luncheon and faced with having to walk her poodle first. When the little animal wouldn't poop, she blew her cool and in an aggrieved voice, demanded that it "shit." The poodle, sensing a control issue, just wagged its tail. That, Professor Hutt concluded, was passive-aggressive behavior. It drew a lot of laughs from the auditorium. He wrote me a great letter sans humor!

Embellishing or padding your resume with research experience was relatively uncommon in the 1950s, but some of us had it figured out even then. John Liddicoat, an undergraduate friend, and I found an opportunity during the school year to work in a research laboratory at Ann Arbor's only private hospital, St. Joseph Mercy—in a small basement room that had been converted into an animal operating facility overseen by Dr. Clarence Crook, a middle-aged, silver-haired, dignified surgeon. Most of the work on which John and I assisted related to cardiac procedures, including assessing a new heat exchanger to cool the body down during heart surgery and a disc oxygenator to add oxygen to blood circulating in an artificial heart-lung machine.

Our work gave us the opportunity to meet Richard Sarns, a young engineer who was helping develop new devices for cardiac surgery. Already successful, he went on to found his own company in 1966. The following year, one of his heart-lung machines allowed Christiaan Barnard to perform the world's first successful heart transplant. Meeting Sarns, and the work we were doing with his devices, sparked my interest in medical research, and I'm sure this extra dimension of my resume was not overlooked when I applied to medical school.

That research lab was the site of many other exciting projects, most often led by a young surgical resident, Edward "Ted" Diethrich, who subsequently trained in Houston with Denton Cooley, becoming a rising star in cardiothoracic surgery and the founder of the Arizona Heart Institute. John and I assisted him on many experimental operations. Our experience may have looked good on our applications, but it was even more important to our final career choices. It was our first exposure to surgery and we sucked up every detail. John pursued cardiac surgery while I became a vascular surgeon.

Two other factors besides college grades, letters of recommendation, and research experience played a role in my medical school applications: Medical College Admission Tests (MCAT) scores, and my personal interviews.

The MCATs were the equalizer that helped admissions boards to see past the differences between grades from colleges and universities of differing academic stature. They measured the candidate's knowledge in four areas: verbal ability, quantitative ability, scientific achievement, and understanding of modern society. I posted way above-average scores in all four categories, but really excelled in the science section. A memorable question the year I took the test was, "What natural resource is of limited supply in Australia?" I don't recall three of the four possible answers, but the forth and correct answer was "Men." The summer before I took the test, *Time* magazine ran an extended article on Australia that made a major point of the paucity of men and its impact on the country's workforce—a scrap of knowledge I never thought would help me get into medical school!

Interviews were another story. I had applied to only two places: Wayne State University in Detroit and what was my favored choice, the University of Michigan in Ann Arbor. The multiple applications and rolling admission policies of today didn't exist then. But I didn't think I needed to apply to more than two schools. Perhaps I was too cocky and self-confident, but medical school seemed like a sure thing, even without my bachelor's degree. Anyway, with an M.D., who needed a B.S. after their name?

I don't believe my father shared my confidence. He never directly addressed the possibility that I might not get into medical school or, worse yet, drop out after starting my medical education, with no degree and a checkered resume to accompany later job applications. Sensing that possibility, however, he intervened twice during my interviews. The first occasion was a benign and subtle test to see if I was doing OK.

The Wayne State Interview

Wayne State invited me for an interview within weeks of receiving my application in the late fall of my senior year. When my father offered to drive from East Lansing to Ann Arbor and take me to Wayne's administration building in Detroit, I thought it was a nice gesture and gladly accepted. Dad knew the Detroit streets better than I. The fact was that I was nervous and enjoyed the short and quiet ride to my first interview. It was on a Saturday morning in mid-December 1959.

The silent winter sky, sparse traffic, and few people about the campus buildings at Wayne State were quickly forgotten once I entered the dean's office suite for the interview. I was greeted by the assistant dean,

Dr. Morton Levitt. He was more vertically challenged than I, perhaps 5' 6" tall at most, a clinical psychologist who had received his PhD at the University of Michigan a little more than three years earlier. Dr. Levitt quickly extended a warm handshake and ushered me into his office.

I was accompanied by another applicant. This was unexpected and caused a modest amount of anxiety: another person like me, a competitor, in the same room and both of us vying for attention and approval. My rival was in a master's degree program at the University of Chicago. As the interview began, I suspected perhaps he didn't have high enough undergraduate grades to get into medical school. But I really didn't know. I did know, however, that he was somehow related to Dave DeBusschere. He dropped that out during his introduction to Dr. Levitt. DeBusschere was an emerging basketball star at the University of Detroit that year. Everyone with any athletic interest in Southeast Michigan knew about his phenomenal career at Detroit Austin Catholic High School. He would go on to play for the Detroit Pistons and New York Knicks, eventually joining the NBA Hall of Fame.

My own name, Stanley, didn't seem to measure up to DeBusschere. But the tables began to turn as we alternated answering Dr. Levitt's questions. Why do you want to be a doctor? What's your favorite subject? What would you do if you don't get into medical school? Then the breakaway question:

"Do you have a hero?"

Leave it to a psychologist to ask such a question. DeBusschere went first, responding, *"Babe Ruth."* No surprise coming from someone with close athletic ties, but Dr. Levitt, looking a little upset, leaned forward

"Why is he your hero?"

"Because he's a good athlete, of course. Don't you know?" was his reply

What followed were several seconds of dead silence. I was stunned: no comments of substance from my competitor about Ruth's drive, how he had made the Yankees what they were, or how he grew up to exceed his family's expectations. My colleague was not doing well. An interest in athletic prowess was not our interviewer's thing.

Rear Admiral Richard E. Byrd was my hero—and I had reasons. He had explored both Antarctica and the Arctic, and as a youngster I had listened to his radio broadcasts from Little America. My father had taken me to a lecture he gave at Fairchild Theater on the campus of Michigan State College when I was nine years old; afterward, I got to shake his hand. That was one of the transforming moments of my young life. Who wouldn't be enthralled to meet a real explorer? I wanted to have his imagination and desire to discover. His book, *Alone*, describing his solitary sojourn in cramped operations quarters on the Ross Shelf in Antarctica, autographed by Admiral Byrd himself, still sits proudly in my library. I wanted to have his courage. Dr. Levitt seemed intensely interested in my hero, or perhaps he just didn't want to revisit Babe Ruth. Byrd wasn't Albert Schweitzer, Madam Curie, or Jonas Salk, but he made my interview.

On the way back to Ann Arbor, Dad reveled in the fact that he had played a role in making my interview impressive. He was the one who had introduced me to Admiral Byrd. Three weeks later, a letter arrived dated January 4, 1960 and signed by Dr. Levitt, announcing that I had been accepted into the next year's freshman medical class at Wayne State. I was going to be a doctor.

The Michigan Interview

I had submitted my University of Michigan and Wayne State medical school applications simultaneously. Unlike the interview notice and acceptance from Wayne State, Michigan sent no word other than a postcard acknowledging receipt of my papers. I wasn't too concerned about my own university's slower process—many of my smartest friends were in the same boat. I wish I could have said the same for my father.

On a quiet day after returning from a quantitative chemistry lab, a note on my chair told me to return a phone call from the University of Michigan Medical School. My heart was racing as I dialed the number.

When a woman's voice said they wanted to set up an appointment for me to come in for an interview, I knew I was on a roll.

Two days later I walked into the dean's office on the 7th level of the Medical Science Building to meet with Dr. Robert L. Hunter, an assistant dean for students and professor of anatomy. He had a PhD and was an exceptional microanatomist. Greeting me, his secretary said she was happy that my father, the "Dean"—as always, Dad went by his middle name, not his first name—had called and that Dr. Hunter had found time to meet with me. It was mind-boggling to me that my father had called the Medical School dean's office. I was angry at what I considered a compromise of my integrity. To put it in the vernacular, I was really pissed.

Dr. Hunter arrived with a pleasant smile and quiet voice and invited me into his office. He started off by saying that my dad had called and simply was inquiring as to where my application stood. Dr. Hunter used those words again—my father, the "Dean"—and I couldn't believe it. He went on to explain that my application was on the bubble and that my admission was likely but depended on just how many students accepted offers already extended. So there I was, having done the best I could, in the middle of the pack, and with my future hanging on someone else's decision. I was furious that my father had exposed me to this meeting. I felt violated. Then something happened that made a difference, to me and Dr. Hunter.

I told him that I was very disappointed my father had called. I may have been stuttering and I'm sure my anger showed. Then I rather proudly told him that I had already been accepted to Wayne State and that I was going to be, by my own measure, an outstanding physician. I informed Dr. Hunter that the top students in any medical school, be it Harvard or East Podunk, were bound to succeed. And I intended to be a top student.

I bragged a little about my academic success in Engineering College and the strides I had taken working on a heat exchanger and a disc oxygenator for the heart-lung machine. At that point Dr. Hunter said that my engineering grades had not caught up with my application, and that he would see to it they were included. That was what we now call a game changer. Dr. Hunter had listened to my opinion that medicine had enough problems with integrity that it didn't need favoritism or cronyism at the entering level. But he also caught that my application was incomplete—due, as it turned out, to the Engineering School's oversight.

I don't know for sure, but I suspect Robert Hunter had strong feelings about cutting corners when it came to Medical School admissions and that my little diatribe was well received. That my father was not an academic dean, he never brought up. I rather believe he had already figured that out. Less than a week later, on March 4, 1960, I received a letter from H. Waldo Bird, a psychiatrist and assistant dean, informing me that I was accepted as a member of the class entering the University of Michigan Medical School that next September. All I needed to do was to send back a signed acceptance form and attach a check for $50. That was easy. I took my first step toward being a member of the Class of 1964.

Acceptance

I was ecstatic, notwithstanding a solemn promise I made to myself that under no circumstances would I ever admit to my father that I knew the basis for the interview that had moved my application to the "accepted" pile. I did speculate about what would transpire if the subject came up—most importantly, I wanted him to know that I intended to be successful on my own. Shouldn't we all? Many times in the ensuing years I've been reminded that while who you know may make a big difference, it is personally worth a lot more when you're judged favorably because of what you know, not who you know.

The remaining few months of my senior year were bright. I no longer was a premed combatant. I came to appreciate even more the role my teachers played in imparting real values to me and my future medical school classmates.

During the summer after my June classes ended, I worked as a surgical technician at Edward W. Sparrow Hospital in Lansing. Two facets of this new job stuck with me. First, the hours: the operating rooms started up early. My day began at 6:30 a.m., well before my friends, neighbors, and parents were on their way to their own jobs. I rather liked being the early bird. It made me feel special, if not important, knowing I was sacrificing a little to do a better job helping someone else. Second, the operating rooms themselves: they smelled of ether and antiseptic wash-downs between cases, and the methodical march through a procedure was captivating. The surgeon's hand movements during an operation, and the sight of this skilled professional changing course when the unexpected occurred, made it like watching the conductor of a major symphony orchestra move from a subtle stanza to a burst of sound that brings the walls down. It was exciting and new.

The next four years were some of the most invigorating of my life. The humility, the hills we had to climb, and the patients I met along the way, will someday be the subject of another memoir; I'll only say here that with the grace of time, the events of those days live on.

The Last Heart Attack

What my father helped me start came to a standstill on the last days of my freshman year in medical school. Returning to my apartment from an anatomy lab, I found my phone ringing. It was Mrs. Cobb, our next door neighbor in East Lansing. My mother had just run to her front door in tears, saying that someone had called her from Wayne County General Hospital to tell her my father had died. It was May 10, 1961, and Dad had suffered a fatal heart attack in the parking lot of Detroit Metropolitan Airport. He had left home a little over an hour earlier after lunching with my mother, and was on his way to sign a municipal bond series in New York City. Nancy and I had dined with my father and mother the evening before when they passed through Ann Arbor on their way home from a business appointment in Detroit. He looked fine that night.

A blood clot had acutely obstructed a major vessel in his heart, the left anterior descending artery. A nurse had seen him collapse near his car and tried to resuscitate him, but to no avail. My father had suffered his first heart attack in 1947. He had outlived the statistics of the day, but couldn't outrun years of smoking when younger or the hypertension that plagued him as he grew older. In 1961, heart attack victims were very vulnerable; there were no lytic drugs to break up coronary artery

My father, Dean Stanley, shortly before his last heart attack in 1960. He was my moral compass and kept me safe and sound as I passed through many difficult boundaries during the 22 years we had together.

clot, no catheters to perform angioplasty and deliver stents, no complex coronary bypasses, no fancy drugs to control high blood pressure. My mother would suffer the same fate on December 6, 1974, before help could arrive.

My father was the anchor in my life; what he taught and inculcated into me, especially the desire not to be average, didn't dissolve the day he died, but merely shifted more fully onto my shoulders. He may have bruised my sense of integrity a year earlier, when he attempted to help nudge along my Medical School application, but he never tarnished his own integrity. I always accepted his advice when it counted and I was not going to let him down.

22

A College Sweetheart

The sexual revolution was still years away in the late 1950s as I entered college, and the pristine moral standards of the day didn't make relating to the opposite sex any easier. But we worked hard to find our way—especially when alone, entangled in one another's arms and legs. New boundaries were frequently approached during those times and how we negotiated them defined our sense of identity and personal value.

New Freedoms

Personal freedom as I entered the University of Michigan in 1956 had many caveats—more for the girls than the boys. Walter B. Rea, better known as "Bud" Rea, was the dean of men. During orientation week he spoke to the boys in the entering class at Hill Auditorium, a place with 4,200 seats in those days. His advice was to keep our noses clean, but if we got in trouble to call him. He seemed very sincere—a guy's guy. The women were treated differently.

Deborah Bacon had been the dean of women since 1950. She was much tougher on the girls. During my undergraduate days, women had to be settled in their dormitories, sorority houses, or university-approved off-campus housing, by 11 p.m. on weeknights and midnight on weekends. The entranceways, doors, and adjacent patios of these residences were cluttered with couples trying to be cool while necking right up to the magic hour when the minute hand pointed straight up and passion was abruptly cut off.

If you were a girl and you broke a rule, and Bacon became involved, your parents would likely receive a phone call. Many of the boys and a few brave coeds thought she was a batty old crone, seemingly on a mission to protect the virtues of womanhood. It was not a surprise that a faculty committee on student affairs recommended that the offices of both the dean of men and women be eliminated before I left campus, an action attributed in part to her behavior. She resigned in 1961 to a collective breath of relief from most students, both boys and girls.

Early in my junior year I had a date with Nancy Norville, who I had met nearly a year earlier when a girl who I was dating set up a blind date between her and a friend of mine from East Lansing. That evening, Nancy, with her long dark hair, penetrating eyes, and friendly smile, caught everyone's attention, including mine.

Nancy

Nancy Norville grew up in Chicago, living with her parents, sister Diane, and brother Tim. Her father, Leo, had worked his way through both undergraduate and law school at the University of Michigan in the late 1920s and early 1930s. He was a proud alumnus, had been the president of the University of Michigan Alumni Club in Chicago, and was a generous university benefactor. His philanthropy honored one of his history teachers, Preston Slosson, and of course the law school.

Nancy had visited Ann Arbor frequently during her youth, accompanying her family for football weekends, and it was no surprise when she arrived in September 1957 as a freshman. She lived at the Helen Newberry dormitory, a small residence on State Street across from Angell Hall, the center of classes in the Literature, Science, and Arts College. Nancy and her roommate, Martha Cavanaugh, both pledged Kappa Alpha Theta. Many times, next door at Sigma Alpha Epsilon, I would see her walking to class, looking like what every guy dreamed would be the cute girl-next-door. Only it wasn't a dream. She really was the cute girl living next door.

Shortly after her sophomore year began in 1958, I asked her to go with me on a grasser. This now-quaint custom involved packing up a blanket, a few beers or soda pop, and going to some grassy place in a park or secluded area where couples could stretch out on the blanket and discuss life, letting nature take its course.

That was our first date, on Saturday, September 20, 1958, at Silver Lake on a knoll overlooking the water. There were four of us—Nancy; myself; Phil Warren, a fraternity brother; and Phil's date. As we got acquainted, it came out that Nancy was Catholic and I was a Protestant—something of a big deal in those days. Nevertheless, Nancy seemed to be everything: kind, sensitive, insightful, and trusting. It was our beginning and our first kiss.

The next few months of my junior year and her sophomore year, we got to know each other better. Nancy was an education major and I was deep in my premed courses. Later we found time to take a Russian history course together. It was taught by Professor Andrei Lobanov-Rostovsky, who entertained the class with anecdotes of his days in the motherland. Although this was the only class we had in common, we arranged our schedules so we could frequently meet at noontime to have lunch at Drake's Sandwich shop—typically a BLT or cream cheese and chopped olive sandwich. These meals were bettered only by our Sunday dinners. Neither Nancy's sorority or my fraternity served supper on Sunday nights, and we would walk hand-in-hand across town, through the "Diag" on campus to the Old German or Pretzel Bell, where could eat with the older townsfolk. Those walks on warm fall days and through the ice and snow of winter gave us lots of time to talk and understand each other.

Visits by the two of us to my home made it obvious to my parents that I was in love and my trips to Chicago to see Nancy and were special—we even celebrated New Year's Eve dining by ourselves in the Empire Room at the Palmer House. Not bad for two kids who weren't even old enough to order a bottle of champagne. But we didn't need the bubbly to make the evening. We were in love.

We spent many weekends at Nancy's parents' summer home in Sawyer, Michigan. It was a rustic but majestic place originally owned by a playwright by the name of Kasper and his wife, built on a high hill with a view of Lake Michigan. There were four bedrooms upstairs and an open deck that looked out over the lake. The main floor incorporated a living and dining room with a beautiful stone fireplace, an adjacent kitchen, and two small writing rooms off the large open space. A screened-in porch ran the full length of the house and provided a spectacular view of the lake.

Nancy's father had purchased the house in 1946 when the previous owner was quite ill. Mr. Kasper had left everything in place with the sale. Later, after he died, we discovered his diplomas, honorary degrees, a silver tea set received as a gift from Swedish nobility, and two Tiffany lamps, all in the attic. It was a special place with an intriguing history. In its former days it must have formed part of a writers' haven—the poet Carl Sandberg owned a house a few doors from the Norvilles'.

A Real Home Away from Home

Nancy and I felt our commitment deepen during my senior year. It was then that I moved from the SAE house. No more listening to loud music and debates in the fraternity that kept you awake all night, but no more regular meals and a bed made by a hired houseman, either. That year, together with three friends—two fraternity brothers and a high school classmate—we rented a private home in a nice part of residential Ann Arbor. It was the home of Samuel Eldersveld, a professor of political science who in 1957 had been elected mayor of Ann Arbor. He was about to go on a sabbatical to India with his family when Ron Gregg, who had roomed with me as a sophomore and had been the president of the student government, became aware that the house was available. Mr. Eldersveld interviewed us, gave us a contract, and we moved in at the beginning of the 1959–60 academic year.

The four of us were a serious bunch. I was headed to medical school. Ron was going to Harvard Law. Bart Burkhalter was finishing up his bachelor's degree in engineering and heading for a PhD in library science—at that time the university's only program in computer technology. Tom Astley was finishing a business degree, intending to return to East Lansing, his hometown, and enter the family business.

There is a side story about the Eldersveld home. A cleaning woman came every two weeks, and the house always seemed well kept and neat.

In addition, twice a semester we rotated between the four bedrooms, forcing the four of us to keep our personal things in order. We respected the house's contents and we didn't have open parties. The fact was that we all had steady girlfriends who would eventually become our wives and we didn't need parties. But apparently we didn't take quite good enough care of the home. When the Eldersvelds returned we were informed we would not get our one month's deposit back. They had to refinish the hardwood floors—and there were a lot of square feet of flooring to be redone.

I saw Professor Eldersveld around town often in the ensuing decades. He became chair of the Political Science Department after returning from India and was well known on campus. I avoided him like the plague: I didn't want him to recognize me as one of those roustabouts who trashed his home.

Our relationship changed in 2005. One Tuesday morning as I sat in my office editing a paper, I received a call that someone was on the way to the emergency room with a ruptured abdominal aortic aneurysm. I was not officially on call, but I was the only one available. I arrived minutes later to find an 87-year-old man in severe pain with a blood pressure under 90 mm Hg—in impending shock. We rushed him to the operating room, with a resident and a nurse pulling the stretcher and me pushing it. Just before we got through the operating room door I asked the nurse his name. She was out of breath, but I recognized it:

"Samuel Eldersveld."

The likelihood of an 87-year-old surviving a conventional open operation after a free rupture of an aortic aneurysm is less than 10%, and the operation was difficult. But Professor Eldersveld left the operating room in one piece. His recovery was complicated by respiratory failure, requiring lengthy treatment. But he was one tough patient with a caring wife, Els, and he eventually regained his health. It took a while for me to finally tell him I was one of the youngsters to whom he had rented his home more than four decades earlier. His response to that news was a quiet,

"Yes, I remember."

Nevertheless, I believe Sam Eldersveld forgave me for messing up his floors—after all, I had saved his life. He invited Nancy and me to his ninetieth birthday celebration, just a few weeks after he had published his twenty-third book, and I had the opportunity to make the opening remarks wishing him a happy birthday—making mention of our earlier acquaintance as well as more recent times. It was a joyous reconciliation. Sam passed away peacefully five years after I operated on him—but not before he had written his memoirs and published a twenty-fourth book. I had a strong affinity for him. It was a special thing: he was a strong survivor and an outstanding academic. Two very admirable characteristics!

The Wedding

As Nancy's senior year approached and I was about to enter medical school, we finalized our plans to get married. During the winter class break at Christmas time, I took the slightly old-fashioned step of formally asked Nancy's father for her hand after a dinner at her home in Chicago. My conversation with him reflected the respect I had for him, and I'm sure the feeling on his part was similar. Later that evening, when everyone in her family had gone to bed and Nancy and I were left alone, I asked her to marry me. A "yes," a hug and kiss, and we were all set with a day picked in the summer when we would be wed.

Nancy's engagement ring diamond came from my grandmother Geist's engagement ring. My mother had saved the ring and we were delighted to inherit it, despite its rather ornate filigree gold setting, which must have been in vogue in the late 1800s when Mom's mother received it from Charles Geist. Nancy and I both had looked at rings in the window of the Harris Jewelers, a small store on South University owned by an elderly couple who treated us like their own. It was there we had my grandmother's diamond reset in a plain platinum Tiffany mount with a matching wedding band

Everything was set. The issue of religion had been sorted out earlier, after lots of Sundays in Ann Arbor, trying out both St. Mary's Catholic Church and the First Presbyterian Church. This joint venture wasn't made any easier by Father Bradley at St. Mary's, who at every service would remind the churchgoers—mostly students—that their faith wouldn't bless a marriage outside the Catholic Church. We wanted to have a common faith and we were trying to find our way. Nancy didn't want to betray something that had been part of her upbringing, and I didn't want to feel like a thief.

Fortunately, a high school classmate, Tom Astley, invited us to St. Andrew's Episcopal Church, and we were taken by its inclusiveness. The minister, Henry Lewis, with his full head of silver hair, was everyone's grandfather type. And one of the assistant ministers was Richard Cockrell, who had been one of my East Lansing teachers in junior high. He was a welcome helper at guiding Nancy and me in deciding where we would go to church. We soon joined the congregation at St. Andrews. It included the best of both our former churches' traditions.

Nancy and I were married on Saturday, August 5, 1961, at St. Margaret's Episcopal Church in Chicago, during a High Mass at noontime. It was pretty catholic in its order—Father Griffen was the parish priest and Dick Cockrell came from Ann Arbor to co-officiate. A sit-down dinner followed in the midafternoon at the South Shore Country Club.

The wedding was a little tough for my mother. Dad thought the world of Nancy and would have been proud of our marriage day, but he had died three months earlier. His brother, Fred, who lived in Evanston near Chicago and had lost his wife to breast cancer a few years earlier, became my surrogate father, and helped my mother enjoy the day. The other important person who wasn't there was my brother, Bob, who was to have been my best man. He was still convalescing from a serious subhepatic infection that had occurred as a complication of gall bladder surgery in New York City. My close college buddy, Phil Warren, stood in his place.

Our wedding was a festive affair, especially the reception and dinner, which included nearly 200 friends and members of our families. When the wedding party walked into the ballroom the orchestra played Mendelssohn's wedding march; then, without a pause, the University of Michigan "Victors" fight song—composed by Louis Elbel in 1898 after Michigan defeated the University of Chicago, 12 to 11, at Chicago's Marshall Field. No question, Nancy and I were "True Blue" kids—Nancy at

21 and me at 22 years of age, pretty close to the average age of couples marrying in those days.

We couldn't have been more excited, surrounded by so many happy guests. But we were dumbfounded when Dick Cockrell approached us at the head table a few minutes after the toasts had been made and said that he and his wife, Joyce, who was a nurse, needed to excuse themselves. And we were worried. They had been staying at the South Shore Country Club.

"Are you OK?" I asked.

"Oh yes, it's just that we have always wanted to play golf here and we have a 2:30 tee time," was his reply.

With a smile on their faces, they were off. Leave it to the Episcopalians to be pragmatic.

After the reception, we left for our new apartment in Ann Arbor, a honeymoon on Cape Cod, and a visit to my brother in New York on the way back. But our new life didn't start without a hitch or two. My best man, Phil, drove us to Midway Airport to catch a plane to Detroit, where we had left our car at the airport for the short, 20-mile drive back to Ann Arbor. Phil had moved his vehicle close to the reception area just in case we ran late: good idea, but he had parked it in a bad location, a restricted area next to the club's kitchen. Someone had placed a full 8.5-by-11-inch No Parking notice on the driver's-side windshield—not under the windshield wiper blade, but glued to the window itself. With a comb as a scrapper, Phil chiseled a small opening in the paper—just enough to see the road—and got us to the airport on time.

Then, as Nancy and I walked out of the terminal and up the stairs to enter the DC-3, I followed behind her. Closed tarmacs didn't exist in those days. Walking behind the girl, when you were a boy, was what the books on etiquette told us: "gentleman should follow behind the lady going up the stairs and proceed in front of her when descending the stairs." Very logical—you could catch her if she fell. The only hitch was that the lady would have to fall backward when going up or forward when going down. It didn't work that way for us. As Nancy reached the top step, she fell forward on her noggin: pillbox hat, corsage, and all. Following behind her, I was useless. As the stewardess helped her up, she glanced at me, smiled, and said something about newlyweds. Nobody was hurt, and neither was our pride. Three hours later we arrived safely in Ann Arbor and spent our first night together.

We left from Ann Arbor on our honeymoon trip the next day in our little red Chevrolet Corvair coupe. We passed by Niagara Falls in the late evening rain and arrived at Woods Hole two days later. We spent two nights there before going farther out on the Cape, to Lewis Bay near Hyannis. It was the high season on Cape Cod, and the newly elected president, John F. Kennedy, was residing at his family's compound nearby. I had made reservations at the Yachtsman Hotel for a week's stay, by phone. Unbelievably, upon our arrival the desk attendant said they had never heard of us.

Nancy, her brown eyes welling up with tears, saved the day. The next thing we knew, we were being escorted to a large group of rooms, including the bedroom, a dining area and screened-in porch. It was Clark Clifford's suite. Clifford was Kennedy's senior foreign intelligence advisor and was not to be there for another four days. The bedside phone with

The Yachtsman Hotel on Cape Cod's Hyannis Bay a few thousand yards from the summer residence of the newly elected President John Kennedy's family.

a direct dial to the "Summer White House" disappeared from the night stand when we returned from the beach later that afternoon. The place was in a whirl. Pierre Salinger, Kennedy's press secretary, held court every day with the media in the hotel ballroom. Later in the afternoon he could be seen at poolside, wheeling and dealing while a young, attractive, red-headed woman assistant, attached to him like glue, took notes.

We had only one embarrassing moment during our honeymoon. Shortly after arriving at Lewis Bay, we went to the Western Union office in Hyannis to send telegrams to Nancy's parents and my mother. My father had been heavily invested in Michigan Republican politics, and one of Nancy's father's good friends was Senator Everett Dirksen of Illinois, who was the sitting Republican minority leader of the Senate, a position he held from 1959 to 1969.

Our telegrams read:

"The rehearsal, wedding, and reception were perfect. However, the honeymoon gives them all a meaning. The weather is wonderful and even the Democrats do not bother us. Love, Jim and Nancy"

We paid for the telegrams and they were sent, but we felt lucky to get out of the office, deep in Kennedy country, without a few words of chastisement.

Nancy and I were more circumspect the rest of the week. We moved to a smaller room our last three days on the Cape, then drove to New York, where we stayed at the Waldorf Astoria and visited my brother and his wife, Marge, before heading back to Ann Arbor in our Corvair—the car that Ralph Nader, a few years later, would classify as "Unsafe at any Speed." But we made it. We had started our new life together.

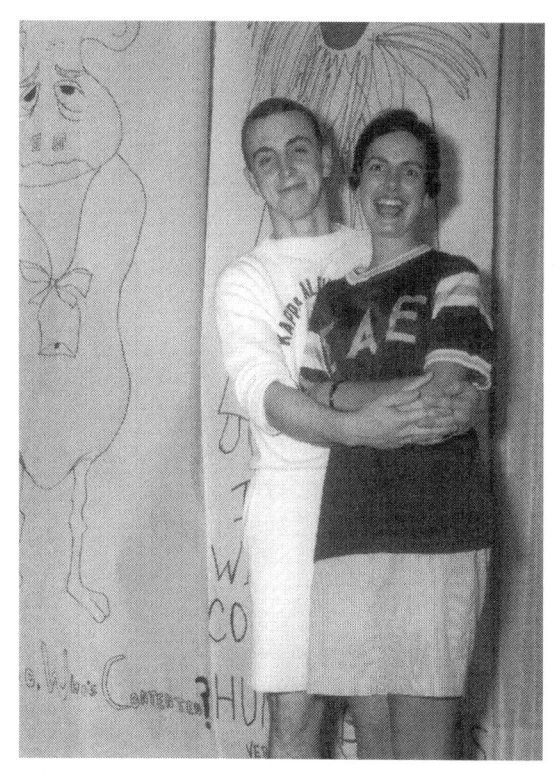

Nancy Norville and I were college sweethearts. We first met when she was on a blind date her Freshman year at the University of Michigan in 1957. She was with someone else, as was I. A year later we had our first date, and many evenings on the town like this dinner together in Florida, 1958.

Nancy and I lived next door to each other for 1 year; she in the Kappa Alpha Theta sorority and me in the Sigma Alpha Epsilon fraternity. At this party we arrived wearing each other's shirts, 1958. Strange doings, but fun.

Nancy and I at her family's summer home on Lake Michigan, 1959.

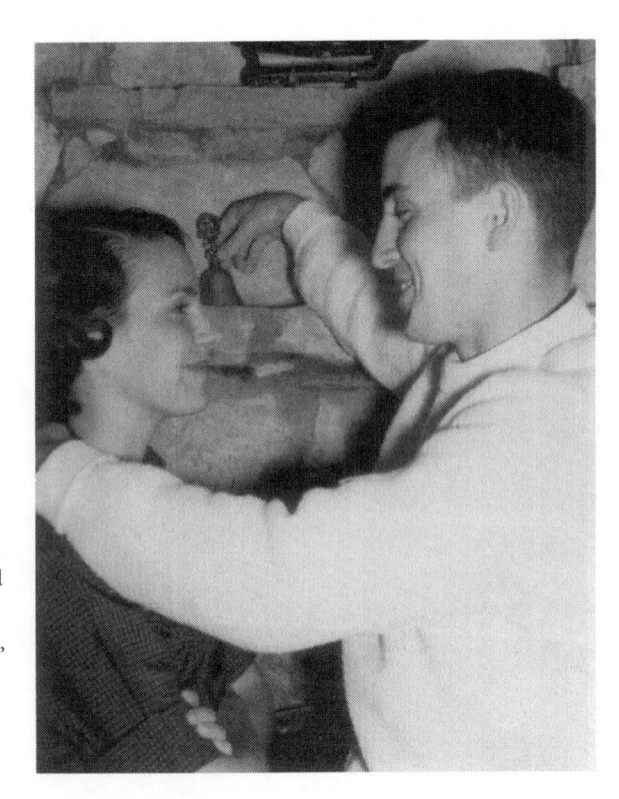

We were trying to look serious as we discussed wedding bells and our upcoming engagement, 1959.

Nancy and I were married on August 5, 1961, and we were a happy twosome on the ride from St. Margaret's Episcopal Church to the wedding reception.

Our wedding party with our families and lots of friends celebrated the day at the South Shore Country Club in Chicago.

Nancy and I a half-century after our first date and first kiss at a "grasser" on Silver Lake.

23

Beginnings: Anew

I don't think I really came of age until my children did. Our three children all arrived healthy and sound: Timothy, born in 1964; Jeffrey in 1966; and Sarah in 1969. Their beginnings were full of joy, and they picked up bits and pieces of the two of us, their mom and dad, as they too found life's boundaries.

Tim and the City of Brotherly Love

Tim was conceived during the mid-fall of my senior year in medical school. Nancy was teaching 4th grade in a small school in Denton, Michigan 15 miles east of Ann Arbor. She was eight and a half months pregnant as we headed for Philadelphia, where I was about to begin my internship at Philadelphia General Hospital (PGH), a 2,200-bed facility caring for many of the city's less advantaged. Wally Jefferies, Nancy's obstetrician at the University Hospital, had been a varsity swimmer at Michigan and like many other ex-jocks in the ob-gyn group, he instilled a lot of confidence in the mothers-to-be. But he had no suggestions as to who should care for Nancy after our move to our new digs in Philadelphia.

Happily, the new chair of Michigan's Obstetrics and Gynecology Department was J. Robert Wilson, who came from Temple University in Philadelphia and knew the city well. His advice was to deliver at PGH:

> "They deliver more than 7,000 babies a year there and they are very experienced."

Nancy and I didn't have the name of a doctor—just PGH. But the day after we arrived we met Sandy Glassman. He was going to be the chief resident on the obstetrics service in July, heading a unit that delivered an average of 20 babies each day—not your typical birthing center. He would be Nancy's doctor. We felt confident.

Ultrasound imaging of the child in utero didn't exist in 1964, and gender identification was a guessing game. Wise obstetricians placed their guess on the prenatal chart as to one gender or the other, and then as the child was about to be born, they would proclaim that the mother's newborn was going to be the opposite sex from what they had written down earlier. If their verbal proclamation turned out to be the case, they looked very wise. If not, they would scratch their heads in disbelief and ask the scrub nurse for the prenatal record, which of course would have the correct gender, and they would say they must not have looked at the right record beforehand—and thus they still looked wise. This slightly devious ploy was one of the tricks of the art of medicine, although it wasn't written down in any text I had read. PGH doctors played the game well.

On a Wednesday, three weeks after our arrival in Philadelphia, we decided to attend a performance of *Carmen* at the Robin Hood Dell, an open-air theater with benches and grassy knolls in the city's Fairmont Park. Nancy had experienced Braxton-Hicks contractions for a week, but nothing more.

Then it started. As we walked to the knoll where we were going to sit, the baby dropped, engaging itself in Nancy' pelvis. Along with that accomplishment by our child-to be was Nancy's unrestrained exclamation:

"*Wow.*"

I had been up all the night before and wasn't too attentive to the opera, but when we got back to our apartment, the contractions started to come every 10 minutes and that got my attention. A quick phone call to PGH yielded the instruction to come in when they reached five- to six-minute intervals. With a hand on Nancy's belly, I fell asleep mumbling something about how well she was doing—clearly, much better than I.

Beginnings: Anew

Nancy stayed awake until the wee hours of the morning, watching the tail end of the Republican National Convention: there was not much else on TV at those hours in the mid-1960s. At 5 a.m. she got up to go to the bathroom and experienced some spotting and the contractions became more frequent. Two quick showers for the two of us and we were off on the 30-minute ride from Drexel Hill, where we lived on the outskirts of Philadelphia, to PGH.

As Nancy's contractions grew more painful, now coming every three or four minutes, I became acutely conscious that our first born might arrive in our Corvair. Then I put my foot in my mouth:

"Wifey, just pretend it's a bad toothache."

She didn't say a word. But a decade later, when for the second time I passed a painful kidney stone, she returned the comment, unaltered and with a wry smile. I remembered and laughed, and I also got the message: he who laughs last may laugh best, but it may be that he is just stupid. I had been stupid.

I got another taste of my foot when we rolled into PGH at the Labor and Delivery entrance, where a pleasant, grey-haired senior obstetrics nurse met us and asked if she could help. When I told her my wife was in active labor, she said she would get a wheelchair.

Then came my second gaffe of the early morning:

"It's OK, she can walk."

Bad move, met with no acknowledgment from either wife or nurse as Nancy was whisked away in the wheelchair. Ten minutes later, after I had parked and entered the building, asking what labor area she might be in, the same grey-haired lady sternly replied:

"Dr. Stanley, she's in the delivery room."

A few minutes more and I was there holding Nancy's hand. She was fully dilated and with a little encouragement from Joel Polin, another chief resident, Timothy James entered the world—a healthy little boy, 7 pounds 6 ounces. It was July 15th and it was not only his birthday, but also the birthday of Nancy's father, who was ecstatic at the news of his first grandchild.

Tim joined the rest of the newborns in the PGH nursery—probably more than 75 children, in random states of sleep and crying. He was easy to pick out when I took my intern colleagues to see him, because for most of his four days in the nursery, he was one of the few newborns not of color. I was proud of his entering a world of great diversity as a minority. There were no boundaries in the nursery.

As Tim became of age, his understanding of complex mathematical science placed him in a league of his own. In retrospect, his grasp of numbers and problem-solving was obvious when he was in 8th, 9th, and 10th grades when he and some of his classmates walked off with first-place honors in mathematics at the Academic Games competition in Kentucky and Georgia. Three years later, as a high school senior, he was in the top 100 of 24,000 high school students competing for the 25th Mathematical Association of America (Michigan Section) prize. Almost as important, Tim ran the family's first marathon in 1992. His determination to finish set a standard for his siblings and me to follow years later.

Tim has come a long way from the city hospital where he was born. Some 50 years later, he has collected B.S. and M.S. degrees, both in computer science and computational mathematics from Stanford, and a 1992 J.D. degree from the University of Michigan Law School—the last year having been completed at Harvard Law. Tim married Stacy in 1990 and they reside in Los Altos, California, a few miles from their principal business office in Mountain View.

Tim's modus operandi is to just do it, and it has worked. He and his wife, also a lawyer, were founders of two major Silicon Valley internet companies focusing on the legal profession, Findlaw and Justia, founded in 1995 and 2003, respectively. Growing up in the university town of Ann Arbor, and perhaps something picked up in the diverse surroundings of his birth, have made him aware that talent trumps outward appearances, and this has served him well in recruiting for his businesses. Tim is much more than the technology guru I never became. Intellectually he has outdone his dad, and I am as proud of him today as I was the day he was born—which is saying a lot.

Jeff and Uncle Sam

Jeff was conceived around Thanksgiving of my first year as a captain in the Army Medical Corps at Ft. Sam Houston in Texas. I had completed my internship at PGH and along with many others, had been called into active duty as the Vietnam conflict escalated. So Jeff entered the world as an army "brat" in the affectionate sense of the term. The turbulence of the war in Southeast Asia, coupled with the growing opposition to the war at home, was causing great unrest.

The stress on service members and their families was palpable, yet Jeff came home to a peaceful duplex dwelling that we shared with another army family at 214 Foulois Road, within the confines of the post. It was an anxious life between the anticipation of my being deployed and the indigestion accompanying my newfound love of refried beans, barbequed beef, and drinking Lone Star beer—Texas style.

Prenatal care was different with Uncle Sam—every bit as regulated as a parade march for the many general officers who had retired to San Antonio. Things always worked, provided everyone showed up and did what they were asked: that was our story. Nancy's pregnancy was uneventful and relatively quiet, but she showed no sign of any contractions, false or real, as her expected due date passed. Because of Tim's quick entrance, her bag had been packed for weeks and we were both waiting.

Two weeks after her due date, on a quiet afternoon, my senior non-commissioned officer, Walter Tyska, on whom I relied for advice on how to stay out of trouble, stopped by our home. He wanted to talk about a swap of supplies with Brooke General Hospital—a not-to-be-discussed exchange he wanted me to know about, but not question. He had been an infantry soldier at the Battle of Anzio in World War II, and he knew how to get things done. I was not to comment further on the matter.

Nancy walked in halfway through his explanation of the transaction.

"I'm in labor."

That got my attention. She hopped in the car while I dropped Tim off with a next door neighbor, and we were on our way. Brooke General Hospital was only a few blocks away and we were there in minutes.

In 1966, fathers were not allowed in army delivery rooms—and that's where Nancy was 15 minutes or so after arriving at the labor suite. I was stuck in the waiting room, cut off from the events inside.

Major Chaney, the obstetrician following Nancy, had been called when we arrived. Nancy knew the baby was on its way, but the attendants, including a resident, did not want to provide an epidural for the discomfort until Chaney got there. By the time that happened, Jeff was on his way—natural birthing without an epidural, and not by choice. Three years later, with the impending birth of our third child, Nancy didn't care who "caught" the baby. A resident would be fine, but don't forget the epidural.

Jeffrey John joined his brother as part of the Stanley family on August 17, 1966, at 8 pounds, 13 ounces: 10 fingers and 10 toes, accompanied by bright red hair and lots of it. His brother, who had just turned two, had blond hair—nearly white from the Texas sun. On a vacation to Mexico, six months after Jeff's birth, we struck up a friendship on the beach with a young couple from Chicago. After a few days, they asked us if our two boys were adopted—Nancy and I both had very dark brown hair in those days—but they were ours.

Some 40 years later I look at Jeff and see a lot of myself, only he's better at many of life's important roles. He has had a balanced life as a medical doctor, practicing in his specialty of otolaryngology, treating diseases of the ear, nose and throat. Jeff followed me in taking his premedical schooling at the University of Michigan, where he received his B.S. degree with honors in 1989. He attended medical school at the University of Illinois in Chicago, where he finished in 1993 as a James Scholar, which allowed him to have outside rotations at many of the finest hospitals in the country in addition to those at his own institution.

Jeff undertook his residency training at the University of Iowa and the University of New Mexico, joining the staff at the latter institution when he finished in 1999. After a period in private practice in the Dakotas and a sleep medicine fellowship back in New Mexico, he and his wife Kate, a pediatrician—a neonatologist—accepted appointments at the University of Michigan in 2010. I couldn't have been prouder.

Jeff met Kate during his days at the University of Iowa, where she was a medical student. In 1999 they were married and set up home in Albuquerque. She and Jeff are the proud parents of Teddy, born in 2005, and Lauren, born in 2008. Both grandkids are sheer fun, with the smiles and intellect of their two gifted parents. Jeff has outdone his old man in many regards, but most importantly he has given more time to being a father than I did.

Jeff is also the musician I never became. He played the trumpet in high school—first chair in the symphony orchestra—except in the fall of his senior year, when he played football. Being somewhat vertically challenged, like his dad, he played safety, getting creamed more than once. But going out for football in a school with more than 400 students in each grade and playing with athletes nearly twice his size taught him—again, like me—about the value of extra effort.

There was no more football for Jeff in college, but he played in the first rank of the Michigan Marching Band his freshman year—no small-time achievement for a first-year, premed major. Jeff plays the piano as well; listening to him in a quiet corner with a glass of wine comes close to perfection for me. He took beginning piano lessons from Jan Fogler in Ann Arbor and for his first recital, talked her into letting him play Paul McCartney's and John Lennon's "*Yesterday*," rather than the chromatic scales the other eight-year-olds performed. Probably a dozen parents with their children attended, and you could have heard a pin drop in the room when he played. Jeff's intonation and understanding of the piece left a stunned father with a few tears in silence as the others applauded.

Sarah and the Moon Landing

Sarah Anne was the third and last to join our family, entering the world on July 19, 1969, the day before Neil Armstrong and Edwin "Buzz" Aldrin landed on the moon. That day the Apollo 11 astronauts were less than 24 hours from leaving their command module to enter the Eagle lunar lander, which was to carry them to the Sea of Tranquility. The first humans to be on the moon's surface in the succeeding days and their photos of the earth from some 240,000 miles away looked so peaceful as to raise our hopes that it would stay that way for our daughter as she grew older.

Nancy's pregnancy was again relatively easy, this time under the care of J. Robert Wilson. Five years earlier he had sent us to the PGH resident staff, but now the circumstances were different. I was in the second year of my surgical residency at the University of Michigan. The families of the resident physicians all were assigned faculty to oversee pregnancies. Dr. Wilson was a tall man, soft spoken and balding, and once he fixed you in his gaze he didn't let go until you understood his message. He was all business with years of preparation, and we were very comfortable in his care.

Our boys, with a little help from us, had also been preparing for the new arrival. Jeff moved into his older brother's room, vacating a small, 8x10-foot room that was to become his sister's—although none of us knew at the time if "it" was going to be a baby girl or boy. The room was just big enough for a lace-covered bassinet that the boys had slept in years earlier, a small dresser with five shallow drawers, and a card table for changing diapers. Instead of today's disposables, these were all soft cotton that you rinsed out in the toilet and kept in a plastic diaper box for pickup by a laundry service.

We defined the new arrival's space by cutting out a picture of Tim in diapers as a newborn from an old snapshot and pinning it securely to the bottom of the bassinet. Daily and sometimes more often, the boys would rush into the room and peer over the edge to see if "it" had arrived— often to their disappointment, as all they saw was the tiny photo on the sheet below. Being only three and five, they hadn't yet figured out that if Mom was in the next room, the new addition must still be in her tummy.

When it was past her due date and Nancy still wasn't showing any signs of labor, Dr. Wilson decided it would be wise to induce her. We arrived at the hospital early on a Saturday morning, but the staff quickly became somewhat overwhelmed with other cases in active labor and Dr. Wilson told us to go home and come back in a few days. I don't recall his exact reasoning, but I know he had a standing game of tennis on

Saturdays that might have figured into the equation. My knowledge of a woman's parturition—labor and delivery—was pretty limited, but I did know from her earlier deliveries that once Nancy commenced labor a breathing baby would not be far away.

Marvin Haig was the senior obstetrics resident on service that day and as he was writing her leave papers, I recited my wife's history. My worried look must have been obvious. He suggested I speak with the "boss," Dr. Wilson. So downstairs I went to the chair's office and in a quiet manner I made a case for Nancy's staying put. My wife had already told him during an earlier prenatal visit that she didn't care if a resident delivered her baby—the memory of waiting and no anesthetic before Jeff's arrival was still there.

Dr. Wilson heard my plea and slowly responded:

"We will see."

Perhaps more importantly, it was raining cats and dogs outside—unfortunate for the doctor's tennis game, but not for us. Within a half hour Nancy progressed from Pitocin-induced contractions unassociated with any cervical dilation, to a rapid delivery.

Dr. Wilson caught Sarah as she quickly entered the world with a quiet statement:

"This is different."

I was holding Nan's hand and didn't pay much attention to his words, but my wife was scared, thinking something was wrong. Not so. Dr. Wilson had a dry sense of humor and what he was saying was that the delivery was faster than he would have predicted. Only minutes old, Sarah was pink, with bright roving eyes and pudgy cheeks. Her entrance at 9 pounds, 1.5 ounces, was just fine.

In 1948, the book *Cheaper by the Dozen* made large families seem like fun. The message was underscored when the book was made into a movie in 1950 starring Clifton Webb and Myrna Loy. Happiness was equated with a full table of kids around dinner, and of course really smart parents. Sometime in the past, Nancy and I had thought lots children would be wonderful—six, perhaps—but with Sarah's arrival our family felt complete.

Our daughter grew up fast, and like her brothers, she was never lacking as a student or athlete. She knew just the right button to push to get my attention, and she pushed it often—but she was also more laid back than her mother. I got a vivid demonstration of that on a Sunday afternoon when she was crewing for me in our 15-foot, 6-inch Snipe sailboat. We were sailing in a race with a dozen other Snipes on Barton Pond, a small body of water behind a dam on the Huron River that flowed downstream through Ann Arbor.

We had been luffed off the starting line by Bill Grabb, a plastic surgeon whose home was on the banks of the pond. Bill knew we were recent members of the Barton Sailing Club, and I think he wanted to joke around a bit with us. He was an expert sailor and with the right of way, maneuvered us to a very unfavorable position at the end of the starting line—just for the sport of it. I was perturbed, but I knew the rules and kept quiet.

Sarah, however, at age twelve was truly angry, and without much thought addressed Dr. Grabb, who was only a few meters away:

"Damn you."

He got it, and so did I.

Cussing at home was a no-no, and at times when I voiced a profane word or two at a bungled football play, Nancy would deliver her standard retort:

"You really don't need to talk like that!"

Words of wisdom from a special education teacher used to dealing with young students—and she was right. Every once in a while, however, I felt a little swearing cleared the air and prevented my heart rate and blood pressure from getting out of control. In fact, it sort of felt good. That afternoon in the boat, Sarah and I laughed at her exclamation: she said what I was thinking, and it was all in fun.

During her early years as an undergraduate at the University of

Michigan, Sarah became a bit of a feminist. When I described a female patient or coworker as "petite" or "cute," she admonished me, noting that I didn't describe my male colleagues as "hulks" or "handsome dudes." My everyday language lost a lot of adjectives as a result. One day, during our Grand Round's teaching conference in 1990, I presented the case of a young child I had operated on.

I started by saying,

"This five-year-old woman was admitted to Mott Children's Hospital."

That brought a laugh from the audience and I quickly explained that my language had been politically cleansed by my teenage daughter.

An outstanding long-distance runner, Sarah encouraged me to get back into shape, as I described in an earlier chapter. She had grown from an adorable infant into a bright and competitive young woman who was a great coach.

Like her siblings, she was also an exceptional academic. Sarah received her A.B. degree in psychology from the University of Michigan in 1991 and a M.S. degree in speech pathology from Northwestern University in 1996. We knew she was a serious student, but were happily surprised when she called one Saturday to announce that she had received a $5,000 scholarship for her second year of graduate school—not based on economic need, but for being the top student in her class that year. She knew how important it was to get the most from her educational opportunities. We were proud.

Sarah married Ray in 2002 and two years later they gave us our first grandchild, Annie in 2003. This little creature, and her brother, Charlie, who arrived in 2006, reawakened our love for the young. Sarah has a deep passion for physical fitness. Just during the past three months, as I am finishing this memoir, she has completed a marathon and two triathlons—setting a high standard for the rest of the family.

Nancy and I with our firstborn, Timothy when a year old. He arrived in 1964 on his grandfather Norville's birthday, July 15th.

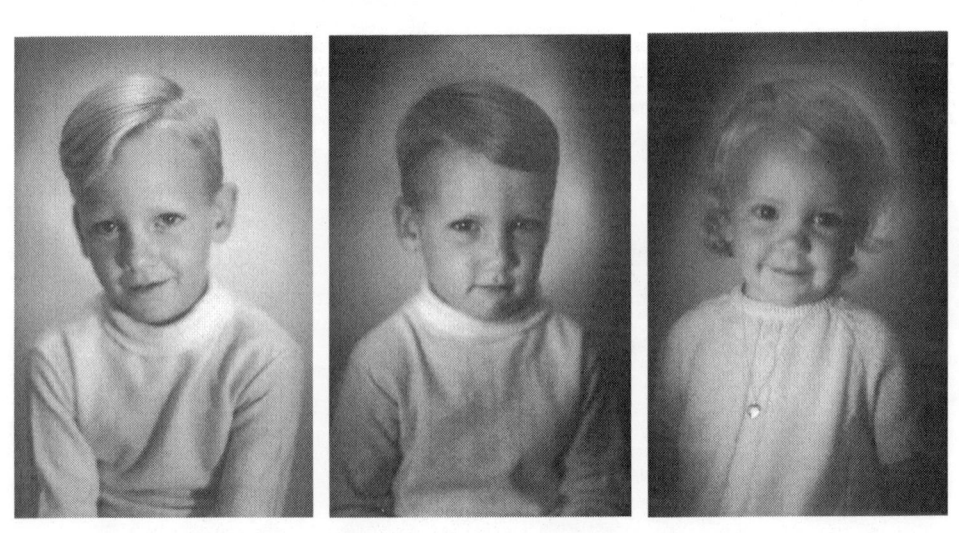

Tim, Jeff, and Sarah in 1972. The pride and joy of their parents both then and now.

Our children as they were growing; longer hair for the boys…a sign of the times, 1976.

Our Children more than a decade away from home; on their own as mature young adults, 1996.

My 60th birthday dinner with Nancy and our children, 1998.

My 70th birthday with our grandchildren…Annie, Lauren, Teddy, and Charlie, 2008.

Balance

My three children have all faced boundaries in their lives, some of which I experienced, others that are foreign to me, and a few I threw their way. Witnessing how well they've done has been exhilarating. Their coming of age satisfies my own. Reflecting on my own past from a vantage point a little more than halfway through my eighth decade, a few simple observations reflect my hopes for those who follow. Here they are:

In my life I have faced many boundaries that defined who I am—more, perhaps, than I'm willing to admit. Some were good, a few decidedly bad.

The boundaries you face can reveal new wonders, depending on how you choose to approach them. Choose wisely.

Remember to leave something behind that will outlive you—a story, a song, a painting, an idea—something of your own creativity that was not bought or borrowed from another.

Embrace the colors and sounds of diversity, for they are the essence of life. Your journey will be brighter for the experience and the world will make more sense.

Seek contentment with those about you, and forgive the loud and callous who just don't seem to get it. At day's end they will be silent, and perhaps the next morning's light will find them in a better place.

Be at peace within your own existence. This may come from your faith or a simple appreciation of life's complexities depicted by the breadth of our DNA origins. You needn't hide your beliefs. Your beliefs will shape your life as much as your life's circumstances will mold your beliefs.

Most importantly, share your love without conditions or designs. You will receive much more in return—without asking.

Life has been good to me. Be it the same for you.

Peace.

Epilogue

My life has been a series of big and small connected moments—some exciting and full of wonder, others routine—all defined by an assortment of boundaries. Many of these, like the limits of the universe, I will never comprehend. Some, like speed limits on the road, were meant to keep me safe or keep me in the game, like the sideline markings on a football field. Most boundaries were there to protect me, but they focused inward—after all, that's where most of the early action in life took place.

The most challenging boundaries encountered, finding something that would make a difference, begged me to look outward. That was where frontiers existed, usually a long distance from comfort and security. Those frontiers are where discovery occurs—and the boundaries there were often not physical ones, but were of thought: biases, beliefs, and judgments. Some were easily recognized, and by choice or chance I got crossed many that would otherwise have prevented me from experiencing the world and understanding myself.

My teachers, family, and friends led me to many frontiers, and they often seemed to have a covenant to protect me so I could ignore my fears of failing. I was lucky. They gave me opportunities to grasp the new and frequently gave me space to improve the old—in both ideas and substance. Risks were always there—I knew that—and at times crossing the boundaries I encountered as I became of age were painful. But that was my choice, to which this memoir is a testament.

Acknowledgments

This memoir would not have come about if the author had not received encouragement from Patricia Foster of the University of Iowa Writers' Workshop, in whose memoir class I was a student for two summers. I could not have asked for a better teacher and mentor. Very special recognition is also due to Paula Newcomb, who helped with editing and formatting of this work, and especially Eric Laursen, who undertook the copy editing of the original manuscript. I am most appreciative of my longstanding administrative assistant, Duwana Villemure for balancing my office and practice, and protecting time for me to write. Christopher Hedly of Michigan MultiMedia proved invaluable in preparing the graphic contributions for this work. Lastly, my deepest and warmest thanks go to my wife, Nancy, and our children, Timothy, Jeffrey and Sarah, who have patiently supported me as I pursued this writing venture.

Made in the USA
Charleston, SC
01 February 2015